Linguistic Criticism

SECOND EDITION

ROGER FOWLER

This book has been printed digitally and produced in a standard specification
in order to ensure its continuing availability

OXFORD
UNIVERSITY PRESS

Great Clarendon Street, Oxford OX2 6DP

Oxford University Press is a department of the University of Oxford.
It furthers the University's objective of excellence in research, scholarship,
and education by publishing worldwide in

Oxford New York

Auckland Cape Town Dar es Salaam Hong Kong Karachi
Kuala Lumpur Madrid Melbourne Mexico City Nairobi
New Delhi Shanghai Taipei Toronto
With offices in
Argentina Austria Brazil Chile Czech Republic France Greece
Guatemala Hungary Italy Japan South Korea Poland Portugal
Singapore Switzerland Thailand Turkey Ukraine Vietnam

Oxford is a registered trade mark of Oxford University Press
in the UK and in certain other countries

Published in the United States
by Oxford University Press Inc., New York

© Roger Fowler 1996

Not to be reprinted without permission

The moral rights of the author have been asserted
Database right Oxford University Press (maker)

Reprinted 2009

All rights reserved. No part of this publication may be reproduced,
stored in a retrieval system, or transmitted, in any form or by any means,
without the prior permission in writing of Oxford University Press,
or as expressly permitted by law, or under terms agreed with the appropriate
reprographics rights organization. Enquiries concerning reproduction
outside the scope of the above should be sent to the Rights Department,
Oxford University Press, at the address above

You must not circulate this book in any other binding or cover
And you must impose this same condition on any acquirer

ISBN 978-0-19-289261-4

Printed and bound in Great Britain by CPI Antony Rowe, Chippenham and Eastbourne

LIBRARY
Acc. No. BB52495
Class No. UCL808OO(4Fow
Date 02-11-12

Preface to the Second Edition

Linguistic Criticism is an introduction to the critical study of discourse; the chief emphasis is on those works of language hailed as 'literary', but I have tried to make it clear that all texts merit this sort of analysis, and that belief in an exclusive category 'literature' or 'literary language' is liable to prove a hindrance rather than a help. I hope this book will be used as a text in courses whose aim is to enrich the whole of students' experience of language in all its modes.

'Linguistic criticism' is not simply criticism of language, but criticism using linguistics. What is entailed in applying a technical model of linguistics is explained in Chapter 1. As for the specific model of analysis deployed, I have used the version of linguistics commonly known as 'functional' rather than 'structural' linguistics: this is based on the theory that the forms of language in texts reflect—and in turn shape—the purposes of communication, and the social dynamics of cultural interaction and cultural knowledge. I have drawn heavily on the functional grammar of M. A. K. Halliday, but adapted it and simplified its terminology as necessary. In addition to the categories of functional grammar, many terms and analyses from traditional English grammar are used. I hope readers will find the linguistics accessible; certainly the model is easier and more familiar than that of Chomskyan generative grammar, which I consider quite unsuitable for the present purpose.

Modern critical ideas form the intellectual background to the argument: the basic concept of *defamiliarization* from Russian Formalism, *foregrounding* from the Linguistic School of Prague (and its powerful linguistic version in the theory and analysis of Roman Jakobson), *polyphony, heteroglossia,* and related ideas from Bakhtin, *point of view* incorporating ideas from

Anglo-American studies of narrative, as well as from Russian and French studies by Uspensky and by Genette. The 'poststructuralist' phase of French structuralism is a rich source of ideas about the dynamic nature of texts, particularly the writings of the late Roland Barthes. Finally, I have attempted to connect my critical linguistic theory with modern literary-critical and psycholinguistic accounts of the role of the reader in reacting to and interpreting texts. The scope and approach of this book are, then, truly interdisciplinary.

Since the first edition of this work was published in 1986, the approach has become well established, developed by myself in other critical works, and, more important, practised and improved by colleagues. When a revised edition came into prospect, I consulted colleagues who had used the book in teaching as to what changes would be desirable. The advice I received was to preserve the existing argument of the book (basically, the exposition of defamiliarization and its techniques) while modernizing it in other ways. The main change of emphasis has been to develop aspects of the argument which relate to sociolinguistic structure and to pragmatics: this being the fruitful direction which linguistic criticism has taken in the last decade. I have made much more use of Bakhtin's theory of heteroglossia, connecting it with Halliday's 'social semiotic' and with 'register': a new chapter (10) on these topics has been provided, and relevant sections elsewhere have been expanded. Sections dealing with the role of the reader have also been clarified and expanded. New, twentieth century, textual examples have been added for analysis and discussion, and a fairly thorough stylistic revision has been carried out throughout the book, aiming to clarify, lighten, and modernize the style.

Finally, in the course of bringing references to sources and other discussions up to date, I have made a substantial change to the way such information is presented. All footnotes have been removed, making reading more straightforward. At the end of each chapter I have provided a section of 'References and Suggestions for Further Reading', annotated as appropriate, consolidating the bibliographical information and locating all references in their proper places. Guidance on reading is thus more explicit and more readily accessed than in the form of a plain list at the end of the book.

Contents

Acknowledgements

FLEUR ADCOCK: 'Street Song' reprinted from *Selected Poems* © Oxford University Press, 1983. Reprinted by permission of Oxford University Press and the author.

W. H. AUDEN: 'The Unknown Citizen' reprinted from *Collected Poems*, edited by Edward Mendelson. Reprinted by permission of Faber & Faber Ltd.

CRAIG RAINE: 'A Martian Sends a Postcard Home' reprinted from *A Martian Sends A Postcard Home* by Craig Raine © Oxford University Press, 1979. Reprinted by permission of Oxford University Press and the author.

HENRY REED: 'Naming of Parts' reprinted from *Collected Poems*, edited by Jon Stallworthy © Oxford University Press, 1991. Reprinted by permission of Oxford University Press.

WALLACE STEVENS: 'Disillusionment of 10 O'Clock' reprinted from *Collected Poems*. Reprinted by permission of Faber & Faber Ltd., and Alfred A. Knopf Inc.

CHAPTER ONE

Introduction

Some of the best twentieth-century literary criticism has been that which has focused on the language of the works being discussed: in Great Britain, William Empson's *Seven Types of Ambiguity* (1930) and the Cambridge tradition of 'practical criticism' which Empson's work and that of I. A. Richards inspired and sustained; in the United States, the 'New Criticism' of the 1940s and 1950s (e.g. Cleanth Brooks's *The Well Wrought Urn*, 1947); in France, the earlier work of the 'Structuralists' such as that of Roland Barthes in the 1960s and early 1970s (e.g. Barthes's brilliant book *S/Z*, 1970). The values and the terminologies employed by the critics in those movements might today seem somewhat quaint, but a general principle of attentiveness to language seemed to be tacitly agreed. These critics routinely anchored their interpretative and evaluative commentaries to specific linguistic constructions within the texts: to distinctive word-orders, choices of vocabulary, patterns of sound and rhythm, complexities and idiosyncracies of meaning, and so on. One might disagree with their views on the texts, but, thanks to the fact that these critics do refer to real structures of language, it is at least possible to query and discuss the claims being made in relation to the evidence being offered.

Informed appeal to the language used in literary texts, and the way it was patterned, much improved the quality of debate between established academic literary critics; they became less inclined to discuss literature in terms of such qualities as their own feelings, or the author's presumed intentions, or abstract aesthetic properties, or simple moral judgements. Even more important, though, was acceptance of the lesson of language within literary *education*. At a very early stage, I. A. Richards's *Practical Criticism* (1929), though linguistically unsophisticated, firmly advocated close attention to the evidence which the text itself had to offer; and his polemical discussion of the practice of criticism was concerned directly with the impressionism and wrong-headedness he found among students reading English at Cambridge, who in their practical commentaries on texts were just not looking at the texts themselves, but rather producing stock responses from their own earlier personal experiences. From the end of the 1930s, a succession of very influential university textbooks was published which brought home to teachers and students the need to make language the focus of literary commentary: the enormously popular *Understanding Poetry* (1938) by Cleanth Brooks and Robert Penn Warren began this tradition of critical textbooks which encouraged the bringing of language into the centre of the literary classroom. By the 1950s and 1960s, it was well accepted that commentary on language was a normal and essential practice within literary criticism: essential for coaxing out the complexity of literary texts, and for validating the claims one wished to make about them. These assumptions were the guiding principles of such brilliant books as Donald Davie's *Articulate Energy: An inquiry into the syntax of English poetry* (1955) and Winifred Nowottny's *The Language Poets Use* (1962). Confirming how the linguistic movement in criticism was being passed on through higher education, one of Nowottny's pupils at University College, London, the novelist David Lodge, published in 1966 a book in a similar mould, *Language of Fiction*. I was also a student of Nowottny's in those years, and had absorbed the message that criticism was improved by the close study of language. But I wished to go further, to incorporate the methods of *linguistics* into the critical practice devoted to literature. My own *Essays on Style and Language* appeared in the same year as Lodge's book. I do not claim that the proposal was original; a number of linguists, British and American, were advocating what was called a 'linguistic stylistics' at that time.

A distinction must be made—it is emerging already—between two ways of studying literature 'linguistically'. On the one hand there is the activity I have just been referring to: granting priority to language and taking a good deal of notice of it. Lodge's first sentence (which surely can be applied to genres other than the novel) sums up the basic assumption: 'The novelist's medium is language: whatever he does, *qua* novelist, he does in and through language' (Lodge, *Language of Fiction,* p. ix). It follows that whatever the writer 'does' can be shown by analysis of the language. But such analysis might not be attached to any particular methodology, and, characteristically, critics like Lodge are methodologically eclectic and untechnical. The alternative position, as advocated by the proponents of 'linguistic stylistics' in the 1960s, is methodologically much less casual. Here, the linguistic study of literary texts means, not just study of the language, but study of the language utilizing the concepts and methods of modern linguistics; the linguist M. A. K. Halliday expresses the position very clearly:

In talking therefore of the linguistic study of literary texts we mean not merely the study of the language, but rather the study of such texts by the methods of linguistics. There is a difference between *ad hoc,* personal and arbitrarily selective statements such as are sometimes offered, perhaps in support of a preformulated literary thesis, as textual or linguistic statements about literature, and a description of a text based on general linguistic theory. (M. A. K. Halliday, 'The linguistic study of literary texts', p. 217.)

In fact, Halliday here implies two differences between the traditional critical study of language in literature, and the newly proposed linguistic study of language in literature. First, he implies, linguistic description is technically superior because it is explicit, systematic, and comprehensive. Second, the literary criticism of language may be prejudiced if the critic makes up his mind in advance and then supports his claims by citing selected aspects of the text as 'evidence'. There are problems in the way Halliday conceives of this second aspect of the comparison—it implies, falsely, that linguistic analysis is an empirical technique for discovering general properties on the basis of scrutiny of verbal details, without an initial hypothesis—but I will return to these problems later, in a more positive context.

The first part of Halliday's contrast is the basic claim that any linguistic critic would make: if we acknowledge that language is the essence of literature, and that verbal analysis is the basis of informed and plausible criticism, it makes sense to deploy the best available methods of analysis. What is best is *not* the critic's imperfect recollections of scraps of school grammar ('participle', 'past historic', 'gerund') eked out with old rhetorical terms ('zeugma', 'oxymoron') and modern value terms used as if descriptively ('complex', 'cohesive', 'polyvalent'). Such random descriptive jargon, when used by critics who practise verbal analysis, will communicate with readers only fortuitously. There may be communication if the critic and the reader of criticism, through coincidence of education, were once schooled into using a grammar term such as 'gerund' in a similar way; or if, by brilliance of exposition, the critic somehow succeeds in conveying to the reader just what a term like 'cohesive' means in his critical discourse.

A linguistic terminology has many advantages over this rather haphazard apparatus. (I am assuming that my readers have, or are acquiring, some knowledge of linguistics: this book is not meant to teach the subject from scratch.) Linguistics is an independent discipline, quite distinct, in its modern development, from literary criticism, and has its own goals and criteria: this independence ensures that linguistic terms, when brought to criticism, have their own established meanings, and are not chameleon adaptations to the needs of the critical discourse. Students can work through a course on linguistics and emerge knowing a set of concepts which are agreed, standardized, at least within one of the major 'schools' which have theorized the subject. (There are, it must be admitted, some differences of terminology between schools.) Terms like 'nominalization', 'parataxis', 'paradigm', 'agent', 'morpheme', 'embedding', and so on all denote stable, well-understood concepts which are readily learned, and readily applied in objective description of texts.

A terminology derived from linguistics has at least two other beneficial properties, which are interconnected; it aims to be *comprehensive;* and to be *systematic.*

First, a linguistic theory aims to be *comprehensive* in offering the methods to provide a complete account of language structure—but note that the linguist or stylistician chooses what aspects of a text to describe for his or her particular purpose: individual descriptions are selective, not exhaustive. Completeness is achieved with orderliness by distinguishing different types of linguistic facts to be accounted for, and assigning them to different *levels of description.* The three 'core' levels are traditional, and are concerned with meaning, word-order and related phenomena, and sound. The *semantic* level of linguistic description deals with meanings: the meanings of words and other expressions, the relationships between them (e.g. the inclusion of the specific meaning of 'cow' within the more general term 'animal', the antonymy of 'wet' and 'dry'), and the combining rules which unite a selection of word-meanings into a properly formed statement (i.e. not a contradiction, not nonsensical, etc.). *Syntax,* traditionally known as 'grammar', deals with the conventional sequencing of words in the phrases, clauses, and sentences of a language; with word-classes; with inflectional matters such as the endings on words which indicate number, possession, tense, etc. (the internal structure of words is treated as a sub-part of syntax called *morphology*). The study of the sounds of language needs to be divided into two sub-levels, *phonetics* and *phonology,* respectively the study of the actual pronunciation of the sounds of speech, the raw data as it were, and the classification and ordering of sounds as they are conventionally used and perceived in a language. In addition to these 'core' levels, further principles of organization are usually proposed. One of these is structure 'above' the sentence (the sentence being the 'highest' unit of syntax). This is the domain of *text-grammar,* which is concerned with the linking of sentences to one another, with the sequencing of sentences in coherent extended discourse, with the distribution of information, themes, argument, story, etc., through a whole text. Another major level of language is *pragmatics.* Pragmatics takes the study of linguistic structure into the realm of the users and uses of language. It is the study of—in one branch—how people make reference to their knowledge of the non-linguistic world in order to make sense of communication; and—in another branch—what actions people perform through their use of language (stating, promising, requesting, etc.).

Two further branches of linguistics, both of them exciting and prolific in research activity, are *sociolinguistics* and *psycholinguistics*. Sociolinguistics is the study of the use of language within society and culture, and treats such subjects as language variation (dialect, sociolect, register, see Chapter 10), communicative competence, speech community, social markers in speech, language and gender, ethnicity, etc. Psycholinguistics is the study of topics in the field of language and mind: the acquisition of language, how the mind works in producing and understanding utterances, the organization of language and knowledge in memory, and language breakdown. Aspects of cognitive psycholinguistics inform important parts of the argument of the present book, for instance the discussion of language and categorization, and the deployment of 'schemes' in the reading process (Chapters 2–3 and 12).

The model of linguistics sketched above is very inclusive, perhaps surprisingly so to those outside the field, and its comprehensiveness means that it allows us to talk about far more interesting topics than the nuts and bolts of syntax. One of the facilities for someone who is confident in the whole set of levels is the ability to switch from one level to another (without being committed to description at all levels.) Suppose a critic has prepared himself or herself linguistically in all of these departments of language. Finding, say, a syntactic feature of interest in a text—perhaps an unusual word-order, an exceptional frequency of adjectives, or whatever—the critic will also be equipped to look for and account for associated features of semantic structure, let us say, or rhythm; and that ability to go from one level to others is important, because the textual features which interest critics very often embrace structure at several different levels of language.

Next, linguistic terminology is *systematic*. It is a first principle of modern linguistics, definitively formulated by the Swiss linguist Ferdinand de Saussure in 1913, that language itself is a system of units and processes (i.e. not simply a list of words and sentences). In recognition of this, the concepts denoted by descriptive linguistic terms are designed to be systematically related; for instance, the syntactic unit 'clause' is a member of the hierarchy of constituents morpheme—word—phrase—clause—sentence; noun phrases and verb phrases are related by a basic rule of the grammar $S \rightarrow NP + VP$; prepositions are integrally related to noun phrases and only indirectly to verb phrases; and so on. The systematic nature of linguistic terminology facilitates textual description, and allows it to be related readily to other texts, the language as a whole, and even Language itself.

The basic purpose of the present book, then, is to argue and to demonstrate the value to criticism of an analytic method drawn from linguistics; these claims stem from my belief that analysis based on the confident use of proper linguistic terms is better equipped for this task than an amateur commentary using only quasi-grammatical terms. (But I shall take the argument beyond this basic methodological purpose shortly.) This is a fairly brief book, and cannot provide an introduction to all of the relevant linguistic techniques; I assume that readers will be consulting other works on linguistic criticism and, even more important, will be preparing themselves independently in linguistic theory and analysis. I have tried to illustrate critical analysis involving all the major levels of linguistic structure, but without attempting to cover every detail of structure within each level. Chapters 2–4 are a discussion of some fundamental semantic processes and their psychological implications, but emphasizing that the meanings we deploy in conversation and in any text are grounded in social process and social practice. Chapter 5 gives a brief overview of linguistic structure within the sentence, and then concentrates on textual structure, particularly the various kinds of cohesive tie which link sentences together into whole texts. Chapter 6 continues with textual construction, focusing on structures which are in some sense additional to the basic linguistic requirements for well-formed texts; in it I stress that the reader is almost as important as the writer in 'producing' extra structure and meaning in literature. Chapters 7–8 explore some aspects of the pragmatic dimension of language: Chapter 7 locates texts within their real or fictional contexts of communication, while Chapter 8 enters the area of interpersonal communication, examining techniques of conversational interaction as they are reproduced in plays and novels; the idea of 'dialogic' structure is introduced. Chapter 9 discusses the 'orienting' devices of language, the means by which the points of view of readers and characters are constructed. Chapter 10 is more sociolinguistic in orientation, using the concept of 'register', the adaptation of style to its setting and purpose. Chapter 11 reverts to semantic topics: to ways in which the linguistic organization of a text suggests a particular ordering of experience, a 'mind-style'. Chapter 12 concludes this book by reflecting on the overall method of linguistic criticism, and its implications for conceptions of the reader, and for the nature of literary education.

Anyone who works through this book, and also follows up the recommended supporting readings in linguistics, should acquire the use of a kind of linguistic toolkit: a system of concepts and terms for analysing the structure of given pieces of language (literary texts). The question remains how to employ this apparatus. Halliday condemns analysis which follows, and seeks to justify, a 'preformulated literary thesis'; so it might be thought that he is recommending the reverse procedure, namely, that linguistic analysis is first applied to the text 'cold', as it were, without prejudice or guess as to the outcome, and from this analysis emerges a critical thesis about the text. Whether or not Halliday intends to commend that sequence of argument (from analysis to thesis), it is an erroneous view both of linguistic analysis and of linguistic criticism. As Chomsky has insisted, linguistics is not a discovery procedure: not an automatic machine which, fed a text at one end, delivers at the other end some significant generalizations about the character of the text. To pursue the machine metaphor, computer programs exist which will run through a text and count, say, instances of nominalizations, or abstract words, or prepositional phrases, or whatever. But that is mechanized numerical analysis, not linguistics (which is concerned with the *nature* of nominalization or whatever as part of a speaker's knowledge); and it is certainly not criticism. A critic switching on the machine would need to have some idea that nominalization (a noun form derived from a verb, such as 'referral' ← 'refer') might be a significant construction and so worth counting; and s/he would need to interpret the numbers that issued as output of the analysis: interpretation which would be guided by the hunch which selected nominalization for study in the first place. This interplay between thesis and analysis is essential to criticism, and it is illustrated throughout the book. I think Chapter 11 provides some of the clearest examples. My discussion of the extract from *Melmoth the Wanderer* (pp. 223–7), for example, concentrates on constructions in which inanimate objects seem to function as agents of action verbs, or as experiencers of human feelings. The significance of these observations does not emerge directly from textual structure itself, but only from our knowledge of the relationship between the text and its literary-historical context, 'Gothic' discourse. Then, as the examples which follow *Melmoth* show, there is by no means an invariant relationship between linguistic structure and critical significance. Purely linguistic analysis cannot reveal this significance: only a critical analysis which realizes the text as a mode of discourse, which recognizes pragmatics and social and historical context, can do so; and treating text as *discourse* stretches the capability of linguistics as presently constituted, taking us towards a theory of language in a full and dynamic sense, language functioning within historical, social, and rhetorical contexts.

While agreeing with Halliday, then, that linguistic criticism ought to be based on concepts drawn from a proper linguistic theory—this being much more efficient and objective than the terms of conventional literary criticism—I must emphasize that linguistics *as such* is not a discovery procedure, and not a critical procedure: therefore, it needs to be guided by some working hypotheses which will be checked against the linguistic evidence, and progressively modified and confirmed, as the analysis proceeds. Critics who are hostile to the use of linguistics in literary criticism have sometimes misrepresented linguistics as a kind of inhuman machine capable only of soullessly dismantling literary works. This is a misleading caricature of linguistic criticism; I hope that this book will do something to reassure critics that it does not work in that mechanical way.

What then are to be the sources of the general hypotheses which are to guide the activity of linguistic criticism? To some extent, parts of the general framework can be drawn from existing literary criticism, and that is what I have done in some sections of this book; but I must insert a general caveat. It is not realistic to assume that all the general premises and values of literary criticism can be maintained intact while linguistic analysis is borrowed and incorporated as an efficient methodological aid. For a start, many of the assumptions with which literary critics work are poorly defined, even mysterious: 'unity', 'tension', 'structure', 'paradox', 'realism', and so on. Many can be improved by illuminating them with the insights derived from a rich enough linguistic theory—one that finds room for text-grammatical and pragmatic concepts, in particular. And there is one fundamental hurdle that must be overcome if linguistics is to influence literary theory fully and productively. It will be evident as my book proceeds that I find fault with the assumptions which critics make about 'literature' being a special and autonomous form of discourse. To propose some special essence for literature, not found in 'other uses of language', is to erect an obstacle in the way of properly understanding literature as language. We will return to this issue and its various ramifications.

There is a second reason why linguistic criticism cannot be just a matter of plugging in an analytic tool at the sharp end of an existing literary theory, like fitting a bit in a drill. Linguistic analysis is not 'just' a neutral method of analysis which is compatible with any theoretical framework. A linguistic model of analysis is a model of language, that is to say, it essentially implies a theory of the nature of language in the process of describing it: such theory may be quite at odds with what is presupposed by a critical model. It is essential to grasp that there is not just one linguistics, but a variety of quite distinct theories, manifesting not simply differences of terminology, but utterly different in their ways of viewing language and the world. For our particular critical purposes, one broad distinction must be drawn, between *structural-generative* and *functional-textual* theories of language. The former are quite unsuitable for linguistic criticism. Generative grammars of the kind pioneered by Noam Chomsky in the late 1950s, and developed by him and by others in a number of versions since, would be the prime example of the first category. A generative grammar is not concerned with actual utterances and texts as such, but is dedicated to accounting for what is *universal* in language: if a syntactic construction in a text is identified as, say, 'centre-embedded', or a 'nominalization', or 'suffixation', or whatever, the generative linguist's main interest is in establishing that that type of construction is one process available within the total set of syntactic possibilities afforded by human language as a whole. (Thus generative grammar is basically psychological in orientation, concerned with the structural possibilities afforded by the human mind.) The text is scanned for data, structures are proposed and checked against speakers' intuitions, and then the text is forgotten. Generative grammar offers no explanation of *why* that structure occurs in that utterance, or what its effect is—precisely the sort of *particular* observation which criticism is interested in. A *functional-textual* model of grammar, on the other hand, of the type employed in this book, is specifically geared to allow individual observations and explanations, so is much better suited to the task. This sort of grammar, which originated in the Prague Linguistic Circle in the 1930s, is today available in the fully elaborated version of functional linguistics which has been developed by M. A. K. Halliday and his colleagues. Functional linguistics respects the integrity and individuality of texts, rather than absorbing their contents into some grander, more abstract, scheme. For every text, a description of its patterns of language can be provided, but the structure revealed is not left as it is: the functional linguist always seeks to understand *why* these particular linguistic patterns are found, in terms of the social and communicative needs which the text is called on to serve. I take it that this curiosity about reason and function is entirely compatible with the explanatory inquisitiveness of literary criticism, so is a natural associate and source of ideas. This does not mean that there are not frictions and tensions, but these should be taken as a source of adaptation and development, not a barrier.

One major set of ideas which I have drawn from literary theory, and have linked with some basic concepts in functional linguistics, are in the area of *habitualization* and *defamiliarization*. These ideas derive from the thinking of the Russian Formalists in the 'teens of this century, especially as expressed by Viktor Shklovsky. Habitualization is, according to Shklovsky, a basic tendency in the psychology of perception (and by extension, knowledge and meaning). If experience is habitual, perception becomes automatic and uncritical. As for language, meanings become firmly established in the minds of members of a society in so far as they are coded in conventional, often used, and familiar forms of expression. Habitualization is staleness of thought and language. Verbal art, for Shklovsky, employs uses of language which 'defamiliarize' experience, restoring freshness and critical alertness. Now Halliday's theory of language as 'social semiotic' provides an account of how different classes of linguistic structure become imprinted with conventional meanings. Then (logically; but thirty years earlier than Halliday) Orwell's widely accepted contention that conventional word-uses render meanings stale, imprecise, and automatic offers a plausible account of the degeneration of social semiotic, and seems to be a perfect linguistic version of Shklovsky's psychological theory of the staleness of over-familiar objects. I proceed to show how various critical and linguistic practices can break the conventional coding and promote defamiliarization. Note that I draw on Shklovsky's idea that language can promote defamiliarization without being committed to his belief that this provides a global theory of Art. The latter extension seems to me unnecessary.

Drawing on Russian literary and linguistic theory again, I have made considerable use of the ideas of Mikhail Bakhtin, whose work has become very influential in the West since it was belatedly discovered and translated in the 1970s. Bakhtin is known for his view that literature is basically *dialogic* in its structure; in our terms, it achieves a critical defamiliarization by juxtaposing different voices and ideologies within one text. The notion of dialogism is introduced in Chapter 8, and the plural or *heteroglossic* text is discussed in Chapter 10.

Another concept found in much literary criticism (under various names) which seems to work well in linguistic terms is *cohesion*. This is the notion—a positively evaluative notion in literary studies—that literary texts are unified by linkings, echoes, and correspondences across sections larger than the sentence. There is the related idea, formulated by Roman Jakobson, that cross-sentence correspondences give rise to extra dimensions of meaning. I have in Chapters 5 and 6 tried to show how these cohesive processes relate to constructive principles of all language, and then applied them in analysis of 'literary' examples.

A further valuable idea which I have drawn from literary criticism is *point of view:* a difficult and rather intuitive category in literary criticism, but well established and apparently indispensable. My interest in this topic stems partly from my belief that point of view ought to be a standard part of *linguistic* theory, if linguistics manages to extend itself beyond the sentence to account for the communicative processes of whole texts. Point of view concerns all features of *orientation:* the position taken up by the speaker or author, that of the consciousnesses depicted in the text, and that implied for the reader or addressee. In Chapter 9 I explore these matters, following quite closely the account of one writer, the literary theoretician Boris Uspensky, who stands usefully between literature and linguistics: I have attempted to render his theory more strictly linguistic. The popular notion of *focalization* drawn from Gérard Genette is also introduced. Chapter 11, 'Meaning and World-View', goes into more detail on one aspect of point of view; and returns us to the semantic topics with which the book opens. It has traditionally been suggested that consistent stylistic choices signify particular, distinctive, orderings of experience; different outlooks on the world. Here I explain how this could work in fictional discourse; I relate the suggested world-views of authors and characters to different linguistic options.

In the last three paragraphs I have picked out some of the issues discussed in this book where general literary notions and the concepts of one linguistic theory—my modification of Halliday's 'functional' linguistics—seem to correspond fairly closely, and to illuminate each other and suggest mutual development.

However, the relationship between the two disciplines is generally less co-operative; a relationship of tension and critique. I must make it clear that I do not regard this as at all a bad thing, since both of the subjects which linguistic criticism puts into juxtaposition are in need of some degree of reform. Here I will just draw attention to one central, crucial, controversy between the two disciplines: this is the debate on the fundamental issue of the status and nature of literature. I reported at the outset that much of the most respected literary criticism this century has been that which grounds its interpretations on objective features of the language of texts; and I suggested that, in this context, the use of linguistic analysis ought to be a natural development towards even greater objectivity. But this suggestion has been vehemently rejected by the critics; and for largely unacknowledged reasons. Careful study of the wording of Lodge's statement quoted on p. 3 above may be revealing. Language is a 'medium' for the novelist, presumably analogous to paint, bronze, or celluloid. This metaphor easily comes to mean '*only* a medium': the real thing is the novel (or poem, etc.) which is conveyed 'in and through' the medium. Thus the substance of literature is shifted into some obscure, undefined, sphere of existence which is somehow beyond language. But for linguistics, literature *is* language, to be theorized just like any other discourse; it makes no sense to degrade the language to a mere medium, since the meanings, themes, larger structures of a text, 'literary' or not, are uniquely constructed by the text in its inter-relation with social and other contexts. This position may be difficult for literary critics to accept, because it appears to remove the claimed special status (and value) of literature, to reduce it to the level of the language of the market-place. But this levelling is essential to linguistic criticism if the whole range of insights about language provided by linguistics is to be made available. We want to show that a novel or a poem is a complexly structured text; that its structural form, by social semiotic processes, constitutes a representation of a world, characterized by activities and states and values; that this text is a communicative interaction between its producer and its consumers, within relevant social and institutional contexts. These characteristics of the novel or poem are no more than what functional linguistics is looking for in studying 'non-literary' materials such as, say, conversations or letters or official documents. Perhaps this is a richer, and thus more acceptable, characterization of the aims of linguistic analysis than literary critics usually expect. But for me at any rate, this is what theorization *as* language involves. No abstract literary properties 'beyond' the medium need to be postulated, for the rhetorical and semiotic properties in question should appear within an ordinary linguistic characterization unless linguistics is conceived in too restricted a way.

On p. 10 above, I raised the question of what might be the sources of knowledge and hypotheses for guiding linguistic analysis in the more ambitious activity of linguistic criticism. I only partially answered this by referring to literary criticism and theory as a source for *some* concepts of a quasi-theoretical kind (point of view, etc.). Other parts of the answer to this question derive from the characteristics of the linguistic model I am proposing. It should be clear by now that I do not conceive of linguistics as a mere mechanical technique for detailing the construction of texts within the narrow bounds of syntax and phonology. The key difference between my approach and, say, the classic linguistic analysis applied by Roman Jakobson to poems (see Chapters 6 and 12), is that the linguistic model which I use makes a serious attempt to include pragmatic, social, and historical dimensions of language. Pragmatics is about relationships between language and its users. It is a part of linguistics which is still very much subject to debate and development, but it is clear that it includes roughly the following topics: the interpersonal and social acts that speakers perform by speaking and writing; thus, the structure not only of conversation but also of all other sorts of linguistic communication as *interaction* (see Chapter 8); the diverse relationships between language use and its different types of context (see Chapter 7); particularly the relationships with social contexts and their historical development; and, fundamentally, the systems of shared knowledge within communities, and between speakers, which make communication possible—this is where pragmatics and semantics overlap.

If linguistics is extended in this way, out into the pragmatics of communication, and incorporates a socially based semantics, then it becomes natural to refer to social structure, history, and the development of ideas as essential parts of a linguistic criticism. These are aspects of the context of literature which traditionally have *not* been attended to very much by those literary critics who have concentrated on language—indeed, the relevance of history and of social context has often been dismissed by critics; and earlier, more formalist, conceptions of linguistics may have encouraged this rejection. But it is fundamental to my approach that the significance of linguistic structures in literature is a function of the relationships between textual construction and the social, institutional, and ideological conditions of its production and reception. Thus history, social structure, and ideology are major sources of knowledge and hypotheses in the framework for linguistic criticism. (Unfortunately I cannot delve into these areas in any detail for all examples analysed in this short book, but I return to the issues, with some illustrations, in my concluding chapter.) On my reading of contemporary critical theory, with its emphasis on discourse, ideology, and history, the present linguistic approach has an even greater contribution to make than stylistics had when it started to make its mark in the more 'formalist' 1960s.

References and Suggestions for Further Reading

The bibliography for this first chapter contains many works of general background and broad interest within the field. More specific readings, including some which are important enough to include here, are listed at the ends of chapters to which they have more direct application. For older works, accessible modern editions are cited, with the dates of original publication added in square brackets.

Traditions of modern *literary criticism* which make close reference to the language of literary texts were established in the 1920s in Great Britain (*'Practical Criticism'*), and the 1930s in North America (the *'New Criticism'*). Pioneer works in Great Britain were I. A. Richards, *Principles of Literary Criticism* (London: Routledge & Kegan Paul, 1963

[1924]) and *Practical Criticism* (New York: Harcourt, Brace & World, 1956 [1929]); W. Empson, *Seven Types of Ambiguity* (New York: New Directions, 1966 [1930]).

The major textbook in the American New Critical tradition is C. Brooks and R. P. Warren, *Understanding Poetry* (New York: Holt, Rinehart & Winston, 3rd edn., 1960 [1938]); a comprehensive theoretical account of the principles of this school is R. Wellek and A. Warren, *Theory of Literature* (New York: Harcourt, Brace & World, 1956 [1948]); and the quintessential critical work in this 'New Critical' mode is C. Brooks, *The Well Wrought Urn* (New York: Harcourt, Brace & World, 1968 [1947]).

By the late 1950s and 1960s, the practical criticism of literature through close reading of language was widely accepted in England and America, and a number of excellent critical studies were published on this basis, for example D. Davie, *Articulate Energy* (London: Routledge & Kegan Paul, 1955); W. Nowottny, *The Language Poets Use* (London: Athlone Press, 1962); D. Lodge, *Language of Fiction* (London: Routledge & Kegan Paul, 1966). An elementary textbook based on the methods of I. A. Richards was C. B. Cox and A. E. Dyson, *Modern Poetry: Studies in Practical Criticism* (London: Edward Arnold, 1963).

The English and American critical tradition created a receptive context for linguistic criticism, but it was not the only model which supported it. Also very influential was the heritage of *Russian Formalism* which flourished in the first two decades of this century, but was not widely known in the West until much later. Key texts are reprinted in L. T. Lemon and M. J. Reis, *Russian Formalist Criticism* (Lincoln, Neb.: University of Nebraska Press, 1965) which includes V. Shklovsky's seminal paper 'Art as technique' (1917); also L. Matejka and K. Pomorska, *Readings in Russian Poetics* (Cambridge, Mass.: MIT Press, 1971). For an account of Russian Formalism see V. Erlich, *Russian Formalism: History, doctrine* (The Hague: Mouton, 1965); T. Bennett, *Formalism and Marxism* (London: Methuen, 1979). References to the work of Mikhail Bakhtin are given below, pp. 108–9; for Boris Uspensky, see Chapter 9 and p. 183.

Formalism was also—with the linguistics of F. de Saussure—one of the major inputs to *French Structuralism* which flourished in the 1960s and in turn influenced linguistic criticism. Introductions to this movement include J. Culler, *Structuralist Poetics* (London: Routledge & Kegan Paul, 1975) and T. Hawkes, *Structuralism and Semiotics* (London: Methuen, 1977). Powerful examples of French structuralist writing include the works of R. Barthes, e.g. *Elements of Semiology* (trans. London: Cape, 1967 [1964]), *S/Z* (trans. London: Cape, 1975 [1970]),

Mythologies (trans. London: Cape, 1972 [1957]). Other specific structuralist writings will be cited as appropriate, below. G. Genette is
particularly important to my treatment of 'point of view': see Chapter 9
and p. 183 below.

At this point I will offer a basic reading list in *stylistics* and *linguistic
criticism*, mentioning books which are popular and accessible, and/or
have had a significant role in the development of the discipline. References on specialized topics will be given later. An indispensable general
guide to the field, for definitions, interpretations, history, and bibliography, is K. Wales, *A Dictionary of Stylistics* (London: Longman,
1989). For an informative analytic review of the field see D. Birch,
Language, Literature, and Critical Practice (London: Routledge, 1989).

Of immense significance in the early establishment of stylistics in the
United States was T. A. Sebeok, ed., *Style in Language* (Cambridge,
Mass.: MIT Press, 1960) which contains a provocative and seminal
paper, 'Linguistics and poetics' by Roman Jakobson, which will be
referred to frequently in this book. Pioneering collections of articles
which facilitated the development of linguistic stylistics in the United
States are S. B. Chatman and S. R. Levin, eds., *Essays on the Language
of Literature* (Boston: Houghton Mifflin, 1967) and D. C. Freeman, ed.,
Linguistics and Literary Style (New York: Holt, Rinehart & Winston,
1970). The Chatman and Levin anthology reprints (at pp. 217–23)
Halliday's article, 'The linguistic study of literary texts', quoted on
p. 3 above.

Two books which helped initiate 'stylistics' in England were R.
Fowler, ed., *Essays on Style and Language* (London: Routledge &
Kegan Paul, 1966) and G. N. Leech's very useful *A Linguistic Guide to
English Poetry* (London: Longman, 1969). For a complementary volume
to the latter, see G. N. Leech and M. Short, *Style in Fiction* (London:
Longman, 1981). Attractive introductions relating stylistics to teach-
ing and to students' experiences appeared in the 1970s, for example
A. Cluysenaar, *Introduction to Literary Stylistics* (London: Batsford,
1976) and H. G. Widdowson, *Stylistics and the Teaching of Literature*
(London: Longman, 1975). A useful anthology of articles is R. Carter,
ed., *Language and Literature: An introductory reader in stylistics* (London:
Allen & Unwin, 1982).

During the second half of the 1970s a significant shift was occurring
in linguistic stylistics, a movement towards what is now known as
'linguistic criticism': stylisticians were becoming less preoccupied with
the formal structures of language in literary texts, and tending much
more to emphasize the relationships between texts and their historical

and social contexts, the interactional aspects of texts, in general terms with *pragmatic* aspects of literature. For representative arguments, see R. Fowler, *Literature as Social Discourse* (London: Batsford, 1981), and for a succinct statement addressed to a literary critical readership, R. Fowler, 'Literature' in M. Coyle *et al.*, *Encyclopedia of Literature and Criticism* (London: Routledge, 1990), pp. 3–26. In the 1980s and 1990s a number of valuable and accessible books in the new tradition of linguistic criticism have appeared. See, for example, M. Birch and M O'Toole, *Functions of Style* (London: Pinter, 1988); R. Carter and P. Simpson, eds., *Language, Discourse and Literature: An introductory reader in discourse stylistics* (London: Unwin Hyman, 1989); R. Sell, ed., *Literary Pragmatics* (London: Routledge, 1991); M. Toolan, *Narrative: A critical linguistic introduction* (London: Routledge, 1988); M. Toolan, ed., *Language, Text and Context: Essays in stylistics* (London: Routledge, 1992). Compatible recent books more in a workbook format are A. Durant and N. Fabb, *Literary Studies in Action* (London: Routledge, 1990); J. Haynes, *Introducing Stylistics* (London: Unwin Hyman, 1989); R. Pope, *Textual Intervention: Critical and creative strategies for literary studies* (London: Routledge, 1995).

R. Bradford, *A Linguistic History of English Poetry* (London: Routledge, 1993) provides a useful historical framework for the discussions of poetry in the present book.

Linguistics—as distinct from linguistic criticism—is impossible to represent in a brief list of introductory reading. It is a vast, inclusive, subject, with many distinct branches and applications most of which have nothing to do with literature or even texts. At present, the authoritative encyclopaedia is the daunting ten-volume, five-million-word *Encyclopedia of Language and Linguistics* (Oxford: Pergamon Press, 1994), ed. R. E. Asher. (This work does, however, include 200,000 words on the subject area Language and Literature—a pleasing recognition that stylistics and linguistic criticism are a valid part of linguistics.) An account of the range of linguistics on a more manageable scale, and most attractively presented, is D. Crystal, *The Cambridge Encyclopedia of Language* (Cambridge: Cambridge University Press, 1987). Two excellent popular books which give a flavour of two distinct schools of linguistics are J. Aitchison, *The Articulate Mammal* (London: Routledge, 3rd edn., 1989) and M. Montgomery, *An Introduction to Language and Society* (London: Routledge, 1986).

Of the major sources of linguistic theory, reference must be made to the foundation of structuralism and of structural linguistics:

F. de Saussure, trans. W. Baskin, with an Introduction by J. Culler, *Course in General Linguistics* (Glasgow: Fontana, 1974 [1916]). The dominant model of structural linguistics in the last thirty years has been the generative grammar first devised by Noam Chomsky: see his pioneering *Syntactic Structures* (The Hague: Mouton, 1957), and for a more recent version, his *Knowledge of Language* (New York: Praeger, 1986). For a readable account of Chomsky's theory and his contribution to linguistics, see J. Lyons, *Chomsky* (London: Fontana, 3rd edn., 1991). However, as I argued in this chapter, structural linguistics in general, even its modern manifestation in Chomskyan generative grammar, is of much less importance for linguistic criticism than is contemporary *functional linguistics*. Functionalism originated in the Linguistic Circle of Prague during the 1920s and 1930s: see J. Vachek, ed., *A Prague School Reader in Linguistics* (Bloomington: Indiana University Press, 1964). The most fully developed functional model of language is that elaborated by the British linguist Michael Halliday: see his *Introduction to Functional Grammar* (London: Edward Arnold, 2nd edn., 1994). More specific references to Halliday's writings will be given at appropriate places below, but it is worth noting one indispensable article which contains an accessible introduction to the theory and an application to a literary work: 'Linguistic function and literary style: An inquiry into the language of William Golding's *The Inheritors*,' in S. Chatman, ed., *Literary Style: A Symposium* (New York and London: Oxford University Press, 1971), pp. 330–65. The paper is reprinted in Halliday, *Explorations in the Functions of Language* (London: Edward Arnold, 1973), and in D. C. Freeman, ed., *Essays in Modern Stylistics* (London: Methuen, 1981), pp. 325–60.

Aspects of Halliday's functional grammar will be expounded in a simplified form and with an attempt to provide a more conventional terminology. This model will be supported by concepts and descriptions drawn from traditional grammar and from modern pragmatics and text-linguistics. Apart from the commitment to functionalism, my approach to practical descriptive apparatus will be quite eclectic. Further linguistic reading is recommended at the end of Chapter 5, pp. 90–1 below, and then more specific references are given later as necessary.

CHAPTER TWO

Language and the Representation of Experience

Literature is a creative use of language—not the only form of creativity in language, as we shall see, but certainly the one that people most immediately acknowledge as creative. What is created, and how? 'How?' is answered in this book's exploration of linguistic technique. In this chapter I begin to explain what is created, starting with some observations on the relationship between language and experience. We need to consider the sources of the habitual meanings of language before we can build on our understanding to see how literature (like criticism and other linguistic practices) unsettles the familiar creatively.

One aspect of literature's creativity is the production of discourse that seems to be 'new' in a special sense. I am not referring just to 'experimental' or 'avant-garde' works. Even traditional kinds of writing can provide the surprise of a new voice, one which seems to be quite distinct from its predecessors and from the mass of language which surrounds us in our everyday lives. A distinctiveness of phrasing, or metre, or metaphor, may be experienced even in works which are not of our time, even texts several centuries old.

But it is not just newness of *language* which we experience when we feel that a literary work is innovative—if that were the recipe for literary creativity, then verbal acrobatics of the most striking kind would guarantee literary success. Verbal tricks are not enough. The important thing that is created is new knowledge. Readers come away from a novel or a poem feeling that they have been given some knowledge which they did not possess before, or, very often, that they have experienced a new insight into some familiar problem or theme. There is a sense of absolute focus and exactness in the presentation of an idea which makes the idea itself unique. Now this is not a result of the claims or assertions that are made directly by texts: 'Beauty is truth, truth beauty', 'The proper study of mankind is Man', 'Brevity is the soul of wit'. The new knowledge seems rather to be a consequence of the way the writer's arrangement of language analyses afresh the topic of beauty or Man or wit. For readers, a new prospect or perspective is opened up, sometimes without their being aware how: the linguistic devices may be quite diffuse or indirect and unobvious, which is one of the justifications for the present book. As a brief example, consider this famous couplet from Alexander Pope's poem *Rape of the Lock* (1712/1714), which, while it gives no tremendously illuminating insight on the nature of life, does nevertheless make a social judgement with devastating precision:

> Not louder Shrieks to pitying Heav'n are cast,
> When Husbands or when Lap-dogs breathe their last.

Pope mockingly attacks the values of fashionable women: Belinda's anguish at the snipping of a lock of her hair exceeds that of women on the death of their husbands. That distortion of values is bad enough, but worse is the equation of husbands and lapdogs, the devaluation of the former and overvaluation of the latter, the implication that husbands are regarded as lapdogs in their living as well as at their deaths. The lines do not state any of this, but the structure of the verse organizes our perception of the ideas concerned precisely, economically, and uniquely.

We may say that Pope has *encoded* this complex social judgement, used language to establish it as an exact concept. The reader who decodes the language acquires it as a concept which is new to him or her. The insight remains fresh nearly three centuries later because of the extreme efficiency and compression of the language, which gives the reader the sense that he or she experiences the concept as Pope invents it and in the exact form in which he conceives it. Notice, however, that Pope has achieved this ironic statement in a kind of two-stage semantic process. The irony would not work unless the habitual meanings of the words 'husbands' and 'lapdogs' were in play (stage 1);

stage 2 links the words through placing them in parallel positions in the metrical structure of the line: 'when husbands or when lapdogs'. This juxtaposition transfers some parts of the meaning of 'lapdogs' into the meaning of 'husbands', defamiliarizing the latter concept, and causing us to regard it in a new light.

The kind of effect illustrated from Pope, which is found on a much more striking scale in other works, is not a defining characteristic of literature, nor is it encountered only in texts which our society treats as literary. The creation of new meanings, and thus new knowledge, is a property of all language, and it happens to be an expected and appreciated part of the texts which modern European and American societies accept as their literatures—so that verbal techniques which facilitate this kind of creativity have been extensively developed in these literatures. Before examining the way in which these linguistic techniques work in literature, we must return to their basic principles as they work in all language. What are the sources of the habitual codings which form the basic semantic stock of our language, and which are played upon by literature in new codings?

We must consider some quite complicated relationships between individual people, social structure, language, and the world. Here is a rather strong, but clear, statement about some of the relationships I have in mind, by the anthropologist Edmund Leach:

I postulate that the physical and social environment of a young child is perceived as a continuum. It does not contain any intrinsically separate 'things'. The child, in due course, is taught to impose upon this environment a kind of discriminating grid which serves to distinguish the world as being composed of a large number of separate things, each labeled with a name. This world is a representation of our language categories, not vice versa. Because my mother tongue is English, it seems self evident that *bushes* and *trees* are different kinds of things. I would not think this unless I had been taught that it was the case. (E. Leach, 'Anthropological aspects of language: animal categories and verbal abuse,' p. 34.)

The 'continuum' is reminiscent of the physicist's 'flux of atoms'. From other things that Leach says in this paper, it seems that he believes that the world has no intrinsic structure, but receives the structure that human beings *think* it has from the influence of their language. Actually, the argument does not depend on Leach or anyone else assuming *no* structure. All we have to challenge is the common but fallacious assumption that the world has a natural structure from which language draws its meanings *passively,* by reflection, as it were. It could well be that the world has one set of structural characteristics, is one set of 'separate things', but that language chops it up into a different set of things. The important point is to acknowledge the active role of language in providing a classification of phenomena and of our experience.

The world human beings live in is complex and potentially bewildering. It is so because our brains make us capable of experiencing it this way: we are always aware of a multitude of factors beyond any present situation in which we are living, we remember a great deal, we make many connections between and discriminations between things and events. The complexity is increased by social organization and by technological activity. We live in large, though loosely linked, social groups, often with large populations packed into small geographical spaces. The material needs of such populations can be provided for only by a complicated division of labour, which generates thousands of functions from bank management to waste disposal. The consequence of living in an industrialized, urbanized society, for the individual, is that s/he is forced to be aware of great numbers of other people, and also to be conscious of their roles. As for technology, this is devoted to transforming the physical (and inevitably, social) environment: to producing new objects, new functions for objects; to extending the range and power of humanity's knowledge about and control over the world. Obvious examples of the way technology increases and diversifies people's contact with the world are television and air travel, but earlier and simpler innovations would still demonstrate the same principle.

Now it is clear that this proliferation of available experience is willed by human beings, and is a product of a drive towards knowledge and discovery which motivates both the preoccupation with creativity with which I began this chapter and the co-operative social organization which helps the individual achieve more than his or her own physical capacity would allow. (This drive has been trivialized as material acquisitiveness and useless competitiveness, in the conditions of industrial capitalism, but that is another matter.) But if the complexity of their world is a privilege for human beings, there is also the penalty that this world can be perplexing and overwhelming. The process of *categorization* that Leach describes is part of a general strategy for simplifying and ordering the world.

The importance of categorization has in recent years been well established and extensively researched in cognitive psychology (as has the relationship between categories and language structure). We make sense of the multitude of separate things and events which we encounter in our daily lives by seeing them as instances of types or categories. This strategy allows infinite variation to be simplified, and irrelevant features to be ignored. Everyone knows what a table or a weed or a pet is. When an instance of one of these categories is encountered, we assume that some central, defining feature is applicable and that other, idiosyncratic qualities are not significant: you can place a book or a cup on a table whether it has four legs or five or one; a weed should be torn up from the garden even if it sports an attractive flower; a pet may be admitted to the sitting room even if it is a cobra. Obviously a snake as a pet stretches the category, and here we may note that categories include both *prototypical* and *marginal* instances. Prototypes of the category 'pet' in our culture would include cats and dogs. If we imagine a category as a circle with its prototype(s) at the centre, then hamsters and rabbits would come close to the centre, goldfish and stick insects slightly further out, snakes and tarantulas near the margin. The social processes involved in the formation of categories and prototypes will be mentioned in a moment.

The economies which follow from this categorizing attitude are very clear. For instance, if you meet someone for the first time and they are introduced to you as a lawyer, a postman, or whatever, you call up the prototype into mind, and assume that the person has had certain experiences typical of lawyers, and so quickly build up a framework of speculative ideas about him which will help you talk appropriately to him even before you know exactly what his life history has been. If someone writes to tell you s/he has bought a bungalow, you don't write back asking whether it has open-tread stairs. Category and prototype allow us to focus on essentials and avoid distraction by what is irrelevant: they allow us readily to know what a thing is.

As we shall see, the economy of types also carries dangers: the prototype, rather than being a provisional hypothesis allowing us to begin to understand a phenomenon, may become a *stereotype*. Stereotypes—oversimplified, automatic interpreta- tions—inhibit understanding; thought becomes routine, uncrit- ical, and discourse becomes prejudicial. Something of this kind can be detected in my sentence introducing the example of 'a lawyer' which unthinkingly drifted into pronouns which denote male gender (I deliberately left them, as an illustration). How- ever, without any categorization, it is doubtful whether we could think or communicate at all—we would be overwhelmed by individual impressions, unclassifiable and therefore incom- prehensible.

It seems, then, that human beings do not engage directly with the objective world, but relate to it by means of systems of classification which simplify objective phenomena, and make them manageable, economical, subjects for thought and action. In a sense, human beings create the world twice over, first transforming it through technology, and then reinterpreting it by projecting classifications on to it. Because classification appears to be natural, members of a community regard their assumptions and types as 'common sense'. It would be more accurate to call these attitudes 'world-view' or 'theory' or 'hypothesis' or 'ideo- logy'. The last of these terms, 'ideology', is often used to accuse a community of holding false or distorted theories of reality. In a sense all theories are 'distortions', since they are interpretations or representations rather than reflections. If one needs to use the terms 'ideology' and 'ideological' pejoratively, it seems better to apply them to unexamined, unselfcritical, routinized presenta- tions of the world, rather than to brand world-views as false.

So far I have suggested that people analyse the world, sort it into categories, impose structure on it, in order to avoid being overwhelmed by its richness. I have implied that this procedure is not deliberate: the widely held notion of 'common sense' suggests that people believe that their theory of the way the world works is a natural reflection of the way the world *does* work. If we look at the sources of categories, we find that some are natural in origin, but the majority are social. Research suggests that a number of basic 'cognitive categories' do arise in individuals naturally, being a product of the way we are constructed biologically. These include basic colour categories, such as black and white, red and green; certain geometrical figures, such as circle, triangle, and rectangle; notions of movement, such as up, down, forward, backward; logical relationships, such as oppositeness, identity, and causation. But the majority of our ideas are *not* natural. My examples 'pet', 'weed', and 'table' will illustrate this. All three concepts are, on reflection, *social* in origin. I have no doubt that there are societies which do not keep unproductive animals in the home, that is to say which divide up the world of animals into different sets than we do—'working animals' and 'animals for food', or 'working animals' and 'food animals' and 'sacred animals' (without 'pets'). Our ancestors cherished for their medicinal properties plants which we would root out as weeds. What counts as an instance of a category is subject to negotiation and revision. Can a lion count as a pet? Yes, the magistrates say, provided it is locked up securely. Clearly the idea of 'pet' cannot be derived from any list of actual animals; it is not a natural feature of certain animals but a property of the culture's system of attitudes towards animals. The idea 'pet' is a cultural category. 'Black' and 'square' and 'upright', by contrast, are natural categories.

The domain of *colour* provides a rich source of material to illustrate many aspects of the argument; it has been much discussed and well researched. It used to be argued that, because human colour vision could distinguish an indefinite number of hues and shades, the colour vocabularies of languages would differ considerably and unpredictably. On the face of it, colour terminologies do seem to differ quite a lot as between languages, presumably reflecting the habitats, technologies, and interests of the societies concerned. This observation used to be cited in support of the *linguistic relativity* argument (part of the notorious 'Sapir–Whorf hypothesis'), according to which there were radical and unpredictable differences in the structures of languages. On closer inspection, in research carried out by Brent Berlin and Paul Kay, a set of basic colour terms emerged, which can be listed as a hierarchy. The order of probability or importance can be expressed in English as:

> black, white;   red;   yellow, green, blue;   brown;   purple, pink, orange, grey.

If a language has two colour terms, they will be terms for the colours named in English 'black' and 'white'; if a language has three colour terms, the third will denote the colour named in English 'red'; if there is a fourth term, it will be one of the set 'yellow', 'green', 'blue'; and so on. The eleven English basic colour terms denote what are known as *focal colours,* colours which are especially salient to human beings given the neurology of the human optical mechanism. We are disposed to notice these, and therefore name them, more readily than colours which appear wishy-washy or indeterminate to us, like beige or ivory. The salience of the focal colours, and the accessibility of the colour terms, are quickly demonstrated if you set a group of people colour-spotting using a comprehensive colour chart such as the one supplied with Berlin and Kay's book. Crucial research corroboration comes from studies of speakers of languages which lack some or most of the basic terms: they easily learn made-up words for focal colours, while non-focal colours present much more difficulty.

There is another experiment which I have frequently conducted with students which reveals a lot more about colour terminology, its organization, and its natural and social sources. I will not disclose full details, since readers may want to try it out—it is entertaining, and if carried out properly, using several subjects, is an excellent basis for discussion. The instruction is simply: 'Write out a list of as many names for colours as you can think of'. The list should be written quickly, at one sitting, and preferably when the subject is alone. When it comes to comparing lists, the group should note how many terms each subject comes up with (usually *c*.15–40), what order they have been written down in, and what terms occur, paying attention to whether they are simple or complex words, native or foreign, what metaphoric fields they draw on (fruit, gems, etc.). Any apparent correlations between an individual's list and gender, age, interests, etc. should be explored. The experiment will tell you something about natural meanings, and something about social meanings.

Returning to the ideas raised in the extract from Edmund Leach, I want to take up his suggestion that language plays a major part in establishing the systems of ideas or 'theories' which human beings impose on the world. I do not think it is true that, as Leach suggests, categorization depends necessarily and exclusively on language. Rather, language is a central part of social process and is a highly efficient medium in the coding of social categorizations. The obvious role of language is the expression of the discriminations which a culture needs to make, but its role goes further than that. Language does not just provide words for already existing concepts; it crystallizes and stabilizes ideas. As the anthropological linguist Edward Sapir said, a

concept does not attain to individual and independent life until it has found a distinctive linguistic embodiment . . . As soon as the word is at hand, we instinctively feel, with something of a sigh of relief, that the concept is ours for the handling. Not until we own the symbol do we feel that we hold a key to the immediate knowledge or understanding of the concept. (E. Sapir, *Language*, p. 17.)

An idea encoded has a clear identity because it has material substance as a sign: it can be spoken and written. Because English has two words 'flower' and 'weed', the ideas are palpably distinct for English speakers, notwithstanding the existence of borderline cases. Words help us remember ideas and, better still, help us store them as *systems* of ideas. The systematic nature of the coding of ideas into words allows us to express distinctions and relationships: 'A square has four sides, a triangle three', 'A weed is a plant', 'Scarlet and vermilion are shades of red'; through such sentences we explore and establish the structure of our community's body of knowledge. Words provide labels to attach to objects in the physical world: 'That's a tree'. Even though, as we have seen, the concept 'tree' is not a single fact of nature but a cultural unit which simplifies the facts of nature, our possessing one word 'tree' assists our belief in the singleness of the concept 'tree'. The same principle caters for abstractions: the ideas 'truth', 'beauty', 'democracy' are not tangible, but then no more is the idea 'table'. All meanings are abstractions. In the case of ideas like 'truth' or 'anger', the existence of words makes them plausible and makes them manageable: the community can use the words to convert the ideas into actions. Sapir asks, rhetorically, 'Would we be so ready to die for "liberty", to struggle for "ideals", if the words themselves were not ringing within us?'

The meanings of the words in a language are the community's store of established knowledge. A child learns the values and preoccupations of its culture largely by learning the language: language is the chief instrument of socialization, which is the process by which a person is, willy-nilly, moulded into conformity with the established systems of beliefs of the society into which s/he happens to be born. Language gives knowledge, and allows knowledge to be transmitted from person to person. Transmission of common sense through language occurs largely in the most mundane discourse. Berger and Luckmann, in a stimulating book called *The Social Construction of Reality*, have argued that the main discursive medium for passing on a community's stock of knowledge is *conversation*, ordinary, unassertive, non-didactic, talk among people. Conversation is so important in the passing on of knowledge through language because it is casual, unexamined, and uncritical: the categories are traded among speakers as if natural and unquestionable. This suggestion is accepted by the leader of functional linguistics, Michael Halliday, and it is important from our point of view because it allows us to suggest that literature is the opposite of conversation: if conversation takes the linguistic coding uncritically, literature opens up provocative questions about the naturalness of the coding—this, it seems, is what the couplet from Pope was doing.

According to Halliday's linguistic theory, language has three functions, which it performs simultaneously and continuously. He calls these the *textual,* the *interpersonal,* and the *ideational* (or 'experiential'). The 'ideational' function concerns us here; aspects of the textual function are discussed in Chapters 5–6, while the interpersonal is broadly the theme of Chapters 7–8. Through the ideational function, says Halliday, 'the speaker or writer embodies in language his experience of the phenomena of the real world'—through it he represents his view of the world (his system of categorization) to himself and to others. The speaker's view of the world, of how it is structured and divided into systems of separate 'things' and 'processes', is obviously carried largely by *vocabulary*: the way 'things' are named and classified, in the manner of the mechanisms we discussed following the ideas of Sapir and of Leach, above. But although vocabulary is the part of language which most obviously sorts experience into concepts and systems of concepts, other aspects of language have this effect, too. Especially, *syntax*: the arrangement of words into phrases, clauses, and sentences. Different syntactic arrangements encode different meanings even though the words may remain the same, even though the 'statement' is the same. This fact will be amply illustrated later in this chapter and elsewhere; here is one example of Halliday's, made up but very plausible and striking:

Imagine that we are out in the open air and that there is movement overhead. Perceptually the phenomenon is all of a piece; but when we talk about it we analyse it as a semantic configuration—something which we express as, say, *birds are flying in the sky.* This is not the only possible way of organizing such a fragment of experience; we might have turned it into a meaning structure—'semanticized' it, so to speak—quite differently. We might have said something like *it's winging;* after all, we say *it's raining,* without analysing that process into components, although it would be quite possible to do this also—there is in fact a dialect of Chinese which represents the phenomenon of rain as 'the sky is dropping water'. (M. A. K. Halliday, *Introduction to Functional Grammar,* p. 108.)

It will become evident as we go on that, as well as vocabulary and syntax, still further levels of linguistic structure are involved in encoding meanings—and in turn, consolidating these meanings and mobilizing them in practical action. I have in mind the 'stylistic' and 'sociolinguistic' dimensions of discourse, the conventions which communicate such features as politeness, formality, genre (novel, ode, Irish joke, official notice, legal document, etc.), membership of social, geographical, and occupational groups, and so on. Many of these conventions will be discussed later on. At this stage I simply want to acknowledge their existence and importance. A great diversity of linguistic structures is involved, and to offer just a few illustrations here would be misleading.

Edmund Leach's examples, and mine too, featured everyday words and concepts which everyone knows. I chose illustrations such as 'table' and 'pet' because I wanted to make the point that not even the most familiar ideas are 'natural', that they are in fact the result of a process of cultural coding. The ordinariness of the examples could mislead in another direction. I do not take the language and the ideas of a culture to be 'what everyone knows'. To look at the issue from another perspective: the culture and the language are fields of knowledge greater than the experience of any individual. We live in an immensely diversified society, and this fact has two linked consequences.

First, the individual is born into, and socialized into, the experience of a particular section of society; factors which bear upon her position include parents' occupation and income, her own education, whether she lives in a city or the country, what her job is, what she reads, where and how much she travels, and so on. A country like Great Britain is multiply divided in these respects. As a result, each person in his or her language expresses experience of one or more *dialect* or, analogously, *sociolect*: the language of a region or of a social group. In using a dialect or a sociolect, we encode knowledge which is peculiar to a certain group, and different from that encoded by other groups. This diversity of language and associated ideology is, on reflection, strikingly obvious when people of different generations, or geographical areas, or genders, or occupations, talk together. (I say 'on reflection' because there is a principle of co-operation in dialogue which works to reduce the visibility of these differences.)

Second, the circumstances in which communication occurs are tremendously varied, and they bring forth very different modes of language and thought. There is variation from the highly ritualized speech of a religious ceremony on the one hand to the loose and free conversation of intimates on the other. Speech and written or printed language require different syntactic organizations and choices of vocabulary. Within each of those two media, style will vary radically depending on purpose, intended audience, the authority of the source, and so on. What is appropriate for newspapers will not suit scientific textbooks. Within the Press, there are striking linguistic contrasts between papers addressed to audiences of different social groups. Scores of other contrasts in the kinds of language used in different circumstances can readily be thought up, and, although the examples themselves may be very diverse, it will emerge that similar causes are recurrently at work. Prominent among them are the status, roles, and occupations of participants; the type of communicative event (personal correspondence, interview, ceremony, school lesson); the medium (speech, writing, script for reading aloud, etc.); the channel (face-to-face, indirect, one-to-many, etc.). The persistence with which such factors recur suggests that communicative events may be systematically classified with reference to them. Linguists have not agreed on a classification, but we can at least say that language-users recognize speech situations as belonging to regular types, and that they assess the situation and produce appropriate words and appropriate responses to other people's words—within the areas of communicative competence which they have mastered, which, as we have seen, is by no means the whole of the linguistically coded knowledge of the community.

Varieties of a language according to the use to which it is being put, and the context in which it is uttered, are known as *registers*. Different registers, like different dialects, carry distinct ranges of ideational meaning. Registers in literature will be the main theme of Chapter 10.

I am now going to move from theory to illustration. In this chapter I have suggested that linguistic expressions 'package' experience of the world and encode different views of the way objects and events are organized. When we speak or write about something, the words we choose, and the structure of our sentences, convey an implicit analysis of the topic, an attitude to it. These attitudes relate to the way we were brought up with language, and to the purpose for which we are using it—these are social, even political, factors. If our reader or hearer shares our beliefs, they may not even notice a certain slanting of the meaning. Newspaper language is a classic example: it is almost a truism that the way a news item is presented conveys a point of view, an ideology. In the example below, we have three headlines on the same event; though they do not seem to differ dramatically in wording, and indeed are syntactically very similar, the details of their language offer quite different representations. I am afraid this is an old example, but it is very striking.

The following three headlines appeared in the *Observer*, the *Sunday Times*, and the *Sunday Telegraph* (respectively) on 12 December 1976:

1. NUS regrets fury over Joseph.
2. Student leaders condemn insult to Keith Joseph.
3. Student chiefs 'regret' attack on Sir Keith.

The headlines stand above reports of a sequence of events involving the conference of the National Union of Students and Sir Keith Joseph, at that time a member of the Conservative opposition party in Parliament. On Friday, 10 December, Keith Joseph had attempted to attend the conference as an observer, was spotted, shouted at, and asked to leave after a voted decision by the delegates that he should not be allowed to stay. All but two members of the NUS executive had voted for his expulsion. The next day, the executive issued a rather tongue-in-cheek statement which might be taken to hint an apology to Keith Joseph. The newspaper reports give a brief account of the scene at the conference, and more space to the Saturday statement and to comments by various protagonists and interested parties.

On superficial examination, these three sentences all seem to say the same thing. Yet they have noticeably different tonal connotations—which are consistent with the political 'lines' usually taken by the three newspapers—and on close scrutiny appear ultimately to offer different analyses of the 'reality' they report.

The different ways in which the participants are named are significant: naming conventions are extremely regular and revealing in English. The *Observer*'s 'Joseph' suggests formality and distance; the *Sunday Telegraph*'s 'Sir' connotes respect while the first name 'Keith' suggests intimacy. The connotations agree with the papers' political characters: the *Observer* claims to be liberal and is not likely to be in sympathy with Keith Joseph; the *Sunday Telegraph* is a right-wing paper likely to admire such a politician. The *Sunday Times*'s 'Keith Joseph' seems to be neutral and non-committal. The *Observer*'s 'NUS' makes it plain that the paper recognizes the National Union of Students as a legitimate organization well enough known to its readership to · be identified by initials. 'Student leaders' and 'student chiefs'— the latter phrase with its implications of savagery or thuggery— are less sympathetic. The syntax of 'student leaders' could mean 'people who lead students' or 'people who are studying to be leaders' or 'students who lead students': the equivocation tends to undermine the status of the people referred to. Also 'student leaders', like 'student chiefs', evokes a range of comparable belittling phrases: 'petty tyrant', 'student nurse', 'junior officer', 'boy king', 'learner driver', etc.

These are fairly simple observations which require very little linguistics for their demonstration. But the fact is that we *do* respond to features such as these: the connotations are not random—they arise from systematic conventions in the way the British handle their language, in this case, the sociolinguistic conventions for naming and referring to persons. Readers who were not faced with the comparison as set out above might well absorb the suggestions of the version chosen by their own newspaper without noticing the process of bias.

There are more powerful differences, which only emerge clearly through critical comparison of the three versions; these follow from the choice and handling of the verbs in the headlines. The verbs 'regrets', 'condemn', and '"regret"' are subtle variants which carry major distinctions of meaning. Though both 'regret' and 'condemn' mean basically 'judge adversely', they differ in a number of important ways. 'Condemn' is an act, albeit an act of speech: 'state condemnation of'. The *Sunday Times*'s 'condemn' merely reports that the NUS issued a statement condemning the insult to Keith Joseph: it does not commit itself one way or the other on the sincerity of the statement. 'Regrets', on the other hand, is *either* an act of speech *or* a mental state: 'state regret' or 'feel regret'. In principle, the *Observer*'s 'NUS regrets' is ambiguous: either the paper is reporting that the NUS issued a statement of regret, or it is reporting that the NUS experienced a feeling of regret. In the latter case, the *Observer* would probably commit itself to accepting the NUS's sincerity: certainly the phrasing allows the reader to assume that the *Observer* believes in the NUS's sincerity. The *Sunday Telegraph* leaves us in no doubt. By putting ' "regret" ' in quotation marks, the paper declares that it is merely reporting an act of speech, and implicitly casts doubt on the sincerity of that act: 'they say that they regret, but we don't believe they really regret'. Another difference between 'condemn' and 'regret' is that the former is transitive and the latter reflexive: one condemns somebody else's actions, but regrets one's own—or at least, one regrets the actions of someone for whom one is responsible: a parent's child, a manager's team, a union executive's membership. The distinction is crucial in relation to the words 'fury', 'insult', and 'attack', because the truncated syntax does not specify *who* was furious, *who* insulted, *who* attacked. We supply the missing subjects on the basis of what is suggested by 'condemn' and 'regret'. The *Sunday Times* suggests that it was someone other than the 'student leaders' who 'insulted Keith Joseph' whereas the *Observer* implies that it was the NUS that was furious, the *Sunday Telegraph* that the 'student chiefs' made the attack.

Finally, note that the preposition 'over' contrasts with both 'to' and 'on': these leave no doubt that Keith Joseph was the object of the insult/attack, whereas 'over' allows him other possible roles, including, principally, the role of the person *responsible for* the NUS's fury. If one goes by the left-to-right order of words, in all three headlines the NUS is the agent of the action, Keith Joseph the object or patient: superficially, it appears from all three that the NUS did something to Keith Joseph, simply because, in English, the noun at the left of the sentence is assumed to be subject and the one on the right object. In 2 and 3, this assignment of responsibilities is reinforced by the objective prepositions 'to' and 'on'. In 1, however, the preposition 'over' suggests a subversive counter-statement 'Joseph made NUS furious':

Subject $\longrightarrow$ *regrets fury over* $\longrightarrow$ Object
NUS   *Joseph*
Object $\longleftarrow$ *fury (cause)* $\longleftarrow$ Subject

I am suggesting that, to put it informally, the *Observer* manages to have it both ways: simultaneously implying the NUS's responsibility in this train of events and justifying the NUS's action by putting the ultimate blame on Keith Joseph. On the other hand, the *Sunday Times* and the *Sunday Telegraph* analyse the facts in a less equivocal way: Keith Joseph is assigned the role of 'patient' in both cases, and there is no hint that he plays any more active role.

One might say that these headlines differ in 'tone', and that the differences stem from relatively minor details of the language, such as the pejorative 'chiefs' and the dissociating quotes around ' "regret" '. It is certainly the case that they differ in that way; moreover, the tones achieved are consistent with the different ideologies of the papers concerned—for the *Observer* the NUS is an unexceptionable fact of life, for the *Sunday Telegraph* organized students are a problem and perhaps a threat. Loyal readers absorb these stylistic overtones, and these ideologies, without noticing them. Questions of the tone and attitude are important enough for critical comment, but in fact there is an even more serious consequence of linguistic structure in the headlines. Closer scrutiny has revealed that they differ considerably in the ways they present the basic structure of the event that is being reported. By subtle means, they convey quite distinct pictures of who did what to whom: they make different attributions of responsibility in analysing the confrontation between the NUS and Keith Joseph. The structures of perception are slanted differently in the three versions. For the majority of the readership, the newspapers provide their only access to the event itself, and so the structure of the event is determined for the readers by the organization of the language. This is to say, in effect, that, whilst the events involving Keith Joseph and the NUS did actually happen in reality on 10–11 December 1976, the language in which they are presented works, for the reader, in an essentially *constitutive* (rather than merely 'reflective') fashion. The headlines construct the event before the reader's eyes, and in doing so they 'package' the events in three different ways, so that the form of the events, and their evaluation, are perceived by each newspaper and its readers according to the way the language structure analyses them.

The constructive mode of the newspaper headlines is essentially different from the 'creativity' of the extract from Pope, but both are extensions of the principle of coding which were examined in such simpler cases as 'bush' and 'weed'. Each of the headlines, separately, deploys the ideational function of language to represent the events of the NUS conference in its own way. The partial nature of each of the three representations, the settled nature of the beliefs of each newspaper, only emerge when the headlines are ranged side by side and analysed critically. The Pope couplet, with its double articulation of meaning, contains its own inbuilt critique of marital ideology.

References and Suggestions for Further Reading

The quotations from Edmund Leach and Edward Sapir are taken from E. Leach, 'Anthropological aspects of language: animal categories and verbal abuse,' in E. H. Lenneberg, ed., *New Directions in the Study of Language* (Cambridge, Mass.: MIT Press, 1964), pp. 23–63 and E. Sapir, *Language* (New York: Harcourt, Brace & World, 1921). The Halliday quotation on p. 31 is from his *An Introduction to Functional Grammar* (London: Edward Arnold, 2nd edn., 1994, p. 108).

For categorization as a cognitive process, and the roles of language in categorization, see E. Rosch and B. B. Lloyd, *Cognition and Categorization* (Hillsdale: Erlbaum, 1978) and especially Rosch's chapter 'Principles of categorization', pp. 27–48. For a good introduction to language and cognitive categories, including some report of Rosch's work and discussion of the 'Sapir–Whorf hypothesis', see H. H. Clark and E. V. Clark, *Psychology and Language* (New York: Harcourt Brace Jovanovich, 1977), ch. 14. The basic source on colour terminology is B. Berlin and P. Kay, *Basic Color Terms: Their universality and evolution* (Berkeley: University of California Press, 1969).

For further discussion of language variation and cultural coding, see R. Fowler, *Language in the News* (London: Routledge, 1991), chs. 2 and 3; support for the linguistic position taken there, and here, is drawn largely from M. A. K. Halliday, *Language as Social Semiotic* (London: Edward Arnold, 1978). The idea that different sociolinguistic varieties encode different representations of experience is fundamental to the concept of *register*, discussed further in Chapter 10. On *conversation* as a primary mechanism for transmitting a community's view of the world, see P. L. Berger and T. Luckmann, *The Social Construction of Reality* (Harmondsworth: Penguin, 1976).

For a linguistic account of the systematicity of semantic structure, see J. Lyons, *Introduction to Theoretical Linguistics* (London: Cambridge University Press, 1968), chs. 9 and 10, or for more detail, the same author's *Semantics*, vol. I (Cambridge: Cambridge University Press, 1977), chs. 8 and 9.

CHAPTER THREE

Official and Habitual Language: The Case for Criticism

Linguistic codes do not reflect reality neutrally; they interpret, organize, and classify the subjects of discourse. They embody theories of how the world is arranged: world-views or ideologies. For the individual, these theories are useful and reassuring, making his or her relationship with the world simple and manageable.

Since language is not just internal and passive knowledge, but activity carried out in extensive speaking, listening, writing, and reading, every day, the sets of ideas encoded in language are constantly affirmed and checked. Linguistic knowledge is not just ideas, but practical knowledge of the most important kind.

It seems natural to think of language-use as a personal activity, and indeed many textbooks present linguistic interaction in terms of talk between individuals, Speaker A and Speaker B, or Jack and Jill. Similarly, linguistic knowledge is regarded as a property of an individual person, for instance Chomsky's 'ideal speaker-hearer' who possesses 'linguistic competence'. Individuals do of course know and use language, but they have remarkably little freedom to invent or change meanings, or to break away from established patterns of discourse. Their language is social and conventional both in its origin and in the rules which govern the practices of speaking and writing. Language is a social practice which is manifested, or realized, in the actions of individuals. (In the production of public media such as newspapers and official reports, traces of the individual's participation may be removed.)

A convention is something shared by people. If you say that John's behaviour is conventional, you are not saying that it is consistent with itself, with his own past behaviour, but that it matches (some) other people's behaviour; perhaps, the behaviour of the majority of the population. A convention is also something relatively stable. In the case of language and other communication systems, obviously we can only communicate with one another if we assume that the meanings of signs do not vary substantially from person to person and from day to day. This need for semantic stability is also vital in the individual's conceptual relationship with the world, as argued in the previous chapter. The conventional—if illusory—solidity of the concepts carried by language stabilizes a person's 'discriminating grid' (Leach) which enables him to experience the world as an ordered, and not anarchic or random, context for living.

In ordinary usage, the word 'conventional' also has strong overtones of 'old-fashioned', 'unadventurous', 'conformist'. Since the notion of convention means basically no more than communally shared knowledge or behaviour, the secondary meaning of 'conformism' is an interesting development. It indicates what seems to be an inevitable by-product of the useful stability I mentioned: the price paid for stability is conformism and resistance to change.

In any abstract, theoretical discussion—for example, science or politics—a writer who intends to develop any innovative ideas encounters a major problem of terminology, and, therefore, according to the theory I am developing in this book, a major intellectual and communicative problem. Such a writer needs to speak about existing subjects without being fettered by the language in which they are already encoded; to reorient people's thoughts on these subjects, without being continually dragged back towards the stock assumptions and classifications which reside in existing terminology. I can give a personal and immediate example. This book could have been described as an introduction to 'linguistic structures in literature', and my readers would have understood that the term 'literature' refers to a collection of texts including *King Lear, Ode to a Grecian Urn, Sons and Lovers, Jude the Obscure, The Waste Land, Beowulf,* etc. I must use the term 'literature' in this book in order to connect my discussion with my readers' experience. However, I need to use this word with extreme caution, because I reject what many of my readers would take for granted: I do not accept that all the texts called 'literature' have the same essential distinctive properties. There are similar problems, in this text of mine, with a whole range of related terms, for example 'art', 'value', 'significance', 'culture', 'criticism', 'interpretation', 'creative'. Existing discussions of linguistic structures in literature are dependent on that vocabulary; if I avoid it altogether, my book will be misunderstood or rejected, but I can use the vocabulary only if I carefully dissociate myself from its conventional meanings. The difficulty is partly overcome by avoidance of tendentious terms: for example, I hardly use the word 'art', and then only to cite other people's opinions; and I try to avoid 'literary text', preferring the more neutral 'text'. Partly by defining terms: for 'text' see Chapter 5. Partly by using a new vocabulary: 'ideational', 'code', 'sociolinguistic', etc.

Writing linguistic criticism is of course a technical enterprise, and requires new, technical, terms. But the care, even scepticism, which is necessary concerning the existing, familiar, vocabulary of literary criticism is no more than one should exercise when handling ordinary words. The familiar and the appropriate need constant scrutiny. These notions of familiarity and appropriateness can be linked to the notion of common sense or ideology mentioned in the previous chapter. Conventional codes such as (indeed, primarily) language encode world-views which are accepted as common sense. This common sense is not natural, but a product of social convention. Distinguishing bushes and trees by giving them different names is not unlike distinguishing spoons and knives by using them differently at the meal-table: both distinctions are social fictions.

Common sense—the sum of the meanings of codes—is very comforting, and it is indispensable to sanity and to working communication. I want now to discuss the negative side of this distinctively human use of codes and meanings, so as to clear the way for justifying *criticism* and *creative practice* (and their relationships). The twin problems with codes and their conventional meanings are the problem of *legitimation* and the problem of *habitualization*.

To take *legitimation* first. Remember that the meanings which an individual has available were not invented by her or him, but were already encoded in the language s/he acquired as a child. It is the language of the society, and not a personal code, which s/he speaks, and through the medium of which s/he sees the world. This language is an 'official' language in the sense that it comprises the structures and the meanings authorized by the dominant interests of the culture. Significantly, infants learn their language first from parents; in effect, from people who are a generation older than they are, and in absolute authority over them. They are exposed to meanings which serve the interests of an older, authoritarian group (*from the perspective of the child,* this is true even if the parents are young and poor). Education carries this process of initiation into the codes of authority further: schools and their staff are authorized by the State, and the codes of behaviour, and associated meanings, that they convey, are directly legitimated by State authority (by means of regular inspection, public examinations, compulsory teacher training at recognized institutions, etc.). The textbooks children have to work with, and the books that are available or allowed in public libraries, are 'standard' texts, approved and usually 'well tried', published by respected, large, and commercially successful publishing houses. As children grow up, they are exposed to an official language of legitimated meanings in newspapers, films, and television, all of these media the products of vastly powerful business and state enterprises. The dominance of legitimated language continues throughout our life. 'Real' language is, in official thinking, that of school, book, radio, newspaper, and government. Our private language is regarded as minimal and mundane and, in so far as it discourses on social, personal, and political topics, it is deeply ideological because of its dependence on legitimated concepts.

From this source come concepts such as 'race', 'equality', 'progress', 'value', 'individual', 'love', 'intelligence', 'communication', 'work', 'law', 'authority', 'property', all the general terms which are essential to our thinking about our selves and our relationships. Writers like George Orwell and Stuart Chase have pointed out the dangers of such terms. They may encourage us to believe in spurious entities—that is a predictable development from the general principle that coded concepts are not natural but conventionally constructed. The danger really is not that such concepts are fictitious (they are after all *necessarily* so—all word-meanings are 'constructed', and abstract terms obviously so) but that they are loaded in favour of the political and economic interests that legitimate them. In our present society, this means the advantage of the holders of political office, the owners and managers of companies, and functionaries such as professors, priests, doctors, judges. It is easy to see that ideas such as 'God', 'sin', 'property', 'duty', are advantageous to some classes of people and damaging to others. If I had space, I could show how apparently innocuous and positive terms—'freedom', 'responsibility', 'independence', 'progress'—are also prejudicial. But the general point should be clear. Meaning in language is not natural but conventional. Linguists say that the coding of meanings is *arbitrary*, by which they mean that any sounds or letters could be used to represent any concept. But what concepts come to be represented is not an arbitrary or accidental matter. Over long periods in the history of a society, a vocabulary and phrasings develop to suit the needs of the society—those 'needs' being the interests of dominant, privileged, groups. These dominant groups control the means of legitimating the preferred systems of meanings—schools, libraries, the media. Language thus becomes a part of social practice, a tool for preserving the prevailing order. It does this not only through propaganda, but also by inertia, the settlement towards stability and resistance to change which, as I said earlier, is a characteristic of codes.

I mentioned *habitualization* as a second major problem in conventional coding. Codes simplify knowledge and behaviour by allowing particulars to be recognized as instances of a category. Take traffic signals, which are clearly based on a rudimentary code. When we approach a red light, we stop and wait. We don't *examine* the signal. Variations in the height of signs, intensity of lights, and so on, go unnoticed. We assume that all other road-users understand and respond appropriately to the signs, so we don't pay much attention to road conditions either. If the light is green, we go straight through, with hardly a glance to right and left. That is, we recognize the meaning of the signal, and obey it, without looking at its context and its specific characteristics. This works reasonably well until something goes wrong with the lights (one sticks on red, the intersecting road stays on green), or the conventions change (you can turn right on a red light in some but not all American states), or we come across a driver who reads the conventions differently. In these exceptional circumstances, we are forced to start *seeing,* rather than just *recognizing.* It becomes obvious very quickly how little we see normally. The traffic code has allowed our behaviour to become habitualized, our perception to become automatic and unanalytic. In this example, the literal dangers of habitualization are apparent. According to the Russian Formalist Viktor Shklovsky, habitualization is a normal tendency in everyday perception, and art challenges this tendency. We will discuss Shklovsky's theory in the next chapter.

Habitualization in language-use may bring analogous hazards. The American linguist B. L. Whorf gave some examples which have become famous. Working as a fire insurance risk assessor, he noticed that people's behaviour towards things correlated dangerously with what they called them. Drums which had contained petrol were referred to as 'empty drums', and were regarded as empty drums: people did not hesitate to smoke near them, ignoring the fact that volatile petrol vapour still lingered in them. A half-covered pool into which waste from a tannery was discharged was called, innocently, a 'pool of water'—it also, of course, was highly explosive because of the gases given off by decomposing animal matter. The label 'water', like 'empty', suggested quite falsely a state of affairs incompatible with combustion. Such observations impelled Whorf to research into the coding of meanings in European and American-Indian languages; as a result of his observations, he claimed that one's habitual thought and behaviour are dependent on what language one speaks:

We dissect nature along lines laid down by our native languages. The categories and types that we isolate from the world of phenomena we do not find there because they stare every observer in the face; on the contrary, the world is presented in a kaleidoscopic flux of impressions which has to be organized by our minds—and this means largely by the linguistic systems in our minds. We cut nature up, organize it into concepts, and ascribe significances as we do, largely because we are parties to an agreement to organize it in this way—an agreement that holds through our speech community and is codified in the patterns of our language. The agreement is, of course, an implicit and unstated one, but ITS TERMS ARE ABSOLUTELY OBLIGATORY; we cannot talk at all except by subscribing to the organization and classification of data which the agreement decrees. (B. L. Whorf, *Language, Thought and Reality*, pp. 213–14.)

Whorf's claim that language influences the categories of thought can be entertained so long as we qualify the argument somewhat. In the first place, the semantic categories are not simply properties of the language, but products of the society in which the language is moulded: I think that will be clear from the preceding chapter. Second, Whorf is usually read (though this is probably an extreme reading) as if he is saying that language inescapably determines thought. This is quite implausible: people can clearly see alternative points of view, alternative meanings, if these are pointed out to them, or if they just think; and the 'new knowledge' given by literature would be impossible if what Halliday calls the 'extreme pseudo-Whorfian position' were correct. As Halliday nicely puts it, 'the speaker can see through and around the settings of his semantic system'. How this can happen will be mentioned at the end of this chapter, and discussed more fully in the next. For the moment, we are concerned with the 'default' state of affairs, in which social meanings are firmly coded in language and are usually transmitted in routine, often official, language in an unthinking way.

The habitualization of meaning and the consequent dulling of thought were a strong preoccupation of the novelist and essayist George Orwell. His views are best known from the very emotive but essential essay 'Politics and the English language': the 'decadence' of our society encourages us to have 'foolish thoughts'; the English language 'becomes ugly and inaccurate because our thoughts are foolish, but the slovenliness of our language makes it easier for us to have foolish thoughts'. Although Orwell suggested that dishonest political language can be used with conscious intent to deceive, his basic complaint was that the intelligentsia and the politicians, through the use of prefabricated jargon, allow language to do the thinking for them. His frequent references to 'slovenliness', 'stale phrases', 'mechanical repetition' confirm that he has in mind a process of habitualization, the automatic production of pre-formed words and phrases leading to a language-use which is at best unthinking and imprecise and at worst a 'catalogue of swindles and perversions'. Orwell gives a dramatic picture of the individual using language in an absolutely habitualized mode:

When one watches some tired hack on the platform mechanically repeating the familiar phrases—bestial atrocities, iron heel, bloodstained tyranny, free peoples of the world, stand shoulder to shoulder—one often has a curious feeling that one is not watching a live human being but some kind of dummy: a feeling which suddenly becomes stronger at moments when the light catches the speaker's spectacles and turns them into blank discs which seem to have no eyes behind them. And this is not altogether fanciful. A speaker who uses that kind of phraseology has gone some distance towards turning himself into a machine. The appropriate noises are coming out of his larynx, but his brain is not involved as it would be if he were choosing his words for himself. If the speech he is making is one that he is accustomed to make over and over again, he may be almost unconscious of what he is saying, as one is when one utters the responses in church. And this reduced state of consciousness, if not indispensable, is at any rate favourable to political conformity. (G. Orwell, 'Politics and the English language,' pp. 166–7.)

This unawareness of the relationship between word and meaning leads, in Orwell's view, to an acceptance of political language which is cynically dishonest:

In our time, political speech and writing are largely the defence of the indefensible. Things like the continuance of British rule in India, the Russian purges and deportations, the dropping of the atom bombs on Japan, can indeed be defended, but only by arguments which are too brutal for most people to face, and which do not square with the professed aims of political parties. Thus political language has to consist largely of euphemism, question-begging and sheer cloudy vagueness. Defenceless villages are bombarded from the air, the inhabitants driven out into the countryside, the cattle machine-gunned, the huts set on fire with incendiary bullets: this is called 'pacification'. Millions of peasants are robbed of their farms and sent trudging along the roads with no more than they can carry: this is called 'transfer of population' or 'rectification of frontiers'. People are imprisoned for years without trial, or shot in the back of the neck or sent to die of scurvy in Arctic lumber camps: this is called 'elimination of unreliable elements'. Such phraseology is needed if one wants to name things without calling up mental pictures of them. (G. Orwell, 'Politics and the English language,' p. 166.)

What I am suggesting is that all language, not just political uses, constantly drifts towards the affirmation of fixed, and usually prejudicial, categories. Criticism, and literature itself, have roles in combating this tendency.

The conditions I have described, all too briefly, create a need for a critical activity associated with the use of language in society. In summary: though language creates knowledge, aids thought, and simplifies perception, this gift has two drawbacks: the categories encoded in language may become fossilized and unconscious; and they may be slanted towards the needs of officialdom and politicians, rather than the needs of the individual person. The task of linguistic criticism is to make as many language-users as possible aware of, and resistant to, these conditions. That sounds negative: and indeed 'criticism' is often regarded as a debunking activity, exposing works and writings as sham and denouncing them. Writers have long complained about the fault-finding of 'carping critics', and there is an image of the critic as totally unconstructive and pettily envious. But the basic motivation for practising criticism is *not* negativity, but a healthily sceptical inquisitiveness. Critics are interested in the conditions of, and the restrictions on, knowledge in their society; in the ways that meanings come about; in the implications of systems of meanings for members of their society; and, therefore, in the relativity and potential creativity of their *own* knowledge.

Criticism is not just judgement, the claim that some work is good or bad. However, the serious critic knows that questions of value are involved—moral and social questions—in so far as the works and meanings s/he explores have emerged from the interplay of individual and society.

Criticism may engage with any of the products of a society which have meaning, and which play a role within the processes or practices by which the society is regulated. This excludes almost no topic one could think of! We are familiar with criticism of books, plays, films, paintings, architecture, and other 'art forms'. Once it is understood that criticism is not exclusively concerned with making judgements on 'aesthetic values', then extending the idea and practice of criticism to objects and activities other than 'works of art' becomes natural. The writings of the French semiotician, Roland Barthes, illustrate this extension admirably. He sees society as a network of codes speaking through all kinds of media, and he interprets and comments upon the significance of cultural objects articulated in the codes: on the meanings of fashions in clothing, cars, popular entertainment, restaurant food, wrestling, strip-tease, and so on. The moral of his analyses is that even the most commonplace objects and activities have, besides their practical functions, symbolic meanings. In fact, the cultural meanings are arguably more important than the practical purposes of objects. We tend to rationalize our possessions and actions in terms of their usefulness, and so do not perceive their primarily symbolic values. Who needs (say) an electric carving knife? It will not do anything that an ordinary knife cannot do. 'Perfect for cutting light sponge cakes—no downward pressure is needed, so you don't crush the cake.' But here the value is to draw attention to the excellence of the cake; the cutting of the cake could be performed by other implements. Civilized man needs an electric carving knife to demonstrate his control over nature, carrying the technology of cooking and eating to an extreme and highly conspicuous level. Man (The Male) needs an electric carving knife to enhance his potency and skill with tools as he dismembers the Sunday chicken, ritually demonstrating to 'his family' his mechanized triumph over the lower animals, as he carves the bird on ritual occasions.

This sort of criticism may at first be dismissed as frivolous, but its seriousness and plausibility increase as analysis penetrates into the *systems* of meanings which constitute a culture. Anthropologists have shown that the conventions and technology of cooking and eating are extremely significant social practices. The electric carving knife is an absurd object, but the example is far from trivial. Cultural criticism displays the absurdity of the object (by defamiliarizing it) and the seriousness of the meanings it expresses. The object is one expression of a part of an entire system of unconscious ideas by which human beings in western industrialized societies arrange their relationships with nature (farming, cooking) and with one another (marriage, the family). Criticism dehabitualizes our perception of the object by pointing out that it is *not* 'just a knife' but an artificial expression of an artificial meaning—which has been legitimated and commercially exploited.

Returning to linguistic symbolization and linguistic criticism, we can now define the role of the latter. Criticism is conscious analysis of the relationship between the signs—words, phrases, etc.—which people produce, and the meanings they communicate. Analysis of this relationship is necessarily an exploration of the social origins of meanings and the social purposes of spoken and written language. Criticism is not a self-justifying or self-contained pursuit, nor is it disinterested. It is a form of social *practice*. I try to teach my students how to practise criticism so that they become better equipped to resist habitualization and to question the structure of the society which benefits from its members' lack of critical consciousness. This practice is also *reflexive*: in so far as the critic is a member of the society whose codes s/he criticizes, s/he uses those same codes, and her/his analysis of them is a critical reflection on her/his own habits of perception and communication.

Linguistic criticism may be practised on any use of language. It neither needs nor offers any special definition of 'literature'. In fact, there are two areas of linguistic usage which are priorities for critical analysis and which would normally be regarded as definitely non-literary. One is public, official, language: the statements of governments, administrators, legal officials, business organizations, purveyors of news, as expressed in communiqués, contracts, company reports, newspapers, etc. Such texts merit critical scrutiny because of their official origins, their direct role in shaping attitudes and meanings within a community, and the passive way in which people necessarily consume them—there is no channel through which a person can respond directly to the driving licence reminder or daily newspaper which comes through his letter box. The second area is personal discourse, talk formal and informal among individuals. What we say to other people, and how we say it, needs to be subjected to critical reflection because personal discourse so easily becomes unconscious and habitualized, and because it is no freer of ideology than public language (indeed, we saw that conversation is peculiarly *un*critical). The particular aim of linguistic criticism in the first case is demystification, demonstration of the practices by which language is used to present partial and slanted concepts as if they were innocent and natural. In the second, criticism aims at self-examination, and alertness to the permeation of our own discourse by social values which we might, on reflection, wish to eradicate or resist. In other books, critical linguists have analysed in detail some examples of real language in these two categories, and discussed the implications of the processes which were uncovered. The 'non-literary' analyses performed elsewhere may be seen as both continuous with and complementary to the discussions of literary texts in the present book.

In the following chapter I will consider a set of literary styles, and an aesthetic theory, which claim that literature is itself a technique of criticism: that literary texts use deliberate devices for defamiliarization. I will argue that defamiliarizing techniques are simply an extreme case of techniques of language which are available to all practitioners of language and which are found outside overtly experimental or shocking texts. I will also show that defamiliarization, though initially startling or amusing, and perhaps revelatory, is itself subject to convention and habit. Thus literary styles, becoming stale, regularly create a need for revolution and replacement (hence the peculiarly important positions of writers like Milton, Wordsworth, and T. S. Eliot), and the revision of conventions; the obscuring of old conventions in the mists of history justifies an activity of critical interpretation to keep the best of them alive and significant for contemporary readers. This is the major justification for the application of linguistic criticism to literary texts. (Another justification, in my view, is that literary texts also tend to become official texts, so there is to some extent the same motive for criticism as I proposed for the critical analysis of non-literary public discourse.)

References and Suggestions for Further Reading

Noam Chomsky's 'ideal speaker-hearer' and his equally idealized 'linguistic competence' can be found throughout his earlier writings, e.g. *Aspects of the Theory of Syntax* (Cambridge, Mass.: MIT Press, 1965). In fact, a person's linguistic knowledge is much more diversified than Chomsky allows, as will emerge in Chapters 10 and 12.

The basic sources for my treatment of habitualization are Victor Shklovsky (quoted and discussed more fully in Chapter 4), Benjamin Lee Whorf and George Orwell. See V. Shklovsky, 'Art as technique' [1917] in L. T. Lemon and M. J. Reis, *Russian Formalist Criticism* (Lincoln, Neb.: University of Nebraska Press, 1965), pp. 5–24; B. L. Whorf, ed. J. B. Carroll, *Language, Thought and Reality* (Cambridge, Mass.: MIT Press, 1956); G. Orwell, 'Politics and the English language' [1946] in S. Orwell and I. Angus, eds., *The Collected Essays, Journalism and Letters of George Orwell*, vol. 4 (Harmondsworth: Penguin, 1970), pp. 156–70. Orwell's views on language are discussed in R. Fowler, *The Language of George Orwell* (London: Macmillan, 1995), ch. 3. See also S. Chase, *The Tyranny of Words* (New York: Harcourt, Brace & World, 1938); G. Lakoff and M. Johnson, *Metaphors We Live By* (Chicago: University of Chicago Press, 1980).

Halliday's comment on Whorf, quoted on p. 46 above, is from 'Linguistic function and literary style', in S. Chatman, ed., *Literary Style: A Symposium* (New York and London: Oxford University Press, 1971), p. 333.

On legitimation, language as a social practice, ideology as belief system, the critical analysis of official language, and related issues, see R. Fowler, R. Hodge, G. Kress and T. Trew, *Language and Control* (London: Routledge & Kegan Paul, 1979); R. Hodge and G. Kress, *Language as Ideology* (London: Routledge, 2nd edn., 1993). See also N. Fairclough, *Language and Power* (London: Longman, 1989); N. Fairclough, *Discourse and Social Change* (Oxford: Polity Press, 1992); N. Fairclough, *Critical Discourse Analysis* (London: Longman, 1995). Supporting political theory on ideology and legitimation for the above books and the opening pages of the present chapter may be found in L. Althusser, 'Ideology and ideological state apparatuses', in *Lenin and Philosophy*, trans. B. Brewster (London: New Left Books, 1971), pp. 121–73. For the term 'ideology' in political theory, see J. Plamenatz, *Ideology* (London: Macmillan, 1970).

Semiotics or semiology is the theory and description of the meanings and uses of signs, both linguistic and non-linguistic, within human society. Its founder was the Swiss linguist Ferdinand de Saussure, whose ideas are expounded and developed in Barthes's *Elements of Semiology*, trans. A. Lavers and C. Smith (London: Jonathan Cape, 1967). See also his popular book *Mythologies*, trans. A. Lavers (London: Jonathan Cape, 1972), for illustrative analyses which are 'critical' in the sense intended in the present chapter. A large but readable and stimulating textbook on the subject is Umberto Eco, *A Theory of Semiotics* (London: Macmillan, 1977). Further references and introductory books are cited at the end of Chapter 1.

I have found the introduction and texts in P. Connerton, ed., *Critical Sociology* (Harmondsworth: Penguin, 1976) very helpful in arriving at the definition of criticism used in this chapter.

Introductions to relevant poststructuralist and deconstructionist ideas are C. Belsey, *Critical Practice* (London: Methuen, 1980); C. Norris, *Deconstruction* (London: Methuen, 1982).

CHAPTER FOUR

Linguistic Practice: Defamiliarization

Language is one of the most important areas of knowledge that human beings possess, since, as we have seen, it is a powerful influence on the way people perceive and adjust to the world outside them. This knowledge has positive and negative aspects: 'Language is not only a key. It can also be a fetter,' wrote Sapir.

Language is not just knowledge; it is also a skill, a *practice*. The practical workings of language can be seen in face-to-face conversation: people talking to one another are performing real actions through speech (asking questions, giving commands, asserting claims of truth, etc.), they are affirming and negotiating status and relationship. Even the basic process of passing meanings from one brain to another is not just an automatic, untroubled channelling of information from A to B, but a process of determining and agreeing upon meanings. Although our common code provides you and me with the core meanings of the words 'food', 'beauty', 'progress', our life experiences have been different, so we have to establish by implicit negotiation what each of us intends when a word is used, and to what extent our usages are divergent or compatible.

The linguistic activities—person-management through language—which are visible in communication between individuals reproduce processes occurring at levels of broader social organization. Institutional utterances such as advertising, news reporting, government statements, company reports, and the like are obviously linguistic acts. They are practices which intervene in social and economic organization, affecting the positions and privileges of individuals and social groups.

The usual tendency of these practices (both personal and institutional) is towards stability, consolidation of socially legitimated areas of knowledge, modes of control and types of relationships. The processes tend to stabilize codes and habitualize perception; thought is guided along existing ruts. I have pointed out the detrimental consequences of this situation in the previous chapter. The question now to be asked is whether there are linguistic practices which resist these tendencies: activities in language which promote exploration, consciousness, change, and creativity, rather than stagnation and repression. The fact that there are creative linguistic practices is my motive for writing this book, and at this point the argument can take an optimistic turn.

From my point of view, any activity is creative which is capable, under the right conditions of production and reception, of reanalysing people's theory of the way the world works. It is a precondition for this kind of creativity that whoever initiates it should expose the artificiality of a prior analysis that is being superseded. Often this questioning of existing conventions is the basic creative act that is being performed: some ideology is convincingly shown to be fallacious or at least problematic. In this case the creative thinker is operating like the critic, revealing a problem which s/he declines to solve, demystifying perception without offering the potentially illusory closure of a replacement theory. In linguistic terms, the processes involve *un*coding—disestablishing the received tie between a sign and a cultural unit—and optionally *re*coding—tying a newly invented concept to a sign and so establishing its validity. The ultimate process in linguistic creativity would be the formation of a whole new code, a system of new linguistic arrangements encoding a whole new area of knowledge. Such global recoding in literary language, usually the language of a particular genre, has been the aim of those writers and critics who have sought to effect stylistic revolutions, to thoroughly change the way literature is articulated. Wordsworth's plea in the 'Preface to *Lyrical Ballads*' (1800) to replace the 'gaudy and inane phraseology' of poetry by 'the language of men' is a particularly clear example; similarly, the goals of the founders of the Imagist movement in early twentieth century poetry; or the actual revolutions in the words and thoughts of literature achieved by, say, Milton in the seventeenth century, Joyce in *Ulysses* in the twentieth.

The revolutionary or revelatory effects sought can be produced by the use of a vast range of very diverse linguistic techniques: metaphor, clashes of style, parody, breaking of syntactic rules, extra syntactic patterning, use of an unusual vocabulary, invention of new words, etc. They may be found in texts of widely differing cultural status, from scientific articles to jokes to newspapers to political speeches. Creativity in language is not limited to 'literary' texts. However, 'art' (including 'literature') has, in the modern period, been given a privileged role in combating the dulling familiarity of conventional codes. The theory of habitualization and defamiliarization has been placed at the centre of their justification of art by many of art's apologists, and in the verbal, visual, and musical arts, pronounced techniques of defamiliarization have been developed by such technical innovators as Apollinaire, Magritte, and Schönberg. Here is a very famous defence of art in these terms by the Russian critic Viktor Shklovsky:

If we start to examine the general laws of perception, we see that as perception becomes habitual, it becomes automatic . . .

We apprehend objects only as shapes with imprecise extensions; we do not see them in their entirety but rather recognize them by their main characteristics. We see the object as though it were enveloped in a sack. We know what it is by its configuration, but we see only its silhouette. The object, perceived thus in the manner of prose perception, fades and does not leave even a first impression; ultimately even the essence of what it was is forgotten . . .

And so life is reckoned as nothing. Habitualization devours works, clothes, furniture, one's wife, and the fear of war . . . And art exists that one may recover the sensation of life; it exists to make one feel things, to make the stone *stony*. The purpose of art is to impart the sensation of things as they are perceived and not as they are known. The technique of art is to make objects 'unfamiliar', to make forms difficult, to increase the difficulty and length of perception because the process of perception is an aesthetic end in itself and must be prolonged. *Art is a way of experiencing the artfulness of an object; the object is not important* [Shklovsky's emphasis]. ('Art as technique,' pp. 11, 12.)

I must say straight away that I disagree with some of these assertions—particularly the notion of 'an aesthetic end in itself' and the associated dismissal of 'the object' as 'not important'.

These claims are part of an aestheticism and formalism in Shklovsky's thought, a refusal to allow literary works any connection with social and historical process for which Shklovsky was attacked by Trotsky among others. However, it is clear that Shklovsky's defence of 'art' is founded on a conception of the psychology (though not the sociology) of knowledge and perception very similar to the one I have sketched. I have acknowledged this affinity by adopting his term 'habitualization'. In what follows I must rephrase Shklovsky's theory in terms which will be compatible with my own ideas; I believe this is fair since the foundation is the same, even if my aims and my social theory differ sharply from Shklovsky's.

Art, for Shklovsky, is characterized by the use of a range of *techniques* or *devices* which promote *defamiliarization* (Russian *ostraneniye*, 'making strange'). When we speak or listen or write or read according to the normal lazy conventions of communication—his 'prose perception'—symbols are transparent, automatic, simplified. Accepting as natural a coding which is in fact arbitrary, we become acquiescent, uncritical, we acknowledge meanings without examining them. Similarly we recognize our friends without really seeing them. Defamiliarization is the use of some strategy to force us to look, to be critical. If the husband emerges from the bathroom one morning without his beard, the wife is provoked to enquire: is that the same man, is it still the category 'my husband'? This is a nice question. The 'sensible' answer (common sense, ideology) is 'of course it is; it's just John without his beard', and the 'sensible' action is to accustom herself to his new appearance so that he quickly becomes the same man. But *is* the man who transformed himself with the razor the same man? After all, he has performed the action of transforming himself. A successful technique of defamiliarization would keep that doubting question alive for as long as possible, to resist the wife's sensible re-habitualization of John as 'the same man', 'my husband'.

The basic principle of linguistic defamiliarization is well captured by another prominent Russian Formalist, Boris Tomashevsky: 'The old and habitual must be spoken of as if it were new and unusual. One must speak of the ordinary as if it were unfamiliar' ('Thematics,' p. 85). There are innumerable linguistic techniques for achieving this unsettling of the relationship between a sign and its concept, this questioning of the naturalness of a coded concept. A pointedly naïve perspective, for example, can be created by withholding the usual term for something that is being described, pretending that the thing is *not* coded in the speaker's mind (cf. the discussion of Benjy in Faulkner's *The Sound and the Fury*, Chapter 9, pp. 168–9 below); this might be called *undercoding*, expressed by *underlexicalization*. One of Shklovsky's examples, from Tolstoy, describes the stage and actors in a theatre in words that suggest the perspective of someone who has not experienced a theatre before, and who does not know what is going on. The conventions gradually dawn on him, and what dawns on us is the absurd artifice of the theatrical conventions which we had accepted as normal:

The middle of the stage consisted of flat boards; by the sides stood painted pictures representing trees, and at the back a linen cloth was stretched down to the floor boards. Maidens in red bodices and white skirts sat on the middle of the stage. One, very fat, in a white silk dress, sat apart on a narrow bench to which a green pasteboard box was glued from behind. They were all singing something. When they had finished, the maiden in white approached the prompter's box. A man in silk with tight-fitting pants on his fat legs approached her with a plume and began to sing and spread his arms in dismay. The man in the tight pants finished his song alone; then the girl sang. After that both remained silent as the music resounded; and the man, obviously waiting to begin singing his part with her again, began to run his fingers over the hand of the girl in the white dress. They finished their song together, and everyone in the theater began to clap and shout. But the men and women on stage, who represented lovers, started to bow, smiling and raising their hands. (From *War and Peace*, quoted in 'Art as technique,' p. 16.)

Swift uses this technique of uncoding by undercoding repeatedly in *Gulliver's Travels*, with devastating irony. Here is Gulliver's first sight of the Yahoos:

At last I beheld several Animals in a Field, and one or two of the same Kind sitting in Trees. Their Shape was very singular, and deformed, which a little discomposed me, so that I lay down behind a Thicket to

observe them better. Some of them coming forward near the Place where
I lay, gave me an Opportunity of distinctly marking their Form. Their
Heads and Breasts were covered with a thick Hair, some frizzled and
others lank; they had Beards like Goats, and a long Ridge of Hair down
their Backs, and the fore Parts of their Legs and Feet; but the rest of
their Bodies were bare, so that I might see their Skins, which were of a
brown Buff Colour. They had no Tails, nor any Hair at all on their
Buttocks, except about the *Anus*; which, I presume Nature has placed
there to defend them as they sat on the Ground; for this Posture they
used, as well as lying down, and often stood on their hind Feet. They
climbed high Trees, as nimbly as a Squirrel, for they had strong extended
Claws before and behind, terminating in sharp Points, and hooked.
They would often spring, and bound, and leap with prodigious Agility.
The Females were not so large as the Males; they had long lank Hair on
their Heads, and only a Sort of Down on the rest of their Bodies, except
about the *Anus*, and *Pudenda*. Their Dugs hung between their fore Feet,
and often reached almost to the Ground as they walked. The Hair of
both Sexes was of several Colours, brown, red, black and yellow. Upon
the whole, I never beheld in all my Travels so disagreeable an Animal,
or one against which I naturally conceived so strong an Antipathy.
(Jonathan Swift, *Gulliver's Travels*, p. 193.)

The Yahoos are of course human beings kept as beasts of burden
by the Houyhnhnms (who are horses). Gulliver first codes them
as 'animals', and describes them in meticulous detail as if they
were a species of animal never before observed: 'Their Shape was
very singular.' What follows is a very straight and literal description in phrases which, we slowly realize, are entirely and accurately applicable to human beings (at least, such human beings as
have been exposed to the elements, and do not trim their nails).
Gulliver makes clear his disgust, and elicits ours. What he and
we are inspecting, with loathing, are in fact human beings, but
our perception has been defamiliarized: they are not *labelled*
human beings, so we fail to make the usual allowances. This is
what people are really like (says Swift) if you see them without
preconceptions, from an estranged viewpoint unfiltered by the
forgiving distortions of 'common sense' and the common terms
of ordinary language.

A comic passage from Joyce's *Ulysses* develops this technique of extremely literal and mechanical description but

adds a historically distanced style. A modest twentieth-century meal of stout and sardines is depicted with the wide-eyed astonishment of a time-traveller from the fourteenth century:

And in the castle was set a board that was of the birchwood of Finlandy and it was upheld by four dwarfmen of that country but they durst not move for enchantment. And on this board were frightful swords and knives that are made in a great cavern by swinking demons out of white flames that they fix in the horns of buffalos and stags that there abound marvellously. And there were vessels that are wrought by magic of Mahound out of seasand and the air by a warlock with his breath that he blares into them like to bubbles. And full fair cheer and rich was on the board that no wight could devise a fuller ne richer. And there was a vat of silver that was moved by craft to open in the which lay strange fishes withouten heads though misbelieving men nie that this be possible thing without they see it natheless they are so. And these fishes lie in an oily water brought there from Portugal land because of the fatness that therein is like to the juices of the olive press. And also it was marvel to see in that castle how by magic they make a compost out of fecund wheat kidneys out of Chaldee that by aid of certain angry spirits that they do into it swells up wondrously like to a vast mountain. And they teach the serpents there to entwine themselves up on long sticks out of the ground and of the scales of these serpents they brew out a brewage like to mead. (James Joyce, *Ulysses*, pp. 369–70.)

The relevance of these examples to Shklovsky's theory should be clear. In all three, perception of the object of description is delayed: in the first and second cases, by withholding the name of the object, in the third, additionally, by parody of medieval English prose, using archaic syntax and a Middle English vocabulary which depicts the struggle of an alien mind to understand such mundane things as a sardine tin and a Guinness glass. We experience the described objects as strange, elaborate, artificial rather than familiar, simple, natural. All three—and the second particularly, because of its provocative subject—encourage us to reflect on the artificiality, the constructedness, of our habitual perceptions. The passages make their impact by deliberate linguistic techniques which disturb relationships between signs and meanings; constructing and encoding new meanings.

Craig Raine published in 1979 an amusing poem which could almost be an exercise on the poetic defamiliarization of the domestic and the routine:

A Martian Sends a Postcard Home

Caxtons are mechanical birds with many wings
and some are treasured for their markings—

they cause the eyes to melt
or the body to shriek without pain.

I have never seen one fly, but
sometimes they perch on the hand.

Mist is when the sky is tired of flight
and rests its soft machine on ground:

then the world is dim and bookish
like engravings under tissue paper.

Rain is when the earth is television.
It has the property of making colours darker.

Model T is a room with the lock inside—
a key is turned to free the world

for movement, so quick there is a film
to watch for anything missed.

But time is tied to the wrist
or kept in a box, ticking with impatience.

In homes, a haunted apparatus sleeps,
that snores when you pick it up.

If the ghost cries, they carry it
to their lips and soothe it to sleep

with sounds. And yet, they wake it up
deliberately, by tickling with a finger.

Only the young are allowed to suffer
openly. Adults go to a punishment room

with water but nothing to eat.
They lock the door and suffer the noises

alone. No one is exempt
and everyone's pain has a different smell.

At night, when all the colours die,
they hide in pairs

and read about themselves—
in colour, with their eyelids shut.

The basic form of the poem is a series of riddles (Caxtons = books, Model T = car, haunted apparatus = telephone, punishment room = WC, and so on). All of the things that the Martian writes home about are very mundane domestic objects or basic human processes: things that we take for granted and understand totally and implicitly, very much the kinds of things that Shklovsky says are subject to habitualization, routine perception without exact knowledge. For the human reader, the fun is not simply solving each riddle, but working out the reasoning and analogies by which the Martian arrives at, and by which he justifies, his 'misconstrual'. The first puzzle, for instance, contains many clues: books are 'Caxtons', named after the pioneer of printing; they are birds because their leaves can flutter like wings, and because the shape of an open book in the hand is like the mark ∿ which represents a bird in the sky in a child's drawing; illuminated books are treasured, and vividly marked birds are admired; books can cause their readers to cry and to laugh with pleasure, though the Martian sees dissolving eyes and hears convulsive shrieks; books do not indeed fly, nor do they literally perch, but in this third stanza they are viewed as a kind of pet being handled. There is so much detail in this representation of a person reading a book, and it is so miscellaneous, scattering loose ends in all directions, that even the reader who gets the answer quickly is detained by the detail, and has to pause to work out the new perspectives on books, reading, and the conventions of tears and laughter.

A fuller analysis than there is space for here would not only work out each part of the representation of human life, but study the variety of technique. The first section is the most puzzling, because the Martian 'gets it wrong', and sows confusion ('Model T' works in a similar way, but by that stage the puzzles are easier to solve). 'Mist' and 'rain', however, are understood, and simply revisualized metaphorically. The telephone is neatly presented as both ghost and baby, approximating a human understanding of the prototypes of both. Like the wrist-watch, the phone is animated. The misconstrual of the lavatory as 'punishment room' highlights a system of taboos about excretion and social misdemeanour: here the Martian is like a budding anthropologist who *almost* puts his finger on a major anxiety of Western culture, and the defamiliarization clearly invites us to think about our habits.

My next example is a poem where defamiliarization is not the guiding principle of a whole poem, repeated over and over using various techniques as in the 'Martian', but is sparked at one climactic point. The example shows that startling reorientations of meaning can be achieved in language using very simple devices. In the last stanza of 'The Right of Way' (1923), William Carlos Williams constructs a brilliant *trompe-l'œil*. These are the final three verses of the 28-line poem:

> Why bother where I went?
> for I went spinning on the
>
> four wheels of my car
> along the wet road until
>
> I saw a girl with one leg
> over the rail of a balcony

Like the car driver who when he is moving glimpses an object from one position then from another, so that the object changes, the reader first assumes that the penultimate line refers to an amputee, and then as he shifts his attention to the last line is forced to reinterpret completely, restoring the leg. The switch from one interpretation to the other is striking partly because it so neatly mimes a visual process appropriate to the narrative of the poem. Partly also because the connotations of the two interpretations are contradictory: the penultimate line by itself suggests pathos, violence, the grotesque, whereas the complete girl on the balcony implies relaxation and confidence. Also the word 'until', coming after a string of insignificant impressions, leads to an expectation of climax: this is what it's all about, the pathos and cruelty of humanity—a climax instantly cancelled when the girl turns out not to be mutilated but just an ordinary person like the figures in the street presented earlier in the poem.

My remarks do not apply to just a first reading. The amputee does not go away even after she has been completed by the final line. The enduring effect is like that of one of those line-drawings of a cube which can be seen either as projecting out from the page towards the viewer or as receding away (a Nekker Cube). The drawing switches from one representation to the other unpredictably; either can be seen, but not both together; but while one representation of the cube is being viewed, the possibility of the other can be held in mind. A similar visual ambiguity has been demonstrated with other figures, for example the famous 'duck/rabbit'. The technique is extensively practised by the fantastic painter Salvador Dali (for example, 'Slave Market with the Apparition of the Invisible Bust of Voltaire', 1940). The effect of such ambiguities is unsettling as well as witty; apprehending one of the two meanings, the reader is always conscious that the cube might switch and impose the second meaning on his attention. The difficulty of perception here is caused by the unstable ambiguity of the sign. This is a very radical kind of defamiliarization which, by insisting that a sign is not tied to *one* meaning, constitutes a critique of the conventionality of signs.

The technique by which William Carlos Williams achieves this particular act of defamiliarization is very simple in its design, quite complicated in its execution. In verse, the sequence of words and phrases can be divided up in two ways. There are the normal syntactic boundaries: between words:

> my / car

between phrases:

> on the four wheels / of my car

between clauses:

> for I went spinning on the four wheels of my car along the wet road / until I saw a girl with one leg over the rail of a balcony

between sentences:

> Why bother where I went? / for I went *etc.*

These syntactic divisions have an intuitive psychological reality for speakers of the language, and are felt to divide up the flow of words into units of meaning. There is a second set of segmentations in verse, the line-divisions. These may or may not coincide with major syntactic divisions. Now if the last word in a line *could* be the last word of a syntactic unit, the line-ending encourages the reader to assume that the syntax *does* end there. In our extract, this is impossible with 'the' and 'until', but quite plausible with 'car' and 'leg'. We are bound to try out the hypothesis that 'leg' marks the completion of a unit of meaning; the hypothesis is disconfirmed by what follows, but the trace of it never disappears. In psycholinguistics, this is called the 'garden path effect'.

Williams did not invent this device of the ambiguous line-ending: it is conventional—Empson in *Seven Types of Ambiguity* has examples from Shakespeare. The question arises how the convention works so powerfully and freshly here, how it avoids the staleness of an old conjuring trick. (All creative practice has this precarious relationship with convention: the twin dangers are diminishing returns and obviousness of technique, both products of the over-use of some conventional technique. The dangers are particularly acute for 'modernist' practitioners like Williams, Dali, Brecht, Apollinaire, Satie, Weill, who systematically exploit and draw attention to conventions of illusion.) To answer the question properly would demand a detailed analysis of the whole poem, which is not possible here, but I can indicate some of the elements briefly.

One part of the answer is that the semantic unit 'I saw a girl with one leg' is *motivated*—it is a reasonable climax in terms of the poem's thematic and narrative structure. The speaker in the poem has been driving along catching sight of some mundane, morally unremarkable scenes; he and we are due for a shock. But the main cause of the success of this device is more strictly linguistic. For various metrical reasons (including the shortness of the lines, the presence of one-syllable words at the ends of many lines, the typographical format which frames the text with areas of blank page), the line-boundaries are either very salient or potentially so. This means that they can readily be used to 'punctuate' the sentence-structure—as happens in the penultimate line. Though the metre tends towards interruption at regular brief intervals, the syntax favours long, cumulative sentences. The syntax is what linguists call *right-branching:* phrases and clauses are added to the right of the main clause one after the other, each dependent on the one immediately before:

> for I went spinning
>> on the four wheels
>>> of my car
>>>> along the wet road
>> until I saw a girl
>>> with one leg
>>>> over the rail
>>>> of a balcony

The syntax carries the reader's attention forward in a large sweep broader than the short lines. Although the constituent phrases are roughly the same length as the material lines, very few of them coincide with the lines, as comparison of the above informal diagram with the text of the poem will show. Not only does Williams avoid matching line-ends and phrase-ends; he also produces a sort of 'negative correlation' by ending some lines with words that demand syntactic continuation, emphasizing forward movement in the reader's attention: 'on the/', 'until/'. There is a background of enjambment (run-on lines) against which any potential coincidence of line-break and syntactic boundary is strongly foregrounded. A related structural feature is the scarcity of lines which are syntactically and semantically complete; exceptionally, 'I saw a girl with one leg' is a complete clause, and its completeness, reinforced by the line-break, claims the reader's notice.

So Williams puts together basically dissimilar and divergent metrical and syntactic patterns, resists coincidence of boundaries so that when they ultimately do appear to converge, the sense of delayed completion is particularly strong. Then, such is the fluidity of the language of this poem that the climax is immediately undone by the final two phrases, which change the reader's over-confident syntactic analysis of the penultimate line. But this analysis—'a girl with one leg'—can never be finally erased: it is validated partly by the potential end-stopping, and also by a property of the right-branching syntax which dominates the poem. In right-branching syntax, modifying phrases are added as 'extras' on the end (the right), and can be removed without damaging the wholeness of what precedes (you can test this by going back to the diagram and stripping away phrases starting from the bottom right). It is as if the added phrases are not really necessary . . . so perhaps 'I saw a girl with one leg' is 'really' complete after all. We can never be sure. The poem is distinguished by the openness of interpretation, the witty anti-dogmatism, which its formal structure encourages.

I want now to return briefly to the couplet by Pope to which only a provisional and informal response was given at the beginning of Chapter 2:

> Not louder Shrieks to pitying Heav'n are cast,
> When Husbands or when Lap-dogs breathe their last.

A social judgement is passed here, an indictment of fashionable women who value their lapdogs as much as they do their husbands, and, by implication, devalue their husbands by giving the same degree of affection to people, who ought to be greatly loved, and pets, which merit less attachment. Readers familiar with *The Rape of the Lock* will know that this judgement is only part of a general attack on the levelling of values—sexual, religious, material, political—the degrading of people, relationships, and standards by taking them down to the lowest level, equating them with trivial material possessions—dogs, jewellery, ornaments. Compare:

> Whether the Nymph shall break Diana's Law,
> Or some frail China Jar receive a Flaw,
> Or stain her Honour, or her new Brocade,
> Forget her Pray'rs, or miss a Masquerade,
> Or lose her Heart, or Necklace, at a Ball;
> Or whether Heav'n has doom'd that Shock must fall.

Or:

> Here Thou, Great Anna! whom three Realms obey,
> Dost sometimes Counsel take—and sometimes Tea.

We are not concerned here with the satirical theme of the poem. The point is that a consistent set of propositions are being implied here, which are not the statements affirmed by the normal linear syntax of the poem: indeed, the implications made between the lines are at odds with the assertions made by the actual sentences. As in 'The Right of Way', the effect is achieved by extra, metrical, operations upon language which are superimposed upon the underlying prose syntax. (Of course, the effects are quite different in the two poems, and the metrical devices are absolutely different, but the overall technical principle is the same.) In the case of Pope, the recoding is done by means of his dominant technique of creating equivalent metrical positions. Rhyming words, or in these examples parallel nouns in equivalent places in the first and second halves of lines, take on *semantic* relationships. The words 'Husbands' and 'Lap-dogs' are both two-syllable words with the same stress pattern; both appear after the lightly stressed 'when'. Their phonetic equivalence (similarity of sound and metrical placing) suggests semantic equivalence (the social concept 'husband' has the same value as the social concept 'lapdog'). Similarly, 'prayers' = 'masquerade', 'counsel' = 'tea', etc. (Techniques of equivalence through extra patterning will be discussed further in Chapter 6.)

Now I want to make a further observation which would not emerge if we took the husbands/lapdogs example just by itself. Pope does not create his insight into degrading matrons of the 1700s autonomously within this particular couplet. The technique of language which is used to express this insight—the sensitization of certain metrical positions so that they establish new equivalences and contrasts of meaning—is a stylistic code which is built up in the poem as a whole, Pope's verse as a whole, and Pope's predecessors in the heroic couplet verse form. This stylistic code is an extra over and above the regular code of the language; and it is a convention. Now a reader cannot get the illumination expressed by the husbands/lapdogs line unless he knows this code. In the same way, readers need to have learned something of the conventional significances of enjambment and end-stopping in order to appreciate the full force of the visual ambiguity in the Williams poem.

We can see that there is a paradoxical process working here. Defamiliarization, or creation of meaning, is achieved by using a stylistic code to criticize the limitations of the existing linguistic code. But, because the technique of metrical balance which performs the critique is itself a code, a set of repeatable conventions, it is subject to the law of diminishing returns, and must decay into a meaningless habit through a drift from convention to conformism. And this is exactly what happened to the various conventional techniques of Augustan verse as the eighteenth century progressed. Through repeated use they became meaningless. For instance, one technique was the frequent use of adjectives to qualify the meanings of nouns, so that it became unusual to use a noun without specifying its meaning further. In principle, this is an excellent critical practice, leading to precision and resisting acceptance of the noun as an unanalysed category. In practice, repetition led to cliché and vacuousness. A poem like 'Ode' by Mark Akenside (1721–70) will illustrate the depths to which the technique sank. The first two stanzas go:

> On yonder verdant hillock laid,
> Where oaks and elms, a friendly shade,
>   O'erlook the falling stream,
> O master of the Latin lyre,
> Awhile with thee I will retire,
>   From summer's noontide beam.
>
> And, lo, within my lonely bower,
> The industrious bee from many a flower
>   Collects her balmy dews:
> 'For me', she sings, 'the gems are born,
> For me their silken robe adorn,
>   Their fragrant breath diffuse.'

The adjective + noun phrases in the remaining six stanzas are as follows:

sweet murmurer, rude storm, hospitable scene, gladsome toils, ambrosial spoils, lowly, silvan scenes, flowery greens, fond ambition, boding raven, unhallowed haunts, horrid glooms, barren waste, lurking strength, noxious thing, insipid nightshade, baneful juice, sordid sting, vernal blooms, blameless wealth, generous task, double boon.

'Ambrosial spoils' (nectar) is a dead metaphorical cliché like the notorious 'finny tribes' (fish), symbol of what went wrong with eighteenth-century poetic diction. Most of these phrases are not of that kind, though. They are, simply, redundant and vacuous: the adjective contributes no meaning, for all bees are industrious, all blooms are vernal, all storms rude, and so on. The phrase 'barren waste' (i.e. desert, waste land) is typical: since all wastes are by definition barren, it adds nothing to say that they are barren. The phrase is a tautology, and one feels that the adjective slot has been filled not for semantic precision but out of a mere syntactic habit. What began, in earlier years, as a device for saying something fresh has become a mechanical pattern with no conceptual force.

One task of linguistic criticism would be to study the atrophy of linguistic techniques from creative illumination to automatic and meaningless pattern. The aim of such criticism would not be destructive—though it would be unlikely to convert modern readers to Akenside. There are a number of interesting historical studies to be done on these periods when patterns of language declined into unthinking habit. However, a more important role for criticism is to keep alive what is permanently worthwhile in the creative phases of particular linguistic codes. There is a danger that Pope's techniques can lose their force, not through any inherent defects, but because our response has been contaminated by our knowledge of the later, mechanical, phase of eighteenth-century syntax and versification. It can happen that we are no longer able to see how Pope's poetic technique creatively criticizes the assumptions encoded in the language of his time; and linguistic criticism comes into the picture with the role of resuscitating the original techniques for the jaded and perhaps cynical modern reader.

References and Suggestions for Further Reading

This chapter continues the presentation of habitualization and defamiliarization (which is sometimes called 'deautomatization' or 'dehabitualization'). Further readings in Russian Formalism and the Prague School structuralist studies of literature are relevant. The article by Shklovsky,

'Art as technique', [1917], in L. T. Lemon and M. J. Reis *Russian Formalist Criticism* (Lincoln, Neb.: University of Nebraska Press, 1965), pp. 5–24, will repay further study and reflection. B. Tomashevsky's paper 'Thematics' is reprinted in the same volume, pp. 62–95; the quotation on p. 57 above is at p. 85. See also the Prague School studies by J. Mukařovský and B. Havranek, respectively 'Standard language and poetic language', and 'The functional differentiation of the standard language', both reprinted in P. L. Garvin, ed., *A Prague School Reader on Esthetics, Literary Structure and Style* (Washington: Georgetown University Press, 1964). Mukařovský's seminal paper, which introduces the idea of *foregrounding* (see Chapter 6) is also reprinted in S. B. Chatman and S. R. Levin, eds., *Essays on the Language of Literature* (Boston: Houghton Mifflin, 1967) and in D. C. Freeman, ed., *Linguistics and Literary Style* (New York: Holt, Rinehart & Winston, 1970).

For Trotsky's attack on Shklovsky, see *Leon Trotsky on Literature and Art,* ed. P. N. Siegel (New York: Pathfinder Press, 1977), pp. 32–7.

For commentaries and analysis see T. Bennett, *Formalism and Marxism* (London: Methuen, 1979); C. Pike, ed., *The Futurists, the Formalists, and the Marxist Critique* (London: Ink Links, 1979); V. Erlich, *Russian Formalism: History, doctrine* (The Hague: Mouton, 1965).

For psycholinguistic discussion of the 'garden path effect', see H. H. Clark and E. V. Clark, *Psychology and Language* (New York: Harcourt Brace Jovanovich, 1977), pp. 80–2.

CHAPTER FIVE

How Texts are Made

This chapter, as its title suggests, is about some really basic aspects of linguistic structure: parts of language, and arrangements of language, which are in use in all our experience of language, written or spoken, in any situation from jokey conversation to high epic. The fact that they are ordinary, constant, background features of language does not mean that they are unimportant in literature. Without the basic devices for constructing texts, none of the specialized techniques which are found in much modern literature would be possible.

Let's start with two fundamental units: *sentence* and *text*. I shall be discussing both types of unit, since texts consist of sentences linked together in ways that are described in this and the following chapter. Details of sentence structure will be mentioned throughout the book, but for proper introductions to syntax, readers are referred to the introductory books on linguistics recommended at the end of this chapter. On the whole, other linguists have concentrated on individual sentences, but we are concerned with how sentences work in longer stretches of text. As a concrete example, I can illustrate some of the processes by reference to the opening paragraphs of the novel *Cat's Cradle* (1963) by Kurt Vonnegut, Jr.:

1. Call me Jonah. 2. My parents did, or nearly did. 3. They called me John.

4. Jonah—John—if I had been a Sam, I would have been a Jonah still—not because I have been unlucky for others, but because somebody or something has compelled me to be certain places at certain times, without fail. 5. Conveyances and motives, both conventional and bizarre, have been provided. 6. And, according to plan, at each appointed second, at each appointed place this Jonah was there.

7. Listen:

8. When I was a younger man—two wives ago, 250,000 cigarettes ago, 3,000 quarts of booze ago . . .

9. When I was a much younger man, I began to collect material for a book to be called *The Day the World Ended.*

10. The book was to be factual.

11. The book was to be an account of what important Americans had done on the day when the first atomic bomb was dropped on Hiroshima, Japan.

12. It was to be a Christian book. 13. I was a Christian then.

14. I am a Bokononist now. (Vonnegut, *Cat's Cradle,* pp. 1–2.)

The fourteen numbered units would be called 'sentences', but it can be noted immediately that they exemplify a variety of structures. The traditional thing to say about a *sentence* is that it 'expresses a complete thought'. This is correct, but vague. This 'thought', from the point of view of linguistics or of logic, is a *proposition*. A proposition is a combination of a word or words which *refer* to, or could refer to, entities in the world ('Jonah', 'my parents', 'conveyances', 'a book') with a word or words which *predicate* an action, a state or a process of the entities referred to ('call', 'unlucky', 'compelled'). The referring words are usually *nouns*; the predicating words usually *verbs* or *adjectives,* though, as we shall see, these are tendencies only, and found in only the simplest sentences. Sometimes the reference + predicate structure of the proposition neatly fits the word-arrangement (*syntactic* structure) of a simple sentence, as in sentence 10:

The book	was to be	*factual*
↑		↑
Referring Expression		Predicate
Object		State

Similarly, sentence 3 joins three referring expressions and a predicate together in one proposition which is expressed in a simple sentence:

They	*called*	*me*	*John*
↑	↑	↑	↑
Ref. exp.	Pred.	Ref. exp.	Ref. exp.
Agent	Action	Object	Complement

Note the terms 'agent', 'object', 'complement', 'state', 'action' in the bottom line of each of the above analyses. They belong to a small and highly important basic semantic vocabulary for analysing the roles of the participants referred to by nouns, and the types of activities and situations described by the verbs that go with them. The structures of meaning which represent kinds of process and the roles of participants in these processes are analysed by Halliday under the heading of *transitivity* (part of the *ideational* function). The importance of this part of the analysis of sentence meanings lies in the fact that agency, state, process, and so on seem to be the basic categories in terms of which human beings present the world to themselves through language. We think of the world, and speak and write about it, as a system of objects with constant properties: some animate, some inanimate, acting, moving, changing, causing change in other things, or just being or continuing in a certain state or condition. Literary writings may confirm such assumptions, or challenge them. We will analyse some aspects of this area of meaning in Chapters 9–11.

To return to the 'fit' of propositions and sentences, this is very often less straightforward than it is in the simple sentences 3 and 10 (or 12–14). Sentence 1 illustrates a characteristic complication in the process of expressing propositions: less than the whole proposition is stated; one of the referring expressions has been deleted, and part of the verb phrase, but our knowledge of English syntax tells us what they must be: '[You will] call me Jonah.' Here three referring expressions, 'you', 'me', and 'Jonah', are linked with the predicate, 'call'. The proposition itself is complete in its meaning; but by a syntactic convention of English, it is not entirely expressed.

Many sentences express more than one proposition. Sometimes the component propositions are clearly visible as separate *clauses*, as for example: 'I was a much younger man' and 'I began to collect material' in sentence 9. Often, however, the syntactic constituents of a sentence are shuffled around and deleted to the extent that the underlying propositional components are barely observable on the surface. (I am not saying that this causes any particular difficulty for readers; this is simply a syntactic fact about sentences, and readers know the syntax and so can 'decode' syntactic rearrangements of propositions which look rather complicated when they are pointed out.) Sentence 5 of our passage, for instance, is formed from a series of propositions which are not distinctly visible as separate clauses in the surface shape of the sentence; roughly:

> Somebody has provided conveyances for me.
> Somebody has provided motives for me.
> Some of the conveyances were conventional.
> Some of the conveyances were bizarre.
> Some of the motives were conventional.
> Some of the motives were bizarre.

Listing the propositions like this, as separate sentences, is meant to display all the semantic components that are dovetailed together in the real sentence, showing all the parts rather in the manner that an 'exploded' mechanical drawing of, say, a car gearbox does. We can see the degree of compression involved in constructing a complex sentence out of several propositions. Ideas that occur twice in the semantic structure ('provided', etc.) are not mentioned twice in the completed sentence; and ideas which are implicit are not mentioned at all—for example, the participants 'somebody' and 'me', which are essential to the meaning, are not expressed in sentence 5; they are specified in the previous sentence and 'implied' in the sentence which follows.

Something else which emerges when one divides a sentence into its propositional components is that these *might* have been fitted together in some different syntactic arrangement; for example, compare another possible wording of 5:

> Somebody has provided both conventional and bizarre conveyances and motives.

This rewriting makes much the same sense as the original sentence. Why then does Vonnegut put it his way rather than some other way? For instance, why does he use the *passive voice* 'conveyances . . . have been provided' rather than the *active voice* which would have been consistent with the previous sentence— 'somebody . . . has compelled me to be certain places . . . Somebody has provided . . . conveyances . . . '? Such questions cannot be answered without extensive and close study of the text, of course. Just to note, however, that an answer to a question such as 'why passive rather than active?' will not be provided by a merely syntactic analysis—nor propositional, since from that point of view the active and passive versions simply mean the same thing. Only a *functional* analysis (see Chapter 1 above) can make sense of this syntactic option: an analysis which attempts to suggest why, in terms of the context and the overall rhetoric of the communication, one option rather than another should be selected. The syntactic facts are the 'input' to a considered functional account.

To recapitulate. A sentence consists of one or more propositions, which may or may not be expressed in full clauses. The semantic function of propositions is *referring* and *predicating:* referring to entities (real or imaginary), and predicating actions, states, or processes of them. Obviously, a proposition is an abstract unit of meaning, and so there is a process of 'realization' or 'expression' between the abstract idea and the concrete speech or written text. One aspect of expression is the choice of *vocabulary* items *(lexis)* to designate the things and concepts referred to, and the properties predicated of them. We have seen in previous chapters that the relationship between words and things is a dynamic or dialectical one. Words are not just inert tokens which get automatically selected to express already determined ideas. Because the vocabulary system encodes a categorization of the world as experienced by language-users (and their culture), vocabulary actively shapes the ideas handled by propositions. Thus, speakers must already have words in mind as they work out the ideas they wish to convey. The other part of expression is syntax, which provides the bones for the 'left-to-right' dimension of messages. Propositions must be expressed syntactically as the regularly ordered sequences of words and phrases which comprise sentences.

Shortly, I wish to consider various aspects of the amalgamation of sentences into whole texts, under the two headings of *cohesion* and *coherence.* Before turning from clauses and sentences to the larger unit of structure, *text,* however, I want to mention briefly three further aspects of sentence-meaning and sentence-form which will be taken up later in this book: *speech acts, modality*, and *deixis*. If we recall the plan of language implied by Halliday's 'three functions' (Chapter 2 above, p. 31), propositional structure, transitivity, and lexical structure belong to the *ideational*, speech acts and modality to the *interpersonal*, and deixis and cohesion to the *textual* function of language.

We have seen that the ideational function concerns the 'cognitive' dimension of language, the way language provides structures for the representation of speakers' experience. The interpersonal function adds to this representation the personal contribution of the speaker to the act of communication: their indication of an individual point of view, their performance of some action by speaking, their assessment of and adjustment to the hearer and to the context of utterance. The interpersonal dimension connects language structure with social and cultural structure and with relationships between speakers. The theory of *speech acts* falls within this area of speaker participation according to social conventions. Quite simply, it proposes that when speakers produce an utterance or a text, they are not simply saying something about the world or their ideas, they are *doing something* by uttering. Sometimes, what they are doing is explicitly signalled in the words chosen:

I promise to pay you back on Friday.
I name this ship *The Lucky Lady*.
I sentence you to life imprisonment.

Often the act of speech is indirectly expressed:

Could you pass the salt? (a request, not an enquiry about the addressee's ability)
It's cold. (in the right context, not a comment but a suggestion to turn the heating on)

In our extract from *Cat's Cradle*, for example, sentences 1 and 7 differ from all the rest in being commands, the others being assertions or representatives through which the narrator begins to relate the story which Vonnegut has constructed out of a series of fictional propositions. The range of speech acts in our extract is limited—there are no questions, for example—but we will look at a greater range in Chapter 8.

The second interpersonal feature to be mentioned here is *modality*. Like speech acts, modality is a part of the speaker's individual contribution—'intrusion', Halliday calls it—to the speech event. In this case, we are concerned with judgements which the speaker makes; judgements of various kinds. For a start, speakers take some stand on the truth of a proposition: to say 'They called me John' (*Cat's Cradle*, sentence 3) is to commit oneself to a belief that the proposition uttered is true. But speakers may indicate various degrees of assurance or commitment, or in the case of future events, may estimate with various degrees of confidence the likelihood of the event taking place (indicated typically by modal auxiliary verbs including 'may', 'might', 'will'). The *Cat's Cradle* extract happens not to be a good source of examples of varying degrees of modality, but the range generally varies from the confidence (but irony) of the famous opening sentence of Jane Austen's *Pride and Prejudice* (1813):

It is a truth universally acknowledged, that a single man in possession of a good fortune, must be in want of a wife.

to the wavering uncertainty of the narrator's reflections on the origin of his fear of closed doors at the beginning of Joseph Heller's *Something Happened!* (1974):

Maybe it was the day I came home unexpectedly with a fever and a sore throat and caught my father in bed with my mother that left me with my fear of doors, my fear of opening doors and my suspicion of closed ones. Or maybe it was the knowledge that ... Or the day my father died ... Or maybe it was the realization ... Or maybe it was the day I did open another door and saw my big sister standing naked ...

Note the words 'must', 'maybe', which are explicit signals of modal judgement; others would include 'may', 'can', 'should', 'certainly', 'possibly', 'unfortunately', etc. Modality includes not only judgements as to truth or possibility, but also desirability, value, and the obligations of participants in a speech event and of people referred to. Cumulatively, the modalities which an author gives to his narrators, or to the speaker in a poem, characterize their authority or 'presence', and, in narrative, the point of view they adopt towards the subject-matter, whether omniscient, confident, or partial, tentative. See further, Chapters 9 and 11.

Finally, in this brief introduction to the major components of meaning and structure in sentences we must add *deixis*. This—the Greek word for 'pointing'—refers to the orientation of a text in relation to time, place, and personal participants. Deictic information is supplied principally by personal pronouns, tense and time adverbs, and adverbs of place and other locative expressions. Suppose you and I are together in a specific place, and I say to you: 'We're going there right now', referring to some other place that we both know about. The deictic parts of the sentence locate the proposition within the real world in which we communicate: 'we' establishes that it is the speaker and the addressee who are the subject of the discourse; 'there' links our destination to the place of utterance, '-'re going' announces future time in relation to the time of utterance, and 'right now' further qualifies it as immediate future time. By these deictic devices the message is made directly relevant to the personal and the spatio-temporal situation of the utterance. In written language there is deixis also, but its force is different from that of the orienting devices of speech, because the source and the addressee do not normally occupy the same place in space and time—except in cases such as a note passed in a meeting. With literary texts there are additional complications: the author does not know who the reader is, the reader usually does not know the author, the author may be several hundred years dead, the 'speaker' or narrator in a literary text is anyway not a real person and not the actual writer. In *Cat's Cradle*, the narrator pretends that there is a common point of time, a 'present', which he and the reader share, and that there is a future for both (sentences 1, 7, and 14)—this is in retrospect reassuring or ironic, since at the end of the novel we know that the narrator has survived the end of the world! Between sentences 1 and 14 several time-levels are indicated: a time before that of the narration, the time of the narrator's parents (2–3); a general past time covering the whole of the narrator's life 'so far' (4–6); and a specific past sometime after 1945; the beginning of the relevant narrated time (8–13) including a prospective future between 'then' and 'now' ('to be', 'was to be', 9–12). There is thus a complicated, and plausible, time-scheme evoked by the deictic elements of this sequence of sentences—and a narratively interesting scheme, because the juxtaposition of 13 and 14 implies that something happened which changed, probably aborted, the hypothetical future indicated by 9–12.

Place is not deictically prominent in this extract. There are no indicators of the location of the speaker or addressee (the narrator speaks of 'appointed places' in the past, but not of his or his readers' spatial position in the situation of utterance). Person is important, however. The imperatives of 1 and 7 strongly (if counter-factually) evoke an individual speaker, an individual addressee, and an intimate relationship between them; this fictive personal link is the beginning of the making of a colloquial and jokey style appropriate to the comic apocalypse of which the novel tells.

The above are some of the main headings under which we describe the structure of sentences, and they are also features of structure which are potentially significant when discussing larger units, texts—this will become obvious in the later, descriptive, chapters. But a theoretical point was made at the beginning of this chapter, to the effect that a text is a different kind of unit from a sentence. A *text* is made up of sentences, but there exist separate principles of text-construction, beyond the rules for making sentences. We now turn to these principles.

Let's begin with an example. It might as well be from this very text: say, this sentence and the three preceding ones. If we extract any single sentence—for example, 'We now turn to these principles'—it can be understood out of its context, but it only makes practical sense within its context. The deictic word 'these' points back to the preceding sentence, identifying which principles are being referred to. Similarly, 'an example' in 'Let's begin with an example' harks back to 'these principles': an example of what? Every example must be an example of something—an example 'of these principles'. Then 'It' in 'It might as well . . . ' refers to 'an example', and, after the colon, 'this sentence' replaces 'It', and so connects back with 'an example'. There are other types of connection in this stretch of text. The word 'principles' is repeated, referring to the same principles. Syntactically, 'We' in 'We now turn . . . ' is implicitly reiterated in 'Let's', and then repeated (with the same reference: the author and his assumed reader) in 'If we extract . . . '. The verb 'turn', in this context, must mean something like 'move to consider a new section of the argument'; this meaning is developed in the next verb, 'begin'. Note that, considered in isolation, the two words have little in common, but in this textual context the second picks up and builds on the meaning of the first.

The processes by which sentences are 'stitched' together into continuous texts are known as *cohesion*; the individual links are *cohesive ties*.

We may now return (note the cohesive ties with the above) to *Cat's Cradle* for a second example, for more instances of structure above the sentence. Sentence 1 is the first sentence of the novel, and obviously does not connect with any immediately preceding co-text. (It alludes to the biblical story of Jonah and the whale, and also to the first sentence of Chapter 1 of Herman Melville's novel *Moby Dick* [1851]—'Call me Ishmael'. These allusions, though important and complicated in their effect, are not textual, but *intertextual*, i.e. they rely on readers' knowledge of other texts.) Sentence 2 could not exist without sentence 1: 2 presupposes (as part of its meaning) 'My parents [called me Jonah], or nearly [called me Jonah].' It seems that omission, or *ellipsis*, is a text-structure device; that what is stated in one sentence may be left unsaid in the next, the silence being a signal of the coherence of the text, its focus on a single topic. Note that 'did' is what might be called a *pro-verb*, standing for the verb phrase 'call me Jonah' rather as a *pronoun* stands for a noun phrase—cf. 'They' = 'My parents' linking 3 with 2, or 'It' = 'The Book' linking 12 and 11. Other straightforward linking devices include lexical repetition: 'Jonah . . . Jonah', 'The book . . . The book', 'places . . . place'; and lexical variation: 'times . . . second'. But there are also some very much more complicated textual relationships in evidence here. How is it that we know that sentences 4–6 develop the same idea, that of the narrator as victim of forces which move him beyond his control?

4. . . . because somebody or something has compelled me to be certain places at certain times, without fail. 5. Conveyances and motives, both conventional and bizarre, have been provided. 6. And, according to plan, at each appointed second, at each appointed place this Jonah was there.

Our assumption of logical and narrative continuity derives partly from syntactic cues, in this case the implied syntax of what is not said. We assume that the deleted agent and patient of 'provided' and 'appointed' are the same as those explicitly given for 'compelled'; the nominal 'plan' has the same implied syntax, implying the presence of a verb and associated participants: 'somebody planned for me'. By association, the idea of compulsion against the will extends from 'compelled' to 'provided', 'plan', and 'appointed'. There are other ties among this sequence of sentences. 'Conveyances', for instance, develops the idea of movement to 'certain places' in the preceding sentence, and looks forward to the repeated 'place' in the following one. We could find further links, but by now the general point is surely clear. Not only do sentences have their own individual meanings and their rules for the possible structures for expressing these meanings, they are also, in texts, linked to one another by a complex network of cohesive ties involving numerous different parts of language structure—vocabulary, pronouns, syntactic ellipsis, etc.

When we read a newspaper article, or a novel, or listen to someone talking, or reading a poem aloud, we bring certain expectations about what counts as 'sensible communication'. Texts are organized in relation to these expectations. We expect texts to be coherent, to stay on one topic and not jump unexpectedly from subject to subject; to take another term from Hallidayan linguistics, we expect *cohesion*. Second, we expect texts not to repeat the same point constantly but to present a developing argument or narrative. That is, we expect the propositions in a cohesive text to be arranged to make a *progressive* sequence of ideas. So strong is this assumption of progression that we normally interpret a pair of sentences as logically or chronologically related even if such a relationship is not overtly stated. For instance, if someone says 'John had flu. He couldn't attend the meeting,' we automatically assume that John's flu started before the meeting, and that he didn't attend the meeting because of his flu. Finally, in addition to cohesion and progression, we expect *thematization*. This is organization of the text so as to draw attention to the most important parts of its content, its themes. There are numerous devices for doing this, including attention-catching rearrangements of word-order: 'I like peas and beans, but *carrots* I can't stand'. Illustrations are difficult without quoting lengthy texts, but any unexpected ruffling of the surface of the text by noticeable phonology, printing, syntax, or vocabulary is potentially thematizing. There are many literary conventions for thematization, some illustrated in other chapters of this book.

Of these three basic aspects of textual structure, I shall concentrate on the one which seems to be fundamental to the organization of texts, *cohesion*. Cohesion distinguishes well-formed texts, focusing on an integrated topic, with well-signalled internal transitions, from arbitrary and inconsequential strings of sentences. It is founded on a very simple principle: each sentence after the first is linked to the content of one or more preceding sentences by at least one *tie*. A tie is made by some constituent which resumes, reiterates, or otherwise recalls something designated by a predicate or a referring expression in a preceding sentence. Thus:

Call me Jonah. My parents did, or nearly did. They called me John.

Call me Jonah. My parents did, or nearly did. They called me John.

Call me Jonah. My parents did, or nearly did. They called me John.

Call me Jonah. My parents did, or nearly did. They called me John.

Call me Jonah. My parents did, or nearly did. They called me John.

Call me Jonah. My parents did, or nearly did. They called me John.

Call me Jonah. My parents did, or [my parents] nearly did. They called me John.

Call me <u>Jonah</u>. My parents did, or nearly did. They called me <u>John</u>.

The diagram shows how many cohesive ties exist even in a very short and simple text. Every part of the third sentence is prepared for by some element of a preceding one. It also demonstrates that ties are of a number of kinds; for example, the link between *did* and *Call me Jonah* is quite different from that between *my* and *me*.

Halliday and Hasan distinguish five kinds of cohesive relationship linking sentences:

1. Reference

A word in a subsequent sentence, usually a pronoun (*he, she, it*) or a demonstrative (*this, that*), refers to some entity or action that has been designated by another term in a preceding sentence (my italics in the following examples):

Stately, plump *Buck Mulligan* came from the stairhead, bearing a bowl of lather on which a mirror and a razor lay crossed. A yellow dressinggown, ungirdled, was sustained gently behind *him* by the mild morning air. He held the bowl aloft and intoned: (James Joyce, *Ulysses*, 1922.)

As to these points, *Jenny satisfied him by the most solemn assurances*, that the man was entirely out of his reach, and was neither subject to his power, nor in any probability of becoming an object of his goodness.

The ingenuity of *this behaviour*, had gained Jenny so much credit with this worthy man, that he easily believed what she told him . . . (Henry Fielding, *Tom Jones*, 1749.)

2. Substitution

Here a word in the second sentence refers, not to exactly the same entity as does the related word in the first, but to some other entity to which the same term would be applicable. Halliday and Hasan's example is:

Would you like this *teapot*?
—No, I want a square *one*.

Here the continuity is based not on two references to the same teapot, but two mentions of the concept 'teapot' referring to two different instances. Substitution works with verbs as well as nouns, the commonest verbal substitutes being 'do' ('did') and 'do so' ('did so'). These may be called *pro-verbs* on the analogy with 'pronouns'. In our Vonnegut example, sentence 2, the pro-verb 'did' substitutes for the whole of the verb phrase 'call me Jonah'. As with the teapot example, the same thing, or event, is not being referred to twice. First it is the reader being exhorted to call the narrator Jonah, then his parents nearly called him Jonah.

3. Ellipsis

An omission of an element recalls a preceding mention. A part of a subsequent sentence which would repeat a phrase or idea explicitly stated in a preceding sentence is omitted, making the second sentence depend for its completeness on the first; in the following, I have reinserted the deleted repetitions in square brackets:

He descended upon North Beach like a chapter from the Old Testament. He was the reason birds migrate in the autumn. They have to [migrate in the autumn]. He was the cold turning of the earth; [he was] the bad wind that blows off sugar. (Richard Brautigan, *The Shipping of Trout Fishing in America Shorty to Nelson Algren*, 1967.)

Ellipsis is a very important cohesive device in dialogue, a guarantee that speakers are concentrating together on a single topic and on the background knowledge relevant to the topic. In fictional dialogue, ellipsis suggests intimacy, intensity. (In the following examples, two passages of dialogue from D. H. Lawrence, I have placed empty square brackets at the points of deletion and not supplied the deleted words, to avoid distorting the text too much. The emphases are in the original text.)

'I know what *you* want,' she said.
'*I* know what I want,' he said. 'What's the odds?'
'Well, you're not going to have it off *me*.'
'Aren't I [ ]? Well, then I'm not [ ]. It's no use crying about it, is it?'
'No, it isn't [ ],' said the girl, rather disconcerted by his irony . . . .

'Where have you been?' she asked, puzzled, interested.
'[ ] to the Empire.'
'Who [ ] with?'
'[ ] By myself. I came home with Tom Cooper.' (D. H. Lawrence, *The Rainbow*, 1915.)

4. Lexical cohesion

The cohesive techniques we have looked at so far have drawn on syntactic processes—substitution of pronouns, pro-verbs, ellipsis, etc. Additionally, fully meaningful vocabulary items—referring and predicating expressions, nouns and verbs—contribute to textual cohesion, in two ways:

(a) Lexical reiteration. This is like reference and substitution, only using full words rather than pronouns or other substitutes. The same word is repeated in a subsequent sentence, either referring to the same object (cf. 'reference') or to another instance of an object of the same kind (cf. 'substitution'). In the passage from *Ulysses*:

Stately, plump Buck Mulligan came from the stairhead, bearing a *bowl* . . . He held the *bowl* aloft . . .

and

from the *stairhead* . . . he peered down the dark winding *stairs* . . .

where 'stairs' varies the 'stairhead' reference as well as repeating it. Variation may be taken a stage further, with the second word being a close synonym of the first. Halliday gives an example from Leslie Stephen:

Accordingly, after a peace-offering of tobacco, in return for a draught of foaming milk, I took leave, and turned to the *ascent* of the peak.
The *climb* is perfectly easy, though I contrived to complicate matters by going the wrong way.

(b) Collocation. Sets of words tend to turn up together in texts because they relate to the same idea: 'ice', 'snow', 'freeze', 'white', 'frost', 'blizzard'; 'electricity', 'amp', 'circuit', 'charge',

'switch'. They *collocate*: members of the same lexical set tend to appear close together in texts because texts tend to be cohesive, to stay on the same topic. 'Frost' goes with 'snow' not only in the vocabulary structure of the language considered abstractly (cf. Chapter 2 on vocabulary structure), but in real texts expressing real meanings:

Outlook: Wintry showers in many places at first, becoming mainly dry in the South. Sunny intervals, cold, with night frost, becoming less cold later (*Guardian*, 29 January 1979).

Collocation is a natural and unnoticed aspect of textual cohesiveness (but no less important for that). In a weather forecast, a very high density of meteorological terms is expected and makes no impact; similarly, a chemist will find nothing abnormal in a scientific article being full of chemical terms, though (and this may be a clue to what happens in literature) a layman may well find that usage extremely defamiliarizing. For the chemist, the high density is usual given the context s/he supplies for the text; but the layman cannot supply exactly the right context, and therefore the text is odd. The defamiliarizing effects of lexical collocation in literary texts result from the fact that the context is *not* given in advance and so the reader has to construct a context which makes sense of the lexical patterns. (On context and meaning in fiction, see Chapter 10, pp. 204–5 below.)

One example of the significance of lexical collocation will serve at this point (the technique is also illustrated in Chapter 6 below). Let us extend the *Ulysses* passage a little:

Stately, plump Buck Mulligan came from the stairhead, bearing a bowl of lather on which a mirror and a razor lay **crossed**. A yellow dressing-gown, **ungirdled,** was sustained gently behind him by the mild morning air. He held the bowl aloft and **intoned:**
—**Introibo ad altare Dei.**
Halted, he peered down the dark winding stairs and called up coarsely:
—Come up, Kinch. Come up, you fearful **jesuit.**
Solemnly he came forward and *mounted* the round gunrest. He faced about and **blessed gravely** thrice the tower, the surrounding country and the awaking mountains. Then, catching sight of Stephen Dedalus, he bent towards him and made rapid **crosses** in the air, gurgling in his

throat and shaking his head. Stephen Dedalus, displeased and sleepy, leaned his arms on the top of the staircase and looked coldly at the shaking gurgling face that **blessed** him, equine in its length, and at the light **untonsured** hair, grained and hued like pale oak.

The words in **bold** type are collocates from the terminology of the Roman Catholic church; those in *italics* are compatible terms suggesting the gravity of a religious ceremony. Buck Mulligan does a parodic imitation of the Mass within the profane context of two very secular young men getting up, shaving, cooking their breakfast in the Martello tower in which they lodge. The mock ceremony is intimated by the lexical collocations as well as narrated by the propositions of the sentences. The half-comic, half-disturbing tone of the scene is a result of defamiliarizing shifts and breaches of lexical cohesion: the intrusion within the religious vocabulary of a clashing lexis of brisk and physical motion—'rapid', 'gurgling', 'shaking', 'shaking', 'gurgling'—and the unexpected metaphor 'equine' which is both grotesque and implicitly blasphemous. Note also the oddity of a *face,* rather than a whole person or the mind or spirit of a person, performing a blessing. Naturally, lexical collocation, its developments and deviations, has a strong influence on the structuring of ideas in a text.

5. Conjunction

Sequences of sentence cohere—and *progress*, cf. p. 82 above—by various semantic relationships between them. As the following example, illustrating *temporal succession*, shows, these relationships hold between the clauses within a sentence as well as the sentences within a text:

I wrote the address down on a piece of paper and pushed the directory back across the desk. The negro put it back where he had found it, shook hands with me, then folded his hands on the desk exactly where they had been when I came in. His eyes drooped slowly and he appeared to fall asleep. (Raymond Chandler, *Farewell, My Lovely*, 1940.)

Besides temporal succession, there are various logical conjunctive relationships which Halliday and Hasan classify into three types:

(a) Additive. A succeeding sentence supplies some additional information about a topic:

The book was to be factual . . . It was to be a Christian book.

He descended upon North Beach . . . He was the reason . . .

(b) Adversative. The second sentence is in an oppositional or contrastive relationship with the first, expressing one of the adversative semantic relationships such as 'yet', 'nevertheless', 'but', 'despite', etc.:

He was totally blind. Yet they had been very happy. (D. H. Lawrence, 'The Blind Man'.)

> Shall I compare thee to a summer's day?
> Thou art more lovely and more temperate:
> (Shakespeare, Sonnet 18.)

The logical relationship between the first two lines of this sonnet is contrastive: there is an implicit 'no' between them, answering the initial question posed but unstated—note that these conjunctive relationships do not need to be expressed in an actual conjunctive word.

(c) Causal. Here the relationships are 'if . . . then', 'because', 'therefore', etc.; once again they may either be stated explicitly in a conjunction, or just implied. Expressed:

Fanny asked her mother numerous small questions, all having nothing to do with the subject, which a wise person would have perceived was occupying her attention. *Consequently,* she received many short answers. (Elizabeth Gaskell, *North and South,* 1854–5.)

Unexpressed causation:

I drove fast. I needed a drink badly and the bars were closed . . .
   I was hungry. I went down to the Mansion House Coffee Shop and ate lunch . . . (Raymond Chandler, *Farewell, My Lovely.*)

There is an implicit 'because' between the sentences in the first example, and a 'so' or 'therefore' in the second. Interestingly, I found it very hard to find clear examples of expressed causal conjunction in *Farewell, My Lovely*. There are a great many implicit causatives in Chandler, like the above examples, and these may contribute to the overall terseness of his style, the impression that the reader has constantly to retrieve unstated assumptions to understand Marlowe's reasoning and motives. There are also numerous equivocal or even paradoxical explicit causatives:

1. I walked along to the double doors and stood in front of them. 2. They were motionless now. 3. It wasn't any of my business. 4. So I pushed them open and looked in.

The conclusion in 4 is warranted by the observation in 2, but is inconsistent with the immediately preceding proposition in 3: more appropriate would be the adversative conjunction 'nevertheless'. Such contradictions as this, ironized by Marlowe, help shape Chandler's characterization of his hero-narrator as reckless, hasty, uncalculating, and humorously fatalistic. Once again, we find an arrangement at the level of textual structure contributing to the experiential meaning of a text: a cohesive device, often repeated, contributes cumulatively but directly to the narrative tone of the novel.

References and Suggestions for Further Reading

Valuable sources for aspects of structure 'above' the sentence are R. de Beaugrande and W. Dressler, *Introduction to Text Linguistics* (London: Longman, 1981) (note the chapter on *coherence*); M. A. K. Halliday and R. Hasan, *Cohesion in English* (London: Longman, 1976). See also Halliday, *Introduction to Functional Grammar* (London: Edward Arnold, 2nd edn., 1994), ch. 9. The three-part distinction between 'cohesion', 'progression', and thematization' introduced on pp. 82–3 is treated under a different terminology in R. Fowler, 'Cohesive, progressive and localizing aspects of text structure', in T. A. Van Dijk and J. S. Petöfi, eds., *Grammars and Descriptions* (Berlin: Walter de Gruyter, 1977), pp. 64–84.

A readable and reliable introduction to syntax is E. K. Brown and J. Miller, *Syntax: A linguistic introduction to sentence structure* (London: Harper Collins, 2nd edn., 1991). The best resource a student of linguistic criticism can have is access to a reference grammar on English syntax.

Highly recommended is the series of grammars, of various levels and ranges, written by R. Quirk, S. Greenbaum, G. Leech and J. Svartvik. The most complete is *A Comprehensive Grammar of the English Language* (London: Longman, 1985). Widely available in libraries is the same authors' *A Grammar of Contemporary English* (London: Longman, 1972). Also based on the same research is Quirk and Greenbaum, *A University Grammar of English* (London: Longman, 1973). Two useful reference books by R. Huddleston are *Introduction to the Grammar of English* (Cambridge: Cambridge University Press, 1984) and *English Grammar: An Outline* (Cambridge: Cambridge University Press, 1988). All of these works provide descriptions of the main areas of English sentence-structure cast in primarily traditional terminology, and are compatible with Halliday's functional account, though Halliday's terminology is more idiosyncratic.

For wider background on the English language in terms of history, use, and variety, see A. C. Baugh and T. Cable, *A History of the English Language* (London: Routledge, 4th edn., 1993); S. Gramley and K.-M. Pätzold, *A Survey of Modern English* (London: Routledge, 1992).

For concepts in pragmatics and discourse analysis, see S. Levinson, *Pragmatics* (Cambridge: Cambridge University Press, 1983); G. Brown and G. Yule, *Discourse Analysis* (Cambridge: Cambridge University Press, 1983); M. Coulthard, *Introduction to Discourse Analysis* (London: Longman, new edn., 1985). More specific references on speech acts, modality, etc., are given in later chapters.

Extra Structure, Extra Meanings

In the previous chapter I introduced some basic features of textual organization which reflect conditions for any 'sensible communication' through language. Whether it be an informal conversation or a formal paper, a text is a sequence of sentences. A sentence is a syntactic unit, but the syntax, the ordering of words and phrases, is semantically based; its function is to make meanings tangible as signs arranged in space (writing) or time (speech). The core of meaning is the proposition, which refers to entities in the world as categorized by the language community, and which predicates properties of these entities. Sentences are used to perform *speech acts* such as stating, questioning, and commanding, and, in more specialized contexts, promising, marrying, betting, etc. The speaker also communicates his attitudes towards the probability, desirability, and so on, of the states of affairs mentioned in the propositions *(modality)*. Additionally, the utterance of a sentence contains indicators of the spatial, temporal, and interpersonal orientation of its content *(deixis)*.

We saw also that, in continuous text, sentences are linked together by an intricate network of cohesive ties. Textual *cohesion* distinguishes a well-formed text from a random list of sentences. Through cohesion, a text stays on its topic, or makes clear shifts of topic; develops a subject rationally; and indicates what are the prominent and the subordinate parts of an argument or a story. A text stuctured in this way will emerge for a reader as *coherent*. The complexity of cohesion and related text-structural devices is only just beginning to be recognized by linguists; their importance, once acknowledged, is evidently very great. The reader can test this importance by taking any text quoted in the previous chapter and jumbling its sentences into another order, noticing the incoherence that is produced, and considering what cohesive ties have been destroyed by the rearrangement. Radical dislocation of cohesion is of course a conventional strategy in some kinds of writing, for example the *nouveau roman;* such writing attains its effect only by virtue of the strength of the cohesive conventions which it disrupts.

The next stage of my argument returns to some topics related to *defamiliarization* (Chapter 3), but it does not depend on any notion of 'disrupting' normal text conventions, or 'deviating' from a standard language. Although it is true that many of the defamiliarizing devices of modern literature do involve breaking the rules, even creating new rules, nevertheless texts can be perfectly regular in the terms of the previous chapter, and still signify more than their propositions literally state. The fact is that a piece of language in real use is *more than* a text put together by the basic conventions which I introduced in the last chapter: a much richer *discourse* than has emerged so far.

To see language as discourse is to study it in its communicative context, as language socially and historically situated. Language structure adapts to the context in which it is used: as well as making statements about the world, performing speech acts, and so on, a text reflects its communicative use in society—an advertisement is different from a scientific textbook, a lecture from an informal conversation on the same subject, and so on. Social meanings are conveyed by these adaptations, and they are communicated to the reader or listener by patterns of linguistic organization additional to those required by the sentence and text structure. The extra structure and extra meanings referred to in the title of this chapter are organizations of language which respond to a text's communicative functions. The structure of discourse, as opposed to the more limited structure of text, reflects the whole complex process of people interacting with one another in live situations and within the structure of social forces. In real communication—written as well as spoken—people are doing more than just transmitting neutral propositions to one another in 'sensibly' formed texts. Their language assumes extra structuration reflecting their personal purposes in communication, their social statuses and relationships, and the nature of the setting within which language is used. A speaker may wish to persuade, to inform, to impress, to justify himself, to bully or attack another person, and so on. These purposes will be expressed in linguistic structure, as also will be the relationship between the speaker and his interlocutor: if speakers are very close and intimate (lovers, siblings) their language will be characteristically different from speech on the same topic between individuals who don't know one another very well, or who occupy disparate social statuses, for example, company director and worker, teacher and pupil. Another influence on the text's further structuring as discourse is the kind of setting in which it is produced and received: a love letter is necessarily different in its discourse structure from a formal lecture, a lecture differs from a face-to-face row, all of them from a newspaper advertisement, and so on. So language *as discourse* expresses, by extra structure, the functions and circumstances of the interactions which it mediates. Looking at language from this perspective, we are entering the area of styles and social meanings. When choices of characteristic discourse structures consistently correlate with similar communicative circumstances, we speak of distinct 'styles' and 'genres'. These generalizations are as applicable outside as within 'literature': it is just as valid to describe the styles of popular newspapers, the genre of the television advertisement, the stylistic conventions used in official notices, the genre 'letters to the Press', etc., as it is to generalize about the genres of Miltonic sonnet, epic, confessional novel, the styles of Augustan verse, seventeenth-century prose, Imagism, and so on, as literary critics do. Once again, we see that the opposition 'literature: non-literature' beloved of literary critics is unnecessary when the uses of language are regarded in a broad enough perspective.

Leaving stylistic generalizations and their interpretations on one side for a moment, in this chapter I shall offer a more detailed focus on a few sample techniques of extra structure which happen to be important in some styles of modern literary discourse. I shall also introduce two major processes which are regularly involved in adding extra structure to texts in the formation of culturally significant discourses.

The extra meanings of additional structure have already been illustrated in a fragmentary way, from the Pope couplet in Chapter 2 to some of the examples of textual structure analysed in Chapter 5. In the Pope, a social criticism was voiced not by the propositions in the text but by the formal arrangement of the verse which placed 'husbands' and 'lapdogs' in metrically parallel positions, implying their semantic equivalence. *Parallelism and equivalence* is one of the two processes to be explained here. The other is *foregrounding*: whenever some item or construction appears in a text with unusual or noticeable frequency and apparently for some valid reason, then cumulatively a distinctive effect emerges. Examples of foregrounding cited so far would include the highlighted tentative modalities—the 'maybes'—of *Something Happened!* (p. 78 above); the adjective-noun combinations in Akenside (pp. 69–70); the collocating vocabulary of religious ceremony in the opening of *Ulysses* (pp. 87–8). Note that parallelism may be an instance of foregrounding: it is so in Pope, in fact, since it is a constant, and constantly significant, feature of his metrical discourse.

The importance of foregrounding and parallelism has been argued in two extremely famous and influential articles, by the Prague School poetic theorist Jan Mukařovský and by the founder of modern linguistic poetics, Roman Jakobson. These theorists are in the tradition of the Russian Formalist school; specifically, both of their proposals can be seen as demonstrations of how language in literature is structured to 'impede' and 'prolong' perception to produce the dehabitualized response described by Shklovsky (see p. 56 above). Although the insights of Mukařovský and Jakobson are profound and constructive, I must immediately dissociate myself from the general aim of their argument: they claim that foregrounding and parallelism are special qualities of 'poetic language' which distinguish it from 'ordinary language'; I maintain that 'poetic language' is not an objective, distinct entity, but an imaginary concept produced by the business of letters by way of publishing, reviewing, criticizing, theorizing, and teaching.

For me, foregrounding and parallelism are bases for a number of linguistic techniques through which texts are made into discourses which are deemed 'poetic' by readers. It happens that certain dominant styles in modern literature depend heavily on these techniques. But other types of discourse use them extensively, for example, advertising, political oratory, rules and regulations, courtroom interrogation, and many others.

Foregrounding uses a visual metaphor to explain a linguistic technique. In painting, this would be any device—contrast of hue or lightness, greater detail or linear precision, manipulation of perspective, paint texture, or whatever—which causes some part of a composition to be perceived as standing out as a figure against a less determinate background. What is foregrounded in language? According to Mukařovský:

In poetic language foregrounding achieves maximum intensity to the extent of pushing communication into the background as the objective of expression and of being used for its own sake; it is not used in the services of communication, but in order *to place in the foreground the act of expression, the act of speech itself.* (Mukařovský, 'Standard language and poetic language', p. 19; my italics.)

Jakobson's assertions about 'the poetic function of language' are very much in agreement with the part of the Mukařovský statement that I have italicized:

The set (*Einstellung*) toward the message as such, focus on the message for its own sake, is the POETIC function of language . . . This function, by promoting the palpability of signs, deepens the fundamental dichotomy of signs and objects [Jakobson's italics and capitals]. (Jakobson, 'Closing Statement: Linguistics and Poetics', p. 356.)

For both of these writers, literary language draws the reader's attention to its own artifices of construction—cohesion or collocation, say, does not function merely as an aid to communication but under foregrounding becomes itself a pattern for independent notice. Signs become palpable, while the objects they designate are backgrounded into subordinate importance. The medium becomes more prominent than the meaning, and that—on the Mukařovský–Jakobson theory—is the reverse of the priorities of ordinary communication.

In my theory, defamiliarizing communication, whether or not it is called 'literature', is discourse in which certain textual structures (of numberless variety) have been made salient by unusual regularity (foregrounded). It is extremely difficult to give any general rules as to what level of repetition and recurrence of structures gives rise to foregrounding, since whether a particular construction is perceived as salient depends on the discourse context in which it appears. For instance, an exceptional number of passives is found in scientific writing, but in that context it is conventional and not noticeable. In the telling of a story, however, even a few passives instead of active sentences are likely to be experienced as an oddity because readers of narrative assume that the essence of the genre is a sequence of actions. I shall not carry these speculations about quantity of foregrounding any further, but let my examples and my readers' intuitions provide further materials for consideration.

As for the motives and functions of foregrounding, the perceptual salience it produces is not, despite our authorities, physical prominence of the expressive medium for its own sake, but extra discourse structure inviting *interpretation*. The significance is additional to the propositional meaning, and often at odds with the latter—as in the Pope example, which speaks of the extremity of grief but implicates the insincerity of those who give vent to it. Once again, the interpretation of foregrounding is easier to grasp through examples than to discuss abstractly.

Mukařovský's 'foregrounding' may be seen as a clarification of Shklovsky's 'impeding perception' in that it suggests that what intervenes between reading and knowledge is a complication of linguistic technique. Jakobson goes a stage further towards specifying exactly what is involved at the level of linguistic structure. For simplicity I have referred to his discovery as 'parallelism and equivalence', but he phrases it in a more careful, complex and only apparently cryptic fashion:

What is the empirical linguistic criterion of the poetic function? In particular, what is the indispensable feature inherent in any piece of poetry? To answer this question we must recall the two basic modes of arrangement used in verbal behavior, *selection* and *combination*. If 'child' is the topic of the message, the speaker selects one among the extant, more or less similar, nouns like child, kid, youngster, tot, all of them equivalent in a certain respect, and then, to comment on this topic, he may select one of the semantically cognate verbs—sleeps, dozes, nods, naps. Both chosen words combine in the speech chain. The selection is produced on the base of equivalence, similarity and dissimilarity, synonymity and antonymity, while the combination, the build up of the sequence, is based on contiguity. *The poetic function projects the principle of equivalence from the axis of selection into the axis of combination.* Equivalence is promoted to the constitutive device of the sequence. In poetry one syllable is equalized with any other syllable of the same sequence; word stress is assumed to equal word stress, as unstress equals unstress; prosodic long is matched with long, and short with short; word boundary equals word boundary, no boundary equals no boundary; syntactic pause equals syntactic pause, no pause equals no pause. Syllables are converted into units of measure, and so are morae or stresses. ('Linguistics and Poetics', p. 358.)

Let us give Jakobson's 'axes' their more usual, and more memorable, names. The axis of selection is the *paradigm;* that of combination, the *syntagm.* The syntagm is simply the linear ordering of sounds and of words constructing a sentence 'left-to-right' as it were; the 'horizontal' dimension of the text. A sentence is one kind of syntagm: 'The child sleeps' is a grammatical sequence of an article plus a noun followed by a verb, or from another analytic perspective a subject followed by a predicate, and from another, a sequence of three lexical items 'the' and 'child' and 'sleeps'. This is also a phonological syntagm: a series of three syllables, the first lightly stressed and the second and third more heavily. A more detailed syntagmatic analysis at the level of phonology would show that each word or syllable is a sequence of phonemes arranged according to the phonological conventions of English: /slips/, etc.

If syntagms are sequences of linguistic elements in actual bits of language, paradigms are the sets of possibilities from which these elements are selected. At each point in the syntagmatic chain, there is a 'vertical' paradigm of other possibilities that might have been selected:

```
        S Y N T A G M
   P  The     child      sleeps
   A  a       kid        dozes
   R  some    youngster  nods
```

A	*etc.*	tot	naps
D		infant	wakes
I		boy	dreams
G		woman	*etc.*
M		*etc.*	

The above paradigms will permit the alternative syntagms 'The kid dozes', 'A woman dreams', etc. The same principle works in phonology: /slips/, /blips/, /slups/, /slaps/, /slaks/, /blaks/, etc. Note that paradigms, being potential resources and not actual pieces of language, are normally 'invisible'—except in grammar books and, on Jakobson's theory, in poems.

By 'equivalent' Jakobson simply means 'substitutable in the same place in a syntagm'; *not* 'identical' or 'synonymous': so not only 'kid' and 'child' are equivalent in his sense, but also opposites or semantically incompatible terms like 'black' and 'white', or 'hot' and 'cold', or 'dove' and 'hawk'. Equivalence includes contrast and other types of paradigmatic relationships.

Jakobson's 'poetic principle' is a kind of foregrounding which includes a vast range of rhetorical techniques, from metrical structure to syntactic parallelism to the semantics of paradox. Its working is very simple. Two or more linguistic units, of whatever kind, which have some paradigmatic relationship, are placed in the sequence of the text in such a way that this relationship is clearly perceptible in addition to whatever syntagmatic relationship the items may have. In this way an extra layer of structure is created over and above the structure of the text as 'sensible communication'. One of Jakobson's examples is the campaign slogan 'I like Ike' /ai laik aik/. Here the principle of phonetic equivalence is carried almost to its limits: each word is only one syllable long, every vowel is /ai/, the second and third syllables end in /k/, and every syllable is strongly stressed. None of these equivalences is required by the meanings of the words or by their syntactic relationships. There is a level of phonetic patterning which is entirely independent of the sentence as *text*. This may seem a trivial example, but its significance is in principle the same as that of the more complex cases I will discuss. Anyone familiar with discourse patterns in English is likely to feel that the matching of vowels and consonants means something in addition to what is stated by the sentence—perhaps, the inherent like-ability of Ike, or the inevitability of 'I' liking him. The fore-grounded sounds are not just a palpable musical texture; they are also an invitation to make meaning.

Jakobson's theory provides (among other things) the basic recipe for the *metrical* structure of verse. Most English verse is constructed on two assumptions of phonetic equivalence. First, a line consists of a fixed number of syllables, the exact number varying with the verse type but in the dominant decasyllabic type of Shakespeare, Milton, Wordsworth, and other major poets, ten syllables. Thus all successive sequences of ten syllables are assumed to be 'equivalent' in Jakobson's sense. To achieve these groupings into tens, syntax has to be carefully arranged, with a fair proportion of major syntactic boundaries (between sentences or clauses or phrases) falling at the tenth syllable. Rhymed verse reinforces the line-endings by extra equivalences—chiming syllables—at those points. The second major structural device in conventional English verse is regularity in the number of strongly stressed, or prominent, syllables per line, and in the number of lightly stressed syllables between the prominent ones. In English, different syntactic classes of word carry different levels of prominence, and within a single word, one syllable will be more prominent than others: for instance, the words 'in', 'and', 'of', and 'a' in this sentence are less strongly stressed than 'English', 'different', 'prominence', etc; and the words 'different', 'syllable', 'prominent', and others always have the strongest stress on the first syllable. Within the verse line, a sequence of words is selected which, conforming to these stress rules of English, disposes the syllables in their expected metrical positions:

Not lóuder Shríeks to pítying Héav'n are cást

Variants on an established pattern are frequent; when they occur, they are felt to be significant, at least for setting the characteristic personal metrical style of a particular poet, and often for creating specific reorientations of meaning:

When Húsbands or when Láp-dogs bréathe their lást

Pope declines the opportunity to stress the fourth syllable of the line ('or'), and so throws the two focal words 'husbands' and 'lapdogs' into a clear syntagmatic parallelism—with what semantic effect we have already observed, but can now explain by application of the Jakobsonian principle: the syntagmatic parallel between the two words invites us to seek a paradigmatic relationship between them, to regard them as equivalent in meaning. Metrical structure, we see, is not an independent, decorative, formal pattern but a discourse convention bringing extra meanings to a text.

Let us look at the interaction between the foregrounded parallelism of metre and equivalence at other levels of language in a complete text. William Blake's 'London' (1794) offers a particularly clear example:

> I wander thro' each charter'd street,
> Near where the charter'd Thames does flow.
> And mark in every face I meet
> Marks of weakness, marks of woe.
>
> In every cry of every Man,
> In every Infant's cry of fear,
> In every voice: in every ban,
> The mind-forg'd manacles I hear.
>
> How the Chimney-sweeper's cry
> Every blackning Church appalls,
> And the hapless Soldier's sigh,
> Runs in blood down Palace walls
>
> But most thro' midnight streets I hear
> How the youthful Harlot's curse
> Blasts the new-born Infant's tear
> And blights with plagues the Marriage hearse.

The repetitions, parallels, and antitheses of this poem can be attributed in part to a metrical motive: constructing one of the childish ballad-like or hymn-like verse rhythms that Blake uses in 'Songs of Innocence' and 'Songs of Experience'. Thus repetitions like 'Marks of weakness, marks of woe' and 'In every . . . in every . . . in every . . . in every' obviously enhance the

regularity of the rhythm—and, incidentally, restrict the vocabulary too, so apparently simplifying the style. But any appearance
of simplicity of meaning is illusory. The extra formal symmetries
of the text draw attention to the lexical paradigms that are
displayed in the poem, and call upon us to interpret the relationships between members of these paradigms, to produce complexities of meaning which, judging from the extremely complicated,
virtually contradictory, phrase 'Marriage hearse' which ends the
poem, are not accidental. Consider line 4:

> Marks of weakness, marks of woe.

Here there is syntactic equivalence between the two phrases
(plural noun + preposition + noun), identity of the first word in
each phrase ('marks'), alliteration of /m/ and of /w/. The conventions of verse discourse encourage the reader to look for a
relationship between the matched but different items, 'weakness'
and 'woe'. These words have two quite different meanings, are
only loosely linked syntactically (the phrases are both objects of
the verb 'mark' in the preceding line), but the parallelism implies
a closer relationship. In itself, 'weakness' is a double-valued
word: weakness is either pitiable or culpable, depending on one's
viewpoint (see further, *multiaccentuality*, below). I suggest that
the parallel with 'woe' resolves the value of 'weakness' as
'pitiable', which is of course consistent with the general ethical
perspective of the whole poem. And it is by processes such as
this that that perspective is built up; not by overt statement.

One foregrounded paradigm is the vocabulary for the vocal
laments and exclamations of the pitiable people whom Blake's
speaker encounters: 'cry', 'cry of fear', 'voice', 'ban', 'cry', 'sigh',
'curse'. The prominence of these cries, by the mere frequency of
the terms, hardly needs comment. It might be asked whether this
is a naturalistic picture of a street scene, with the first 'cry'
(line 5) referring to someone crying his wares, the 'ban' a public
proclamation, and so on. But the distinctness of the cries seems
less remarkable than the way they merge and their meanings
develop: the simple word 'cry', in itself neutral as to value,
accumulates overtones first of pain and suffering, and then rage
and malediction. The complex values of the 'cry' paradigm make

sense in the context of the last two stanzas. The sentences about the chimney-sweep, the soldier and the harlot are syntactically difficult, but their general sense is clear: the sufferings of these exploited people are a public indictment of the legitimated forces of oppression—religion, monarchy (or, less specifically, state power), and marriage. Syntactic and metrical parallelisms encourage this interpretation: lines 9, 11, and 14 are syntactically equivalent, as are 10, 12, 15, and 16, so that their central lexical items are placed in a symmetrical set of oppositions:

> Chimney-sweeper: Church
> Soldier: Palace
> Harlot: Infant
> Harlot: Marriage

It is implied that these are antagonistic relationships, and contradictory ones: it is a paradox that the Church, claimed source of spiritual comfort, is part of the set of economic forces which, to sustain their power and privilege, subject children to degrading and dangerous employment. The powerful contradiction 'marriage hearse' has a similar interpretation: the institution of marriage is one part of a sexual institution which also contains child prostitution as an integral part, and in which the production of children is as appalling an outcome as the transmission of sexual diseases ('blights with plagues'). This contradiction 'marriage = death' is only one of several which emerge when one realizes that ironic paradox is a strategy of this discourse. At the beginning of the poem, the repetition 'charter'd street', 'charter'd Thames', might go unnoticed on a first reading, might be accepted as merely an ingredient in the sing-song rhythm. A chartered street is presumably a street whose residents have been granted some privilege; the privilege is recorded in a document, a charter. Can a river be chartered in this sense? Hardly, since a river is a natural but inanimate force not properly under man's control. Society's claim to charter the Thames is arrogant presumption. If we think about the meaning of the word 'charter'd' in these terms, the presumption reflects back on 'charter'd street' as well, and we are bound to consider what is involved in the granting of privilege by authority. The paradox is of course that a freedom which is officially *licensed* is no freedom at all, and that is a version of the paradox that runs through the whole poem: the oppression of the individual by an apparently benevolent official society. This is nowhere stated in the poem, but will be clear to any experienced reader of verse who understands the paradigmatic relationships foregrounded in the structure of the poem.

One effect of repetition and parallelism in Blake's 'London' is to *problematize* the meanings of words: words such as 'weakness' and 'chartered' are foregrounded in such a way as to cause the reader to query their singleness of meaning. The poem exposes paradox and contradiction residing in the 'official' meanings of words. According to the Russian theorist Mikhail Bakhtin, all words are inherently double-voiced or double-valued: he calls this *multiaccentuality*. But the tendency in ordinary speech, and especially in official discourse, is to use words as if they had only one meaning: to suppress critical and paradoxical values in favour of the meaning which is convenient for the ideology of the current discourse (so that words become *uniaccentual*, and discourse *monologic*). Critical and creative uses of language, in this theory, defamiliarize by restoring and highlighting multiaccentuality. Bakhtin's theory may be compared with some well-known approaches in Western poetics: with Empson's insistence on the multiplicity of meaning in poetry (*Seven Types of Ambiguity*, 1930), or with the preoccupation with semantic tension and paradox in New Criticism (e.g. Cleanth Brooks, *The Well Wrought Urn*, 1947).

This process of reinterpreting the syntagm by foregrounding paradigms works in prose as well as verse. In an illuminating discussion of D. H. Lawrence's story 'The Blind Man', Anne Cluysenaar—whose *Introduction to Literary Stylistics* makes very constructive use of the Prague notion of foregrounding—points out that the parallelism in the first paragraph leads the reader 'to suppose that Isabel favours Bertie over her husband' (p. 96):

Isabel Pervin was listening for two sounds—for the sound of wheels on the drive outside and for the noise of her husband's footsteps in the hall. Her dearest and oldest friend, a man who seemed almost indispensable to her living, would drive up in the rainy dusk of the closing November day. The trap had gone to fetch him from the station. And her husband, who had been blinded in Flanders, and who had a disfiguring mark on his brow, would be coming in from the out-houses.

Cluysenaar displays the parallelism but, though her interpretation is doubtless correct, she does not explain how it produces the evaluation.

This is the very opening of the story, and the sentences are first and foremost narrative sentences, identifying the main participants and setting the scene. At the level of discourse structure, however, the syntactic parallels of phrase and clause say much more. Note that in each of the paired phrases below, 1 refers to Isabel's friend, Bertie, and 2 to her husband, Maurice:

Isabel Pervin was listening for two sounds—

1. for the sound of wheels . . .
2. and for the noise of her husband's footsteps

'Sound' and 'noise' are near-synonyms from the same lexical paradigm, but the first is neutral as to evaluation, the second negative—noises are unpleasant. This is the origin of the hinted negative evaluation of Maurice. The system of oppositions henceforth depends on conventional cultural associations and the way we relate them to the characters. 'Wheels' connotes mobility, 'footsteps' the limitations of man unassisted by the technology of travel.

1. on the drive outside
2. in the hall

The drive means access to the wide world outside, travel etc., and fits with Isabel's cultivated and cosmopolitan background; the hall connotes containment, the restrictions of domestic life perhaps.

1. Her dearest and oldest friend
2. and her husband

The paradigm 'friend/husband' is introduced oddly here, the friend being both mentioned first and hyperbolized, and the husband referred to second and neutrally, implicitly reducing the status of the husband; the opposition is immediately continued:

1. a man who seemed almost indispensable to her living
2. who had been blinded in Flanders, and who had a disfiguring mark on his brow

Readers who bring to the text conventional assumptions about marriage and its emotional exclusivity must find the 'friend/husband' paradigm unnaturally inverted. Prospectively, this inversion is disturbing in the light of the following paragraph in which Lawrence has Isabel reflecting on the intensely satisfying and private intimacy of her marriage with Maurice.

1. would drive up . . . from the station
2. would be coming in from the out-houses.

The same opposition as before: with Bertie is associated travel, mobility, the world at large; with Maurice, the meaner parts of the farm buildings (Isabel's fear of and distaste for the farm are quite evident later). In the general terms which might be used by anthropologists, Bertie is analysed as a representative of *culture,* Maurice represents the other term in this powerful opposition, *nature.*

Through various subtle hints, we are told that these evaluations are in Isabel's consciousness: it is she who is named right at the beginning; she is given a verb of active perception, 'was listening for'; the other characters are introduced in relation to her, rather than as individuals—'her husband', 'her friend'. The internal perspective is confirmed by the mixed tenses of the first sentence of the next paragraph—'now' in a past tense sentence conventionally signals entry into a character's consciousness—and by the existence of many sentences in a style which could reasonably represent Isabel's reflective thoughts. (See Chapter 9 for a fuller discussion of point of view in narrative.) But there is much in this continuation which indicates a troubled and complex perspective:

He had been home for a year now. He was totally blind. Yet they had been very happy. The Grange was Maurice's own place. The back was a farmstead, and the Wernhams, who occupied the rear premises, acted as farmers. Isabel lived with her husband in the handsome rooms in front. She and he had been almost entirely alone together since he was wounded. They talked and sang and read together in a wonderful and unspeakable intimacy. Then she reviewed books for a Scottish news-paper, carrying on her old interest, and he occupied himself a good deal with the farm. Sightless, he could still discuss everything with Wernham, and he could also do a good deal of work about the place—menial work, it is true, but it gave him satisfaction. He milked the cows, carried in the pails, turned the separator, attended to the pigs and horses. Life was still very full and strangely serene for the blind man, peaceful with the almost incomprehensible peace of immediate contact in darkness. With his wife he had a whole world, rich and real and invisible.

They were newly and remotely happy. He did not even regret the loss of his sight in these times of dark, palpable joy. A certain exultance swelled his soul.

Foregrounded here is a vocabulary of *extremes*—extremes of sensation or emotion or evaluation:

totally blind, very happy, handsome, entirely alone, wonderful, unspeak-able, intimacy, a good deal, everything, very full, strangely, incom-prehensible, immediate, whole world, rich, real, invisible, remotely, happy, joy, exultance, swelled, soul.

Most of these words and phrases are positive, including, of course, 'entirely alone' in this context. The general message given by these judgements is that the Pervins' marriage is exceptionally happy, that they are intensely and exclusively in love. However, the foregrounding is so dense that it might be felt to be an overstatement—a symptom that the love is less solid than is claimed. What is more, some of the words—'unspeakable' for instance—are potentially negative in their connotations once one concedes the possible insincerity of the context. That has already been hinted in the opening paragraph with its suggestion that Isabel's love for her husband is less secure than her affection for her old friend. And it is explicitly confirmed in the fourth paragraph, which speaks of Maurice's 'devastating fits of depres-sion', and Isabel's consequent dread and sense of burden. So this overblown, hyperbolic, vulnerable language seems justified by the narrative situation.

(There is, however, a radical problem with this technique in Lawrence, namely that he foregrounds the vocabulary of sensa-tion and evaluation indiscriminately, not differentiating the dic-tion according to particular characters' points of view, and often intruding his own judgements into characters' thoughts: the language in which Isabel's thoughts are put is at times violent and out of character; for example, she attributes 'stupid hatred' to her husband. This compositional defect is beyond the scope of the present chapter, but I believe it could be approached through the analysis of foregrounded lexical paradigms.)

References and Suggestions for Further Reading

The foundations for this chapter are the classic articles by Jan Mukařovský, 'Standard language and poetic language', and Roman Jakobson, 'Closing Statement: Linguistics and Poetics': for bibliographical references, see pp. 71 and 18 above. For other modern linguistic approaches based on parallelism and equivalence, and foregrounding, see G. N. Leech, *A Linguistic Guide to English Poetry* (London: Longman, 1969); A. Cluysenaar, *Introduction to Literary Stylistics* (London: Batsford, 1976). An empirical linguistic study of foregrounding is W. Van Peer, *Stylistics and Psychology: Investigations of foregrounding* (London: Croom Helm, 1986).

For the distinction between *text* and *discourse* made on p. 93 and the subsequent stress on discourse, see R. Fowler, *Literature as Social Discourse* (London: Batsford, 1981) and 'Literature', in M. Coyle *et al.*, eds., *Encyclopedia of Literature and Criticism* (London: Routledge, 1990), pp. 3–26. See also A. Easthope, *Poetry as Discourse* (London: Methuen, 1983).

The paragraph on metre is not an attempt to give a complete linguistic account! Metre was one of the first literary topics to be studied linguistically, and it has been extensively treated elsewhere. See S. Chatman, *A Theory of Meter* (The Hague: Mouton, 1965); M. Halle and S. J. Keyser, *English Stress: Its Form, its Growth, and its Role in Verse* (New York: Harper & Row, 1971), W. K. Wimsatt, ed., *Versification: Major Language Types* (New York: New York University Press, 1972); R. Fowler, 'What is Metrical Analysis?' *Anglia*, 86 (1968), 280–320, reprinted in Fowler, *The Languages of Literature* (London: Routledge & Kegan Paul, 1971), ch. 10; T. V. F. Brogan, 'Meter', in A. Preminger and T. V. F. Brogan, eds., *The New Princeton Encyclopedia of Poetry and Poetics* (Princeton: Princeton University Press, 1993), pp. 768–83; D. Attridge, *Poetic Rhythm: An Introduction* (Cambridge: Cambridge University Press, 1995).

Bakhtin's most influential work is *Problems of Dostoevsky's Poetics*, trans. C. Emerson (Manchester: Manchester University Press, 1984

[1929]); for a more theoretical linguistic work, written under the pseudonym V. N. Voloshinov, see his *Marxism and the Philosophy of Language,* trans. L. Matejka and I. R. Titunik (New York: Seminar Press, 1973 [1929]). On Bakhtin's work and ideas, see M. Holquist, *Dialogism: Bakhtin and his World* (London: Routledge, 1990); T. Marshall, 'Dialogism', in R. E. Asher, ed., *The Encyclopedia of Language and Linguistics* (Oxford: Pergamon Press, 1994), vol. iv, pp. 908–14. J. Hartley, *Understanding News* (London: Routledge, 1988) is useful on *multiaccentuality.* For the application of *heteroglossia* and *monologism* to fiction, see R. Fowler, *The Language of George Orwell* (London: Macmillan, 1995).

CHAPTER SEVEN

Text and Context

In previous chapters, I have discussed aspects of the linguistic patterning of texts, including the various 'cohesive' constructions for tying sentences together into well-formed wholes; also the semantic implications of cohesion, and of some deviations from, and additions to, regular conventions of cohesive patterning. Textual structure is of great importance in the traditions of verse literature with which readers and teachers in our culture are mainly preoccupied, and also in rhetorical prose writing such as the Lawrence story which we discussed: such writers constantly foreground the 'mechanics' of their compositions, the basic constructional devices. By doing this (whether through parallelism, foregrounded collocation, or however), writers make available to readers extra levels of meaning over and above the meanings of the component sentences—often, meanings which are in ironic tension with sentence-meanings, as we have seen, and thus defamiliarizing.

Important as textual patterning is, it is only one part of the structure and process of linguistic communication—and a linguistic criticism which attended exclusively to this part would have its limitations. We can now add more dimensions of structure to our linguistic model, and hopefully more strings to our critical bow. For instance, we will look again (Chapter 11) at the structures and meanings of sentences in themselves, as distinct from their relationships in texts. Before doing so, however, there is much to say about the dynamics of texts as *interpersonal* communication in contexts, and this will take us well beyond consideration of texts as formal objects.

In linguistic criticism, it is customary to indicate a change of perspective at this point in the argument by distinguishing between *text* and *discourse*—a distinction for which we prepared in Chapter 6. To look at language as text entails the study of whole units of communication seen as coherent syntactic and semantic structures which can be spoken or written down. Roughly speaking, texts can be regarded as the *medium* of discourse (remembering of course that in the literary traditions from which I have drawn my examples so far, the medium is given a highlighted substantiality). Discourse is the whole complicated process of linguistic interaction between people uttering and comprehending texts. To study language as discourse requires, therefore, attention to facets of structure which relate to the participants in communication, to the actions they perform through uttering texts, and to the contexts within which discourse is conducted. All of these 'extra-linguistic' factors are systematically reflected in the structures of the sentences (and thus texts) which speakers utter. Or, to put it the other way around, the form of a language develops, in response to its discourse functions, so as to provide the means of expression for all the personal actions, interpersonal relationships, and connections with context that are mediated through discourse. Halliday acknowledges this shaping of a language according to its social functions:

The particular form taken by the grammatical system of language is closely related to the social and personal needs that language is required to serve. ('Language structure and language function', p. 142.)

In terms of the three functions of language which Halliday distinguishes (p. 31 above) we are here concerned primarily with the 'interpersonal function'.

Through the interpersonal function of language, text is connected with context. Now 'context' is mentioned frequently in literary theory, sometimes as something outside the scope of literary enquiry: literary works are said to be free of any context, or, alternatively, to 'create their own contexts'. Therein, it is claimed, lies the difference between literature and 'ordinary discourse'. There is a cluster of differences at issue here, including predominantly the fictionality of literature and also its alleged static or non-kinetic quality, that is to say its alleged failure to excite readers to practical action in the real world. These claims involve quite complicated and abstract problems; to think about them productively, we need to clarify what we mean by 'context'. At least three useful meanings can be distinguished, all of them relevant to our present discussion: *context of utterance, context of culture,* and *context of reference.*

In the first place, there is the immediate *context of utterance,* the situation within which discourse is conducted. This comprises: the physical surroundings or 'setting'; the distribution of the participants *vis-à-vis* one another, whether they are two people talking face-to-face, one person addressing a large audience, two people speaking by telephone, a group of informal conversationalists scattered through a large room, or whatever; the channel employed, whether aural, visual, electronic, etc., which will determine the 'mode' as some variety of speech or of writing. It might seem that contexts of utterance may vary in character almost as widely as the number of occasions of utterances, that is, indefinitely. However, human communication is not as random as that, and contexts of utterance tend to fall into types. For a start, there is a fundamental distinction between contexts in which participants are together at the same time and in the same place, and all 'split' contexts of utterance: for example, telephone, or live broadcast, in which the message is produced and received (virtually) simultaneously, but in different locations; letters, written and received at different points in space and in time—as is the case with most written or printed communications. Whether, and how, the context of utterance is 'split' has a profound influence on what deictics of time and place can be used (see pp. 79–80 above) and on what they mean: consider, for instance, the different selections and meanings for words like 'here' and 'now' in face-to-face discourse and in a telephone conversation—these are basic words for locating a discourse in context, but used quite differently according to differences of contextual type. A second systematic difference between types of utterance context involves personal deictics— 'I', 'you', etc.—depending on whether the participants are identifiable individuals or not. On the one hand, we have Mary Smith talking to Fred Smith; on the other, an unidentified 'I' speaking as the narrator in a nineteenth-century novel or a Renaissance love-poem—not the author speaking in his own voice—addressing an unknown mass readership or a pretended mistress respectively. In the case of the Smiths, the 'I' and the 'you' are real, whereas in the novel and the poem they are imagined and constructed. The latter type of utterance context is highly characteristic of literary texts; I will discuss how the fictional 'I' and 'we' are constructed below.

A third point needs to be made about the regularities of contexts of utterance. Although every utterance (or reception thereof) is a distinct historical event with its own idiosyncracies, there are strong and recognizable recurrent features which group distinct utterance contexts under clear categories or *situation types.* These classifying recurrences are the consequences of cultural conventions which sort the objects and activities of societies into categories with their distinct significances. I discussed this process of cultural categorization in Chapter 2, suggesting that it is an essential device for simplifying and making recognizable the material and social world, and that language plays an important part in stabilizing the categories. Although my discussion in Chapter 2 dealt principally with vocabulary, the principles apply to situation types too. As far as contexts of utterance are concerned, the settings and participants come to be recognized as stereotypes. The places where discourse occurs are perceived, not as individual sites, but as instances of institutions or routine settings like 'church', 'classroom', 'sitting room', 'television studio', etc. As for people, they communicate not just as individuals but in accordance with ascribed roles and statuses deriving from their functions within social structure: 'clergyman', 'teacher', 'child', 'salesperson', 'boss', and so on. People's behaviour is strongly affected by their roles, and by those of others, and by the conventions imposed by settings—and this conventionality of behaviour is characteristic of apparently intimate and informal contexts as well as of more rigid and ceremonial settings. There is ample evidence in the writings of sociolinguists and discourse analysts that the structure of verbal behaviour differs predictably from one situation type to another, and that these variations can be attributed to social and economic factors which extend beyond the immediate setting to the broader structure of society.

Thus our first sense of the word 'context', *context of utterance,* needs to be related to a second sense, *context of culture*: the whole network of social and economic conventions, all the institutions and the familiar settings and relationships, constituting the culture at large, especially in so far as these bear on particular utterance contexts, and influence the structure of discourse occurring within them. The distinction is an important one, particularly in the light of some literary-critical discussions, which define fictionality as lack of context, or unreality of context. It may be plausible to say that the context of *utterance* is peculiar in some literary genres (for example, the Renaissance love-poems already mentioned, or Keats's *Odes*); but all discourse has a definite context of *culture,* which may—I would say 'ought to'—be studied as an influence on the linguistic structure of literary texts, and as a guide to their interpretation. The relationships between literary discourse and cultural contexts are referred to informally throughout this book.

So far I have discussed two kinds of context which influence the structure of discourse: the immediate, but nevertheless conventional, context of utterance, and the broader, highly structured, context of culture, which may be seen as determining the possible types of utterance contexts (*situation types*)—and thus, indirectly but substantially, influencing the kind of discourse which may be used on specific occasions. The fitting of discourse to situation type, within the context of culture, will be the subject of Chapter 10 under the heading of *register*.

The third context is what I shall call *context of reference*: the topic or subject-matter of a text. (The subject-matter which is referred to is often known in linguistics as the *field* or *domain* of a text.) Now one of the most remarkable features of human language, distinguishing it from most other animal communication systems, is the relative independence of subject-matter from the contexts of utterance and of culture. This freedom, often called *displacement,* is the capacity of human speech to refer to things and events which are removed in space and time from the immediate context of utterance. Whereas the calls of animals, and the speech of infants, relate to the directly present circumstances of utterance, fully developed human language characteristically refers to contexts outside the here-and-now. The context of reference and the context of utterance do coincide when language is being used to demonstrate or comment on some present activity or object: explaining the controls of a new car—'This is the indicator switch'; commentary on one's own actions—the policeman's 'I'm now approaching the suspect' over his portable radio; cooking or chemistry demonstrations—'Add the contents of this jar to this one'. More often, however (and almost always in written discourse), discourse concerns displaced contexts: when we are telling a story, for instance, or making generalizations or predictions, we are invoking remote contexts of reference. It can be readily seen that displacement is a prerequisite for narrative and fictional discourse; and that both are entirely natural linguistic practices.

Finally, I must mention the relationship between context of reference and context of culture. Once more, there are various possibilities. Non-fictional discourse refers to any individual entities and activities which are both familiar, and known to exist, within the society referred to by the text. Fictional discourse may refer to such entities, but also adds references to imaginary individuals and events which have not existed (or it is immaterial whether or not they existed). Now these fictional creations may be more or less compatible with the norms of the context of culture. At one extreme we have, for instance, the classic nineteenth-century realist novels, the works of Balzac, George Eliot, Flaubert, Hardy, Zola, in which the fictional world is constructed to approximate closely to a known cultural context. Defamiliarization occurs when the context of reference introduces elements which in any way deviate from the expected cultural context. There are numerous techniques by which this can be effected. They include, for example, the introduction of sociologically deviant characters with discourse styles at odds with the norms of the narrative voice (the circus people in Dickens's *Hard Times*); children, idiots, and primitives whose world-views are defective or skewed compared with ours; in animal fantasies such as *Watership Down* or *Animal Farm*, the appropriation of 'our' context of culture for beings who are not normally thought to enjoy it; in science fiction, or fantasies such as *The Faerie Queene* or *Gulliver's Travels*, the creation of contexts of reference which are systematic transformations of our world—possible worlds understandable on the basis of our ideology and technology, but not factually experienced, including, for example, beings with brains and motives like ours but dissimilar bodies, or the other way around; finally, there are texts in which the poet attempts to construct a world which is a logical denial or inversion of the experiential norms supplied by the context of culture.

Let us now explore further how deictic and interpersonal features of language are used to construct fictional speech situations and domains in a number of printed texts. All are 'unnatural' in one way or another, in each case implying a speech situation markedly different from the normal conventions of print. However, I assume that experienced readers of poetry and stories develop ways of accommodating the fictional context of utterance, of naturalizing it while knowing that it is an artefact. As usual, we will progress by examples.

Very many of the poems of W. B. Yeats (1865–1939) begin with, or contain, the first-person deictic pronoun 'I'. A considerable number of these texts refer to events in Yeats's personal life, or to political issues about which, to our knowledge, he had passionate views, or to aesthetic and philosophical positions to which we know he subscribed. To what extent these poems are autobiographical, or may be said to be Yeats speaking, does not concern us. At least there is the implication that the poems transcribe *a* voice, and in each case it is up to the reader to work out what kind of a speaker this is, in what kind of utterance context: the reader cannot take the literal utterance seriously— Yeats writing sixty years ago, the poems printed, read in 1996— but must construct an artificial context.

Often a title will frame the poem as discourse. The title 'An Irish Airman Foresees his Death' refers to the poem's speaker in the third person, thus indicating the presence of another speaker presenting or quoting the first-person speech in the poem. Note also the verb for a mental process, 'foresees', announcing that the utterance is going to be reflective, not dramatic. The poem opens:

> I know that I shall meet my fate
> Somewhere among the clouds above;

In the sixteen lines of the poem, 'I', 'my', or 'me' appear ten times, and there are numerous other places where the first-person pronoun is implied, but does not appear on the surface of the text:

> I balanced all, [I] brought all to [my] mind

There are a good many third-person references—'Those that I fight', etc.—but no address to any second person ('you'). There are, in fact, no speech acts such as questions or commands which would involve an addressee in any more active capacity than that of mere 'listener'. The speaker makes a series of assertions, all of them about his own feelings and judgements:

> Those that I fight I do not hate
> Those that I guard I do not love; . . .
>
> A lonely impulse of delight
> Drove to this tumult in the clouds;
> I balanced all, brought all to mind . . .

The discourse is that of an individual reflecting on his own motives and decisions; verbs of thought and sensation abound, from 'know' onwards. It is a context of isolation, as is surely appropriate to the subject-matter: inner personal experience, rather than interaction. Note also that the discourse is scantily provided with deictics of place and time. 'The clouds above' does not mean that the speaker is standing looking up at the sky, nor does 'this tumult in the clouds' imply that he is actually in airborne combat at the time of utterance; helpfully, these two deictic phrases taken together are contradictory, so that we realize they cannot be interpreted literally as referring to the speaker's immediate location, but must refer generally to his characteristic activities. As for time reference, that is unfixed: it is psychological, rather than historical. The speaker reflects on his emotions at the moment of speech, recalls the period of decision which led him to assume the situation he is in, speculates on his probable future (death in action) and on the alternative future he has rejected (life with inactivity). The real historical background which enabled and inspired Yeats's poem, the service of Robert Gregory in the Royal Flying Corps and his death on 23 January 1918, is a potential context of reference which Yeats has declined to specify in detail within the fictional context of utterance of the poem: the consequence of this choice is that he has produced an effect much admired in poetry, the universal generalizability of an experience which *could* be felt as intensely specific.

Readers may wish to compare the treatment of deixis and reference in a more complicated poem by the same author, 'Among School Children', which I will discuss only briefly. The title and the opening stanza evoke a different kind of utterance context from that of 'An Irish Airman'.

> I walk through the long schoolroom questioning,
> A kind old nun in a white hood replies;
> The children learn to cipher and to sing,
> To study reading-books and history,
> To cut and sew, be neat in everything
> In the best modern way—the children's eyes
> In momentary wonder stare upon
> A sixty year old smiling public man.

Here the printed poem context is more definitively supplanted by the impression of a speaking voice. The crucial difference begins with the present tense action predicate 'walk', which contrasts with the mental state 'know' of the other poem. 'Know' implies no determinate point in time; 'I walk' must mean either 'I am now walking' or, less plausibly in this very particularized context of reference, 'I habitually walk'. All the specific details in this stanza suggest a particular scene within which the speaker is walking and commentating on his own actions and the responses of others: the locative deictic expressions 'Among School Children', 'through the long schoolroom'; the particular nun, and the expression in the children's eyes; the precise qualifiers 'long', 'white hood', etc.; the report of the nun's speech including a phrase which sounds like her own idiom, 'In the best modern way'. I suggest that this discourse of the opening of the poem, though printed and necessarily indirect, is constructed to mime not only a spoken context of utterance, but moreover a context of reference, or domain, which corresponds to the implied context of utterance. But if you study the corresponding discourse features in the rest of the poem, you will find that the context of reference shifts away from the implied context of utterance as the speaker's attention moves away from the classroom (in which we presume him still to stand) to meditate on youth, beauty, age, wisdom, and art. The effect of removal from context, a change to a displaced domain, is produced not only by esoteric and distant references ('Ledean body', 'Quattrocento', 'Plato') but also by basic discourse features: for instance, the frequency of verbs denoting thought and other inner processes—stanzas 2–4 begin 'I dream of a Ledean body', 'And thinking of that fit of grief or rage', and 'Her present image floats into the mind'. The discourse moves into the contemplative mode of the 'Irish Airman', implying an isolated thinker who asks rhetorical questions but needs no respondent—there are no 'you'-involving speech acts.

Let us now consider a different kind of example in which the printed text suggests a speech context. The *dramatic monologue,* a form perfected by Robert Browning (1812–1889), aims to imitate speech in an immediate context of utterance. In his writings in this genre, by an extreme foregrounding of the interpersonal and deictic parts of language, Browning creates not only the illusion of a speaking voice, but also the impression of an addressee towards whom the voice is projected, and a sense of location and movement within a physical space. There are no 'stage directions', no dialogue; all this is done through the utterance of the sole speaker. The opening and closing lines of Browning's 'My Last Duchess' will illustrate the processes which produce these effects. The speaker, an Italian Duke, talks to an emissary from a Count whose daughter the Duke intends to marry; the marriage arrangements are to be discussed, but first the Duke shows the messenger a painting of his late wife, and

speaks of his suspicions of her infidelity. The thirty or so lines
which I have omitted from the middle of the poem (at ' . . . . ')
give the Duke's account of his Duchess's 'trifling' and of her
punishment by death.

> That's my last Duchess painted on the wall,
> Looking as if she were alive. I call
> That piece a wonder, now: Fra Pandolf's hands
> Worked busily a day, and there she stands.
> Will't please you sit and look at her? I said   5
> 'Fra Pandolf' by design, for never read
> Strangers like you that pictured countenance,
> The depth and passion of its earnest glance,
> But to myself they turned (since none puts by
> The curtain I have drawn for you, but I)   10
> And seemed as they would ask me, if they durst,
> How such a glance came there; so, not the first
> Are you to turn and ask thus. . . .
>
>   There she stands
> As if alive. Will't please you rise? We'll meet   15
> The company below, then. I repeat,
> The Count your master's known munificence
> Is ample warrant that no just pretence
> Of mine for dowry will be disallowed;
> Though his fair daughter's self, as I avowed   20
> At starting, is my object. Nay, we'll go
> Together down, sir. Notice Neptune, though,
> Taming a sea-horse, thought a rarity,
> Which Claus of Innsbruck cast in bronze for me!

The poem starts with a deictic (pointing word) 'That's', and
contains many others: 'that piece', 'there', etc.: all refer to the
portrait of the Duchess, or its position, or some aspect of what
is pictured in it. All are distancing deictics, indicating an object
at some remove from the speaker (contrast 'this', 'here'). They
function to indicate that the speaker and the portrait occupy
determinate and related points in space, but no doubt psychological distance is suggested too. Consistent distancing deictics
seem usually to have an alienating effect. The setting is elaborated in a few locative phrases, adverbs, and especially by verbs
of placing and movement. Actually, there are few locative

adverbs or phrases: 'on the wall', 'below'. The main indicators
of space, other than the deictics proper, are verbs of motion or
location: 'stands' (twice), 'turn' (twice), 'sit', 'rise', 'go down',
plus one or two other verbs which imply change of position, such
as 'drawn', 'meet' (= go to meet). The preponderance of verbs of
motion over adverbs of location has the important effect, in this
poem in which an inert printed text enacts the speech gestures of
a person, of suggesting that the Duke, and the Count's emissary,
are interacting dynamically, rather than being fixed within a
statically described scene.

Indicators of time also have some importance. The action
takes place at a significant 'now': not just the narrative 'now' of
a storyteller recollecting the past, but the dramatic 'now' of a
wife-murdering Duke, a silent messenger, and an absent prospective bride. The ominous relationships between time-spheres are
already indicated in the first line, with its startling juxtaposition
of present and past, and its implications of a fateful future.
The past tense of 'last' makes it clear that she is *not* alive,
but present only in a painted image which serves as a warning
to 'triflers'; since 'last' in this context means 'previous' and
not 'final one of a series', we and the messenger must sense
the threat to the future bride. Moving from deictic to interpersonal features, we notice that, as might be expected, there is a
high density of personal pronouns. 'I' (and variants), referring to
the Duke, occurs 19 times in the complete poem; 'you', referring
to the messenger, 6 times, with another 3 in which 'you' is
ambiguously either the messenger or the generalized 'you'—
'anyone'; 'we' links the Duke and the messenger twice; 'she'
referring to the dead Duchess or her picture occurs 23 times—
and there are numerous other noun phrases that refer to her. The
frequency of first- and second-person pronouns obviously contributes to the sensation of a face-to-face discourse between
persons; the large number of 'I' forms is an index of the Duke's
self-importance and potential for tyranny; the 'she' pronouns
hint at the strength of his obsession for the woman he has had
killed.

Finally, the dramatic tone of the poem is heightened by—
among other conversational features of style—a large variety of

speech acts. More precisely, there is a large variety of speech acts which depart from the neutrality of statements and narrative reports. The poem opens with a demonstrative 'That's' which implies an accompanying wave of the hand. 'I call . . . ' is an act of judgement. 'Fra Pandolf's hands . . . ' is a narrative report, followed by another demonstrative 'and there she stands'. 'Will't please you . . . ' is an indirect command phrased with sham politeness; it recurs at the end of the poem, with other indirect commands—'Nay, we'll go . . . '—and a plain imperative: 'Notice Neptune . . . '. In the body of the narration, the Duke interrupts himself with questions and exclamations: '—how shall I say?—'. Frequently the Duke draws attention to his own acts of speech, as if emphasizing the power of his words: 'I call . . . ', 'I said . . . ', 'I gave commands', 'I repeat . . . ', 'as I avowed . . . '. These vocal gestures, which are essentially alien to the printed page, dramatize the speaker and the scene, and, of course, *characterize* the Duke at the same time: authoritarian, indeed tyrannical to the point of committing ducal murder, self-centred, maniacal perhaps in his erratic switches between highly diverse acts of speech.

In discussing these three poems, I have concentrated on ways in which deictic and interpersonal parts of the printed texts suggest three different modes of discourse: a reflective discourse; the speech or thought of a man first conscious of his situation in a classroom, and later withdrawing into his own reflections; and the speech of one person addressing another in direct interaction: in all of these cases, a spoken context of utterance is fictitiously built out of a written text. As we reconstruct the dramatic situation, and begin the activity of interpreting the discourse, we start to draw upon features which relate the language to a context of culture, a social and historical context in which people interact through varieties of discourse which reflect their social roles and statuses. So, for instance, Browning's—and our—characterization of the Duke depends on assumptions about how power, authority, and manipulation are encoded in English. (Though the context of *reference* is vaguely antique Italian, the linguistically relevant context of *culture* relates to Browning's only slightly archaic English.) We assume, for example, that a polite, modalized invitation spoken by the Duke, a social superior (lines 5 and 15), is not polite and considerate at all, but actually a strong and only hypocritically polite command. We make this assumption on the basis of our knowledge of the way power-relations and language intersect in the sociolinguistic conventions of English, and we constantly bring this sort of sociolinguistic knowledge into play when we reconstruct the cultural meanings of texts.

I shall end this chapter with an example of the importance of sociolinguistic structure, taken from a very familiar play, Shakespeare's *King Lear*. This will, incidentally, illustrate not only the linguistic relevance of context of culture, but also another argument which was introduced at the beginning of this book: the function of linguistic criticism in reactivating for modern readers patterns of language which may have lost their force through historical changes in the language, and/or the familiarity of the literature. In this case, the dramatic power of a scene from a classic play is enhanced if we twentieth-century readers can respond to the social nuances of some sixteenth-century pronoun usages which are no longer current in modern English.

In Act I Scene 2 of the play, the old King Lear is in the process of dividing up his kingdom among his three daughters, Goneril, Regan, and Cordelia, in proportion to their professed love for him, which he requires them to declare publicly. Goneril and Regan co-operate with their father, but Cordelia is unwilling to participate in what she seems to regard as an act of emotional blackmail in which her sisters have colluded hypocritically. The Earl of Kent supports her, attacks the king for making this irrational and unfatherly demand; thereby places himself in a state of rebellion against the king, incurs Lear's wrath, and is banished. The text criticizes Lear for giving the formal powers of monarchy expression in an inhuman demand which overrides both the personal bonds of family, and the loyalty and affection of Kent. One of the ways in which this tension between the personal and the formal is signalled is through the forms of address—names and pronouns—which the characters employ with one another. The linguistic patterns involved are not peculiar to this play, but refer to sociolinguistic conventions which apparently still had some force in Elizabethan English, though probably weakening. The relevant *pronoun* usages have now disappeared from English, though our language uses different forms of address through variable *naming* to systematically express types of personal relationships (first name versus title and last name, etc.). These relationships are still clearly encoded in the personal pronoun systems of other modern languages, for instance the choice between *tu* and *vous* in French, and between *du* and *Sie* in German. The relationships concerned are power and subordination; distance and solidarity or intimacy. Two social equals may indicate their similar status, and the lack of closeness in their personal relationship, by addressing one another as 'Mr Smith', 'Miss Jones', or in French by the pronoun *vous;* an intimate relationship, for example, family or close friends, or a solidary relationship, for example, young people together, may be indicated by mutual *tu* in French, or mutual first names in either language. *In*equality of status, however, selects from the same set of linguistic forms, but the meanings are different in the changed social circumstances. A superior (manager, aristocrat, judge, teacher, etc.) may express power or control over a subordinate by using *tu* or first name, while the person of lower status must reply with *vous* or title alone, or title and last name (*Doctor, Doctor Finlay.*) A range of extremely important social meanings is encoded in a very economical set of linguistic forms, whose use is subject to severe restrictions, which of course apply more strongly to the inferior of any pair of people. In a tight linguistic system, deviation from the rules is extremely noticeable: for instance, the use of a familiar form such as *tu,* or a first name, by someone of lower status when addressing someone of higher status makes a potentially suspect and rejectable claim of equality and intimacy. Also, these sociolinguistic systems often contain more meanings than there are terms to express, so that some utterances are disturbingly ambiguous: for instance, *tu* spoken by someone of high status (A) to someone of lower status (B) may either be an assertion of the power difference and of A's right to condescend to B, or it may be a gesture of solidarity with B. The ambiguity creates unease:

if my doctor calls me 'Roger', can I return his first name (if I know it)?

These two instabilities—challenge to authority, and the nature of a claim to authority—are central to what is happening in the narrative and the thematic development in the scene from *Lear,* and they are expressed and reinforced in the language of address: pronouns, names, and titles. The pronoun system, on which I shall concentrate, is very simple. There were two options (with variants) which one person could use to address another: *thou* (*thee/thy/thine*) and *you* (*your*). They functioned like *tu* and *vous* in French, or *du* and *Sie* in German: *thou* was used either 'downwards' by a superior, in which case it encoded status, or 'sideways', reciprocally, between intimates; *you* was deferential when used 'upwards' by a subordinate (who must not use *thou* in that situation), but distant if respectful, perhaps neutral, between non-intimates of any rank.

The situation in this scene is formal and serious, and, as we would expect, the address forms begin by following the conventions strictly. Lear marks the ceremonial of the occasion by using the royal *we:*

> Know that we have divided
> In three our Kingdom.   (37–8)

He asks his three daughters in turn 'Which of you shall we say doth love us most?' (51) First Goneril replies with the polite, deferential *you,* emphasizing her public, rather than family, relationship with her father:

> Sir, I love you more than word can wield the matter;
> Dearer than eyesight . . .
> Beyond all manner of so much I love you.   (55–61)

Lear responds with the *thou* form:

> Of all these bounds . . .
> We make thee lady: to thine and Albany's issue . . . (63–7)

Note that it is impossible to tell whether Lear is using the *thou* of condescension or that of family intimacy in this context, but it does not matter, because the interaction between the king and his eldest daughter is, from their point of view, proceeding smoothly.

Identical non-reciprocal address (Lear *thou*; Regan *you*) is found in the parallel exchange with the next daughter (67–82). But a shift occurs as Lear moves from Regan ('To thee and thine . . .' 79) to Cordelia ('what can you say . . . ?' 85). Cordelia is about to decline to declare how much she loves her father, and Lear's two *yous* (85, 86), by contrast with the *thou* he is entitled to use, and has just used in addressing Goneril and Regan, may show an anticipatory nervousness. For twenty lines, Lear and Cordelia's dialogue employs reciprocal *you* frequently and consistently. Cordelia's *you* is the expected pronoun of deference:

> [I] obey you, love you, and most honour you. (98)

whereas Lear's *you* suggests distance, the refusal of intimate *thou*:

> Mend your speech a little,
> Lest you may mar your fortunes. (94–5)

Suddenly he shifts to *thou*, and begins to use it consistently in addressing Cordelia; in the first instance (105) affectionately as a father, then (108 onwards) harshly and dismissively: his exploitation of the threatening ambiguity of this pronoun is part of the way Shakespeare's text builds up an impression of dangerous capriciousness in his character:

COR. Sure I shall never marry like my sisters,
   To love my father all.
LEAR. But goes thy heart with this?
COR.   Ay, my good Lord.   105
LEAR. So young, and so untender?
COR. So young, my Lord, and true.
LEAR. Let it be so; thy truth then be thy dower.

After a succession of venomous curses, he concludes by dismissing her as 'thou my sometime daughter' (120). At this point Kent tries to intervene on Cordelia's behalf, but he is silenced by Lear, who goes on with his business of dividing his kingdom between Goneril and Regan, excluding Cordelia. Kent manages to speak in line 139, and, significantly, attempts to placate Lear by invoking his own relationships of subordination to the King. When Lear threatens him again, Kent's language changes completely; in saying that Lear has abdicated his authority as a king, and lost his reason, Kent explicitly announces his personal rebellion by addressing Lear with no less than 16 insubordinate *thou*s in twenty lines:

KENT.   Royal Lear,
  Whom I have ever honour'd as my King,   140
  Lov'd as my father, as my master follow'd,
  As my great patron thought on in my prayers,—
LEAR. The bow is bent and drawn; make from the shaft.
KENT. Let it fall rather, though the fork invade
  The region of my heart: be Kent unmannerly   145
  When Lear is mad. What would'st thou do, old man?
  Think'st thou that duty shall have dread to speak
  When power to flattery bows? To plainness honour's bound
  When majesty falls to folly. Reserve thy state;
  And, in thy best consideration, check   150
  This hideous rashness; answer my life my judgment,
  Thy youngest daughter does not love thee least . . .

These *thou*s are an affront to the King, who in a series of furious speeches rages against Kent's insolence, and finally consigns him to exile. Naturally, he addresses Kent with *thou,* the *thou* of contemptuous power. As Kent leaves, he gives Cordelia one intimate *thou,* indicating the affection of an elder who recognizes her sincerity and has her dearest interests at heart: 'The Gods to their dear shelter take thee, maid . . . ' (182).

The second-person pronouns are part of a set of interpersonal linguistic features (including naming and speech acts) which build up the characterization, narrative, and themes in this early scene of the play. The interpersonal tensions and shifts of behaviour and affiliation which unfold here are very precisely controlled by the structure of the text: Lear's instability, the destructive effects of institutional power (monarchy), obliterating personal allegiances and family obligations; the personalities of the main protagonists as the text constructs and explores them. But it cannot be emphasized too strongly that it is not this particular text alone which by its own unique structure creates the opening position in *King Lear*: rather, it is the relationship between the textual structures and the cultural context which in

Elizabethan England, and now, gives the text meaning. The main structures that are active here are interpersonal forms of language, which signify only by virtue of the society's assumptions about how people relate. The cultural context supplies systems of beliefs about the rights and responsibilities of monarchs, parents, subjects, children, their relationships with one another and the ways these relationships are monitored and managed. The audience or reader of the play needs to bring these assumptions to their understanding of the play as its text unfolds, and the text's language (here, pronouns, etc.) instructs the reader towards analysis of and reflection on the values that are at issue in the play.

References and Suggestions for Further Reading

The quotation from Halliday on p. III is taken from 'Language structure and language function', in J. Lyons, ed., *New Horizons in Linguistics* (Harmondsworth: Penguin, 1970), p. 142.

Reference to 'context' is virtually taboo in structural and generative linguistics, but it has attained a position of fundamental interest in anthropological linguistics, particularly that branch known as ethnography of communication; and in functional linguistics. See B. Malinowski, 'The problem of meaning in primitive languages', in C. K. Ogden and I. A. Richards, *The Meaning of Meaning* (London: Routledge, 1949 [1923]), pp. 296–336. Malinowski demonstrated that the full meaning of utterances could not be understood without reference to what he called the *context of situation,* an idea which was taken up by Halliday's mentor J. R. Firth (see Firth's *Papers in Linguistics 1934–1951* (London: Oxford University Press, 1964). The influence of context on language choice and meaning is fundamental to Halliday's discussion of *register:* see Chapter 10 for references. For the detailed study of context in American sociolinguistics of an ethnographic slant, see J. J. Gumperz and D. Hymes, eds., *Directions in Sociolinguistics* (New York: Holt, Rinehart & Winston, 1972).

On *deixis* see S. Levinson, *Pragmatics* (Cambridge: Cambridge University Press, 1983), ch. 2; J. Lyons, *Semantics* (Cambridge: Cambridge University Press, 1977), ch. 15.

There is an extensive discussion of 'My Last Duchess' in R. Pope, *Textual Intervention* (London: Routledge, 1995), based on some very suggestive rewriting exercises designed to defamiliarize the poem.

Introductions to sociolinguistics include W. Downes, *Language and Society* (Glasgow: Fontana, 1984); M. Montgomery, *An Introduction to Language and Society* (London: Routledge, 1986); S. Romaine, *Language in Society* (Oxford: Oxford University Press, 1994); P. Trudgill, *Sociolinguistics* (Harmondsworth: Penguin, revised edn., 1995).

On pronouns and forms of address, see R. Brown and A. Gilman, 'The pronouns of power and solidarity', in P. P. Giglioli, ed., *Language and Social Context* (Harmondsworth: Penguin, 1972), pp. 252–82; S. M. Ervin-Tripp, 'Sociolinguistic rules of address', in J. B. Pride and J. Holmes, eds., *Sociolinguistics* (Harmondsworth: Penguin, 1972), pp. 225–40.

Line numbers in the extract from *King Lear* refer to the Arden edition, ed. Kenneth Muir (London: Methuen, 1957). Pronoun usage in Shakespeare's English can be looked up in E. A. Abbott, *A Shakespearean Grammar* (New York: Dover, 1966 [1870]).

Some Aspects of Dialogue

The previous chapter encourages a view of texts as *discourses,* as interactions between speakers and addressees who might be real, implied, or fictional. In my opinion, this is a most important emphasis, a corrective to the older view in linguistic criticism that literary texts are just formal structures of language; and to the traditional claim in literary criticism that texts are objects rather than interactions: 'verbal icons', 'monuments', or 'well-wrought urns'. The latter phrase is taken from a poem of Donne's by the critic Cleanth Brooks, and applied to all poetry: we are meant to recall Keats's silent Grecian Urn, an unspeaking but meaningful artefact. But 'literary' texts, like all texts, *do* speak: they participate in society's communicative practices, and are an important means of influencing world-view and social structure. In this chapter, I want to examine some aspects of linguistic structure which concern interaction directly: *dialogic* structures.

I am going to explore dialogic structure in two senses; the first is the ordinary sense of the word 'dialogue', in which characters talk to each other. The second is an extended sense, whereby there is implicit dialogic interaction within the straight text—i.e. within a passage of prose or verse with no quotation marks, no alternating speeches, perhaps even little indication of voice. Implicit dialogue in texts may be an exchange or interaction of points of view between the author and the reader, the narrator and his characters, even—without speech, note—between characters. This extended sense of the dialogic comes from the work of Mikhail Bakhtin.

First, we look at dialogue in the conventional sense, the fictional representation of conversation or shared, alternating, speech. The study of conversation has advanced considerably in recent years, after decades during which linguistics was dominated by a preoccupation with the structure of the single sentence. This area of linguistics is variously known as *conversational analysis* and *discourse analysis*; aspects of it also fall within part of the field of *pragmatics*. It is emerging that the structure of conversation is very much more complex than that of sentences taken singly, or even cohesive but monologic texts; a battery of techniques have been identified which make up this complexity. I cannot explain or illustrate the whole range of conversational features that have been proposed, but will pick out three that seem to be relatively promising when applied to dialogue in literature: *sequencing, speech acts,* and *implicature.*

Sequencing is the ordering of contributions to conversations. There are elaborate conventions for arranging the openings, developments, and closings of conversations; conventions for holding the floor, for interrupting, and for turn-taking. They vary according to the setting, the statuses and relationships of the speakers, and the topics of discourse. Who speaks first? What is an appropriate opening move in a particular setting? Given A's first remark, what possibilities are open to B? Must B simply respond with a 'yes' or a 'no', and expect A to carry on controlling the dialogue, or may B assume the stage, begin a new topic and develop it, reserving the initiative to himself? The types of greetings used, the forms of questions asked, even the speed and intonations of contributions, intricately manage the sharing of a conversation between participants. Even a tiny interchange uses structure very precisely to govern what happens, how much is said, and who says it. Take, for instance, the following short telephone call which interrupted my writing of this paragraph:

☎ 1. * * * *
A 2. Hello?
B 3. (Pause) Hello, is that Roger Fowler?
A 4. Yes.
B 5. Oh it's Ian Jones here; 6. have you got a couple of minutes?
A 7. Yes, sure. (Waits)
B 8. Have you got a couple of minutes in, say, five minutes' time?

A   9. Yes, do you want to come down here?
B   10. OK, five minutes.
A   11. See you then, bye-bye.
B   12. Bye-bye.

The first move occurs (1) through the ringing of the phone (the type of ring, incidentally, signalling that this is an internal call from within the University, thus narrowing the range of potential callers, and predicting some possible institutional speaker-roles). I respond minimally, not identifying myself (2). The caller does not recognize my voice, pauses, and checks my identity (3); notice that he does this through a yes/no question, which severely restricts the range of reply options which are available to me (4). In this way, the caller keeps the advantage, reserving his right to begin the informative part of the call. He identifies himself (5), and maintains a high voice pitch level as he moves to a request for my attention (6). Again, this is a yes/no question—to which the answer 'no' would be very difficult! By this time I have identified the caller, and guessed that he wishes to tell me something confidential, and to ask my advice. I wish to get back to my writing as quickly as I can, and the silence labelled 'waits' is intended to tell him to get it off his chest there and then. The caller rejects this move by repeating his wording of (6) in (8), with the additional phrase 'in, say, five minutes' time'. This is an absurd question at face value, so I am obliged to interpret it as a request for a private interview. I, having the status, nominate my office as meeting-place (9); B confirms, indicating, by repetition, insistence (10). There is nothing more to say, so I initiate a farewell sequence (11), which B promptly closes (12).

This conversation worked well partly because the participants knew each other, and the kind of topics on which they had spoken in the past: even casually acquainted people draw on pre-existing common knowledge to help their conversations proceed smoothly and meaningfully. But, in large part, the efficiency stems from the fact that the conversation unfolds according to a plan. I do not mean that the speakers consciously calculate what they are going to say at each point in the dialogue. As usual in language structure, such plans are abstract blueprints which are known unconsciously. The speakers have confident experience of how such calls proceed, and at each point in the sequence they produce types of utterance which progress the conversation in a manner which is appropriate to the type of interaction, and to their relationship and purposes. The Americans Schegloff and Sacks have proposed rules for openings, closings, and sequencings, with particular attention to what they call 'adjacency pairs', interlocked or interdependent consecutive utterances. Sinclair and Coulthard of Birmingham University have proposed a complementary scheme classifying the types of acts and moves performed through smaller and larger parts of conversations. More on sequencing follows in the analyses below.

We next introduce two concepts drawn from pragmatics. The first is the most important approach to speech as action, the theory of *speech acts* or *illocutionary acts* originally proposed by J. L. Austin, and developed by J. R. Searle. The basic insight is that language-use has an extra dimension which has been somewhat neglected by logicians and linguists: a performative dimension. Linguists and philosophers have traditionally been preoccupied with the propositional and semantic functions of language. The linguist is interested in how language encodes meanings, and in such semantic properties as well-formedness, ambiguity, contradiction, tautology, etc.; the logician, in the conditions for the truth or falsehood of the propositions expressed in languages (including the artificial languages of symbolic logic), and in the logical relationships between propositions in terms of truth criteria. Our speech-act philosophers, however, observed that language has a *performative* as well as a propositional function: utterances are used to perform actions, in addition to communicating propositions true or false. This principle is easy to grasp in connection with utterances containing certain special performative verbs such as promise, declare, name, baptize, request, order, guarantee. Consider the sentences:

I promise to pay you five pounds.

I declare this fête open.

A person uttering one of these sentences conveys a proposition about a financial promise, or about opening a fête. But in addition, the utterance of the sentence actually constitutes the action referred to. It is literally a speech act, not just saying something, but doing something through speaking. Notice that the logical test of truth doesn't apply in these cases. The criterion for the success of these is not whether they are true, but whether they are appropriately uttered. A successful speech act of promising, for instance, requires that several conditions be fulfilled, including that whatever is promised must be a future act of the speaker; that he is capable of doing it; that he intends to do it, and intends his utterance to commit him to doing it; that he would not do whatever he promises in the normal course of events (otherwise there would be no point in promising); that he believes the person he is addressing would prefer him to do it ('I promise to burn your house down' would only be a successful promise if we were conspiring to commit an insurance fraud). Presumably, all speech acts have their conditions of appropriateness, differing widely from case to case: only marriageable people—not dogs or babies—can be declared man and wife; you cannot consecrate a supermarket. Defamiliarization can occur if a speech act is spoken in inappropriate circumstances—a deliberate source of verbal humour, for example: 'I name this cat "The Skylark".'

Speech acts can be based on constructions other than explicit performative verbs. Rather than saying 'I order you to shut the door', one would be more likely to say 'Shut the door', or even 'Could you shut the door?': although this looks like a question about the addressee's physical ability, in the right conditions it is likely to be taken as an *indirect speech act* of ordering. Finally, when we consider that an order may be successfully communicated by an apparently simple descriptive statement 'The door is open', or 'It's cold in here', it becomes clear that there is no direct, predictable link between a specific type of linguistic construction and a specific speech act. The important thing to note is the prevalence of speech acts in discourse: the fact that speakers in dialogue continuously engage in a series of illocutionary acts such as requesting, undertaking, challenging, asserting, warning, and so on. This is the chief mechanism by which conversation is maintained as a practical interaction as well as a channelling of ideas.

The third aspect of dialogue which I want to maintain is important for linguistic criticism is *implicature*: roughly, what is said 'between the lines'. This relates to the traditional notion that one can say one thing and mean something else (for example, irony, metaphor, *double entendre*). Neglected in linguistics until recently, discussed by literary critics with no great clarity, these obscure processes have been studied with insight by the philosopher H. P. Grice, to whom we owe the term 'implicature'. An implicature is a proposition emerging from something that is said, but not actually stated by the words uttered, nor logically derivable from them. It must therefore be a product of the relationship between utterance and context; and a vital part of context would be the knowledge and motives of speaker and addressee. It is in the latter area that Grice's suggestions are most interesting. He suggests that conversation takes place under the guidance of a *co-operative principle* which binds speakers to express themselves in such a way as not to impede interpretation—and hearers to assume that whatever is addressed to them is designed to make sense, so that they make an effort to find an interpretation, even when the language does offer difficulties. The speaker's obligations are summarized by Grice under four *maxims*:

1. Quantity

(*a*) Make your contribution as informative as is required (for the current purposes of the exchange).
(*b*) Do not make your contribution more informative than is required.

2. Quality

Try to make your contribution one that is true.
(*a*) Do not say what you believe to be false.
(*b*) Do not say that for which you lack adequate evidence.

3. Relation

Be relevant.

4. Manner

Be perspicuous.
(*a*) Avoid obscurity of expression.
(*b*) Avoid ambiguity.
(*c*) Be brief.
(*d*) Be orderly.

Conversational implicatures characteristically arise when a hearer judges that the speaker has deliberately flouted one of the maxims. Suppose A and B are talking about X, a bank manager who, both agree, is exceptionally tight-fisted when it comes to lending money. A comments: 'He's absolutely the most generous, tolerant manager in the whole history of banking.' A has flouted maxim 2(a) by saying something which both A and B know to be false. A *implicates* the reverse of what he says: he is being ironical. What is more, he pads out what he says in excess words and phrases: his hyperbolic expressions—flouting either maxim 1(b) or 4(c)—draw attention to the fact that there is something unstraightforward about the statement, and they invite B to interpret it. And B, the addressee, is bound by his side of the co-operative principle to attempt to make sense of the utterance, so he recovers the implicature.

Although the theory of implicature was expressed by Grice in very informal terms, and remains fuzzy in its details, it enriches our view of how discourse works, and promises numerous insights for linguistic criticism. As far as dialogue is concerned, the technique of flouting maxims and raising implicatures is central to dialogic structure in a good deal of elliptical, allusive modern drama, such as Harold Pinter's plays; and to dialogue in witty, or ironic, or stylized, novels. My analysis of the Fielding passage, below, could be rethought in terms of implicature, though that is not the terminology which I have chosen on this occasion.

Digressing for a while from the topic of dialogue, there is another important link between the flouting of the conversational maxims and the argument of the present book. As we have seen, writers can deliberately flout the maxims and still make sense, in the knowledge that their readers have tacitly agreed that deviations are purposeful, intended to provoke a search for meaning. Thus, literary writers are permitted to say less (Imagism), or say more (Faulkner, Proust) than might be expected (maxim 1); utter what is known to be false or unevidenced (fairy-stories, science fiction) (maxim 2); create unexpected transitions between discrepant subjects (Joyce, *nouveau roman*) (maxim 3); be obscure, ambiguous, verbose, disjointed (*Finnegans Wake*, Symbolist poetry, Dylan Thomas) (maxim 4). In 'literary' works, such breaches are not just tolerated, but even applauded as producing aesthetically or conceptually agreeable verbal effects. The best book of literary criticism in this century, William Empson's *Seven Types of Ambiguity* (1930), extensively justifies and celebrates breaches of maxim 4(b). I have no doubt that, if the classification of maxims could be made clearer and more discriminating, it would greatly assist the understanding of the traditional 'poetic' figures such as metaphor, metonymy, hyperbole, litotes, etc. This book is not devoted to a detailed survey of poetic figures; but it is worth pointing out a more general link: between the breaching of the maxims and the whole process of defamiliarization.

Breaches of the maxims have exactly the effect that Shklovsky detects in 'artistic' language: they 'make forms difficult . . . , increase the difficulty and length of perception' (p. 56 above). The linguistic peculiarities found in 'literary' texts, like those breaches of the maxims that produce implicatures, are *motivated*: there is a reason for the deviation, and it is up to the reader to figure out that reason; then, guided by the structure of the text and its relation to implied context, the reader arrives at a new perspective on what is being expressed. The structures stemming from deviations from the maxims correspond closely to 'literary' figures, and these are, of course, the figures which give rise to defamiliarization.

Many of the defamiliarizing examples quoted earlier in this book can be understood in the light of motivated breaches of specific maxims. Briefly, the description of the Yahoos quoted from *Gulliver's Travels* (pp. 58–9 above) can be explained as a breach of the maxim of quantity: by withholding of the information that these are humans, Swift gives less information than might be expected, so producing an ironic surprise when the penny drops. Tolstoy's description of a stage quoted above (p. 58) has the same effect. The opening of *Pride and Prejudice* (p. 78 above) deliberately flouts the maxim of quality for ironic purposes: Jane Austen makes her narrator claim as a truth universally acknowledged a proposition which is manifestly not so. Chandler's detective Marlowe is pointedly inconsequential, flouting a maxim of manner (p. 89). Many more of my examples of defamiliarization can be regarded in the light of the maxims, and readers may care to look at other passages in this book, and consider how the maxims might be refined so as to shed a more focused illumination on the techniques of defamiliarization.

The co-operative principle embodies not just a willingness to be mutually helpful, but an agreement to bring to the comprehension of utterances bodies of shared knowledge (ideology, belief systems, in the terms of Chapters 1–2 and 12). That which is implied 'between the lines' may not be created afresh—which is what the theory of implicature and defamiliarization suggests—but may be conventional and expected. In a masterly explication of the implied propositions underpinning a psychotherapeutic interview, Labov and Fanshel have demonstrated how conventional knowledge is an essential element in the interpretation of discourse. Their work may provide a model for thematic criticism. The implicit themes and preoccupations of a text, or an author, or a genre of discourse, or the significance of a particular passage, might be approached by way of a study of recurrent, repeated, general propositions. I have tried this informally with *Look Back in Anger*, below, and the extract from *Tom Jones* analysed at the end of this chapter. Questions of shared knowledge are particularly interesting and problematic when, as in the modern reader's relationship with Fielding, one is trying to decode older works after major ideological shifts have occurred.

Returning from the extension of dialogic concepts to the study of literal dialogue, I want to show how sequencing, speech acts and implicature are deployed to create a verbal illusion of interaction in plays. First, I have chosen the opening of John Osborne's *Look Back in Anger* (1956). Three characters dominate this part of the action: Jimmy Porter, his wife Alison, and their friend and co-lodger, Cliff. In his introductory stage direction, Osborne speaks of 'the uneasy polyphony of these three people'. Polyphony in music is the simultaneous voicing of several separate musical lines—strands which are not in unison. Certainly, these three characters speak in very distinct tones, and they are often discordant. Much of the dialogue consists of Jimmy's verbal harassment of Alison and Cliff, and their attempts to evade his attacks. Jimmy is outrageous and rude, but not only as an effect of his abusive vocabulary; rather, the whole manipulative strategy of his conversation characterizes him as a destructive, self-pitying, childish, bully.

Here is the text of the opening of the play:

1. JIMMY. Why do I do this every Sunday? Even the book reviews seem to be the same as last week's. Different books—same reviews. Have you finished that one yet?
2. CLIFF. Not yet.
3. J. I've just read three whole columns on the English Novel. Half of it's in French. Do the Sunday papers make *you* feel ignorant?
4. C. Not 'arf.
5. J. Well, you *are* ignorant. You're just a peasant. [*To Alison*] What about you? You're not a peasant are you?
6. ALISON [*absently*]. What's that?
7. J. I said do the papers make you feel you're not so brilliant after all?
8. A. Oh—I haven't read them yet.
9. J. I didn't ask you that. I said—
10. C. Leave the poor girlie alone. She's busy.
11. J. Well, she can talk, can't she? You can talk, can't you? You can express an opinion. Or does the White Woman's Burden make it impossible to think?
12. A. I'm sorry. I wasn't listening properly.
13. J. You bet you weren't listening. Old Porter talks, and everyone turns over and goes to sleep. And Mrs Porter gets 'em all going with the first yawn.

14. C. Leave her alone, I said.
15. J. [*shouting*]. All right, dear. Go back to sleep. It was only me talking. You know? Talking? Remember? I'm sorry.
16. C. Stop yelling. I'm trying to read.
17. J. Why do you bother? You can't understand a word of it.
18. C. Uh huh.
19. J. You're too ignorant.
20. C. Yes, and uneducated. Now shut up, will you?
21. J. Why don't you get my wife to explain it to you? She's educated. [*To her*] That's right, isn't it?
22. C. [*kicking out at him from behind his paper*]. Leave her alone, I said.
23. J. Do that again, you Welsh ruffian, and I'll pull your ears off. [*He bangs Cliff's paper out of his hands*]
24. C. [*leaning forward*]. Listen—I'm trying to better myself. Let me get on with it, you big, horrible man. Give it me. [*Puts his hand out for paper*]
25. A. Oh, give it to him, Jimmy, for heaven's sake! I can't think!
26. C. Yes, come on, give me the paper. She can't think.
27. J. Can't think! [*Throws the paper back at him*] She hasn't had a thought for years! Have you?
28. A. No.
29. J. [*Picks up a weekly*]. I'm getting hungry.

Let us first look at sequencing: how the dialogue introduces, develops, and changes topics, how the speakers share their contributions. The main point is that it is Jimmy who controls what is spoken about, and, to a large extent, how Cliff and Alison join in the conversation. For their parts, Cliff and Alison—engaged in reading and in ironing—attempt to avoid involvement, to say as little as possible, and so to give Jimmy the least opportunity to turn what they say against them. This strategy of reticence is not very successful, for Jimmy is very adept at turning their least words to suit his purposes. Through this conversation, Jimmy asserts and implicates a series of judgements and prejudices which begin to build an impression of a 'character'.

Jimmy's opening question is rhetorical: there is no sensible answer to it. Notice the specific 'do this': in order to understand this remark (i.e. 'read the Sunday papers') we have to be aware of what in fact Jimmy is doing, and so he is assumed to be the focus of attention. He hints at the tedium of Sundays ('every', 'same'), and introduces the subject of book reviews, which are indistinguishable from week to week and then (3) pretentious and obscure. The shift which Jimmy makes in 3 and 5 is characteristic. The contrastive stress on *you* implies that Jimmy himself is made to feel ignorant by the reviews, and so he might continue talking about his reactions to them; instead, he turns the word 'ignorant' into an insult to Cliff, expanded as 'peasant' in the metaphorical sense of a person who lacks knowledge and experience. Jimmy persists with this abuse in 17 and 19; Cliff concedes that he is 'uneducated' (20), a deficiency he seeks to remedy by reading the papers (24). In the interests of peace and quiet, he accepts Jimmy's judgement, but just as a plain fact about his education. Jimmy, however, nags away with the insult: 'Welsh' (23) = 'provincial' = 'peasant'.

Going back to 5, Jimmy uses the word 'peasant' a second time, to initiate an attack on Alison: 'You're not a peasant are you?' Here he uses the word in a more literal sense: Alison is not asked to confirm that she is not ignorant, but, literally, that she is not a member of the peasant classes. It may not be clear yet, but this is a taunt: Jimmy holds Alison's upper-middle-class background against her, and ceaselessly reviles her and her parents in these terms (11, 'White Woman's Burden', 21 'educated', etc.). The allegation which Jimmy is starting here is that Alison is mindless despite and/or because of her middle-class advantages: it is implicit in 11—the women of colonial administrators such as Alison's father have no opinions—and an explicit insult in 25–7, where Jimmy twists the meaning of Alison's and Cliff's 'think': 'She hasn't had a thought for years.' The effectiveness of Jimmy's strategy illustrates the economy of conversation between people who can make ready inferences. The one word 'peasant' allows him to launch dual, but different, assaults on Cliff and Alison. He sustains and develops his tirade by two devices. There is the technique of leaping on someone else's words and twisting them; and the starting of a verbal hare of his own, pursuing it relentlessly, and appropriating others' remarks as he goes along. In the opening sequence about the Sunday papers, the groundwork is laid for a critique of intelligence and opinions; Jimmy turns this critique against Alison by an intricate sequence of helter-skelter transitions:

7. not so brilliant after all   (i.e. despite your education and upbringing.)

10. busy
11. talk . . . talk . . . express an opinion . . . impossible to think
12. I wasn't listening properly
13. you weren't listening . . . talks . . . sleep . . . yawn   (Breaking the maxim of Relation, Jimmy implicates, through a dead metaphor, that Alison is inattentive and bored.)

15. sleep . . . only me talking
16. trying to read
17. can't understand
19. ignorant
20. uneducated   (Jimmy digresses from Alison to resume the 'ignorant' attack on Cliff; but takes care to maintain reference to Alison:)

21. Why don't you get my wife to explain it to you? She's educated.
24. trying to better myself
25. I can't think!   (A major tactical error by Alison, allowing Jimmy to climax his condemnation of her.)

26. She can't think
27. Can't think! She hasn't had a thought for years! Have you?

Alison's answer is characteristic of the way she avoids confrontation with her aggressive husband: 'No.' Subjected to this verbal battering, her safest course is to be compliant, and brief;

to give Jimmy the least possible excuse for further abuse. On this occasion he is not interested in persisting with this line, but immediately takes up the right he has assigned himself to be the one of the three who introduces new topics, and to be utterly self-centred: 'I'm getting hungry.'

Jimmy uses another important dialogue technique, akin to implicature, to broaden the scope of his attack on Alison. This is the implying of what Labov and Fanshel call 'general propositions': beliefs or moral principles which underpin discourse and constitute ideology, but are only hinted at on the surface of the language. A system of ideas about marriage is implied from 13 on: Jimmy appeals to the general proposition that wives should be supportive of, and more specifically, attentive to, their husbands. Alison unwittingly sets Jimmy going on this theme in 12 when she says 'I'm sorry. I wasn't listening properly.' Even if she means simply 'I was only half listening', the linking of the · apology 'sorry' with the moral adverb 'properly' suggests that Alison acknowledges an obligation to listen attentively to Jimmy. He seizes on this implication, and reinforces it in 13 and 15 with the accusation that she is bored by his talking, and, as his wife, should not be bored. This latter implication comes from the names which he chooses to refer to himself and to her, emphasizing the marital relationship—'Old Porter/Mrs Porter' in 13, the belittling husbandly endearment 'dear' in 15, and 'my wife' in 21, when he has changed the subject, but evidently still has this preoccupation on his mind. His tone through this sequence is brutally sarcastic, as if he believes that he has grounds for accusing her of failing in her obligations, while he is fulfilling his by talking. The interest of this sequence, apart from illustrating the technique of implied propositions, is that it reveals a contradiction in Jimmy's ideology: he is berating her for breaking a convention of the bourgeois institution of marriage, an institution which he himself continually condemns and reviles. Or is he doing something more complex, mocking her for subscribing to this system and for allowing herself to be condemned by someone who does not uphold it?

I would like to comment on one more dimension of this dialogue: Jimmy's use of questions in order to maintain his control of the conversation. Because it is so one-sided, this passage is, of course, less of a conversation than a discontinuous tirade. Jimmy gives vent to a series of general assertions, judgements, and insults. His questions—which are never genuine requests for information or even action—serve the purpose of demanding attention, while restricting the contribution of the others.

Three main types of question structure are available in English:

1. *Wh-questions*, introduced by a word such as why, where, when, how, which. Such questions request new information. Not surprisingly, Jimmy uses few of these, since they would have the undesired effect of admitting Cliff and Alison into the conversation, allowing them to offer their opinions and explanations. When Jimmy does use wh- questions, they are either unanswerable (1 'Why do I do this every Sunday?') or quickly followed up by another comment (17 'Why do you bother? You can't understand a word of it.'). Jimmy uses wh- questions not to open up the conversation to other people's participation, but to frustrate interchange by posing vacuous questions which he believes he has the sole right to answer.

2. *Yes/no questions*, such as 'Have you finished that one yet?', request either the answer 'yes' or the answer 'no', and allow the person questioned little other freedom of reply. They are very much a feature of interrogatory discourse—for example, job interviews, doctor-patient consultations—where the interviewer is of higher status than the interviewee. Because they so severely restrict the response of the person questioned, they are felt to be impolite, and would therefore be used sparingly in domestic conversation. Jimmy's yes/no questions are not only abrupt as such, they are also highly unfair, because they contain a complexity of implication which is difficult to cope with in a one-word answer: e.g. 3 'Do the Sunday papers make *you* feel ignorant?' in which the complications of the stressed *you* have already been noted, or 7 'I said do the papers make you feel you're not so brilliant after all?' The difficulties of coping with this utterance by a simple 'yes' or 'no' are formidable: 'I said' suggests that the question is in some way a paraphrase of 5 'You're not a peasant are you?', while 'after all' implies that,

though Alison assumed she was educated because she was middle class (not a peasant), the Sunday papers show that she is uneducated (a 'peasant' in the sense in which Jimmy applied the word to Cliff). It is very difficult for Alison to work out what criticisms of herself she might be agreeing with or denying by whatever answer she might give, so she responds only to the most superficial meaning of the utterance: 'you have asked me a question about these papers' (wilfully misinterpreting 'the' as referring to today's Sunday papers rather, than any Sunday papers) 'which I cannot answer because I have not read them yet'.

3. *Tag questions.* These are a peculiar form with a declarative sentence as the basis, and a copy of the auxiliary verb and the subject tagged on to the end, with the 'polarity' of the verb changed: if the main sentence is positive, the tag is negative, and vice versa. Jimmy uses this form several times: 5 'You're not a peasant [*main sentence*] are you? [*tag*]', 11, 21, 27 (with pronoun change). Tags can be very demanding, pointedly requesting confirmation of an assertion which has been made in the main part of the sentence. Teachers use them a lot. They could be regarded as part of the characterization of Jimmy as a person who is aggressively demanding assent, who is seeking to subject his wife and his friend to his system of values. But a quite different account of the function of tags has been offered by Robin Lakoff. She claims they are a characteristic of women's speech, and that they indicate the reverse of aggression, in fact lack of confidence and a need for male confirmation of timidly held opinions. These are opposite characterizations, but they might both be relevant to Jimmy's utterances: his tags might be intended to denote aggression, but additionally, they may connote lack of confidence. Is the bravado real? Might not the insecurity alleged of women's tags underlie Jimmy's tagging of his absurd and insulting statements? Osborne's opening stage direction invites us to look for contradictions in the Jimmy whom his text has created. Further dialogic analysis of the kind begun here would, I believe, reveal how the language constructs and foregrounds these contradictions.

Look Back in Anger is a 'realistic' play: a fictional text in which conversational conventions evoke an illusion of recognizable

people interacting through language. The language is deliberately constructed to make the dialogue seem like an overheard
conversation. The assumption of realistic depiction of talk is the
starting-point for the reader's or audience's engagement with the
play. But this is not to say that the language is neutral, a mere
representation of how people speak. The dialogue is loaded with
evaluation and interpretation, the product of foregrounded
structure which draws the reader or playgoer to recognition of
the significant areas of the text's meaning: I have tried to show
that Jimmy's ways of controlling other people, and the implied
propositions to which he appeals, delineate a character of
offensively aggressive behaviour, but with a vulnerably contradictory system of values. How this presentation through dialogue meshes with the play's overall commentary on British
1950s society is a matter for further exploration. But the
starting-point, as I have shown, could easily be an analysis of the
peculiarities of dialogue which at first sight looks little out of the
ordinary.

A very different dialogic technique is found in another classic
play of the same vintage, Samuel Beckett's *Waiting for Godot*
(1955). In this enigmatic work, two tramps, Vladimir and Estragon, wait in a barren landscape to meet a certain 'Godot'—who
does not materialize, and who is, as far as one can gather, a
stranger to Vladimir and Estragon anyway (if he exists). Their
wait is futile, their lives are absurd and pointless, they have
nothing to do, or to talk about. But they talk throughout the
play, interrupted only by the two incursions of Lucky and Pozzo,
and the two brief visits of the Boy. Their conversation is
vacuous, and often at cross purposes; in these respects it enacts
the futility and meaninglessness of their existence, and, by
implication, the pointlessness of human life in general.

Our apparatus for conversational analysis should, then, show
failures of communication in the areas of structure where, in the
other text, meaning was communicated with clarity and detail.
In *Waiting for Godot*—as in many other of Beckett's works, such
as *Endgame*—misfiring speech acts, misunderstanding, and
incoherence are rife. In particular, Estragon doggedly

misunderstands, or pretends to. In order to 'pass the time', Vladimir tries to tell about the thieves who were crucified with Christ:

VLADIMIR. Two thieves, crucified at the same time as our Saviour. One—
ESTRAGON. Our what?

Estragon's 'what?' instead of 'who?' claims a radical incomprehension: it refuses to acknowledge that the phrase 'our Saviour' refers to a known human being.

V. Our Saviour. Two thieves. One is supposed to have been saved and the other ... [*he searches for the contrary of saved*] ... damned.
E. Saved from what?
V. Hell.
E. I'm going.
    [*He does not move.*]

'Saved from what?' continues a questioning which fixes on single words, and queries the application of their literal meanings. In effect, for anyone who knows the Christian narrative, the pointed contrast which Vladimir makes with 'damned' forces the interpretation 'saved from hell', so Estragon's ignoring this implies his rejection of the terminology and the ideology of Christianity: cf. earlier: Vladimir: 'Suppose we repented'; Estragon: 'Repented what?' Estragon follows Vladimir's reply with the threat 'I'm going', which in its lack of fulfilment—*He does not move*—is typical of a whole class of failed speech acts of both characters: a pledge to do something, followed by a failure to do anything.

Vladimir attempts to continue his story, now concentrating on the fact that 'of the four Evangelists only one speaks of a thief being saved':

V. One out of four. Of the other three two don't mention any thieves at all and the third says that both of them abused him.
E. Who?

Vladimir's highly compressed account presents real difficulties of understanding, particularly for someone who—as Estragon protests he is—is ignorant of the story. Out of eight noun phrases in Vladimir's two sentences, seven are based on numerals or pronouns, words whose referents can only be identified by looking back to previous noun phrases. Since Vladimir's story has been proceeding for some time in a scrambled fashion, with off-putting interruptions, this elliptical speech is bound to cause problems of cohesion (see Chapter 5). Estragon's response is so condensed that it gives Vladimir difficulty: 'Who?' could be asking the identity of the person(s) referred to by any of the seven unspecific noun phrases. Common sense might suggest that the last word, 'him', is most likely to be the queried noun phrase (the third Evangelist or someone else?) but clearly the speaker, who knows what he means, cannot recognize the difficulty:

v. What?
e. What's this all about? Abused who?
v. The Saviour.
e. Why?
v. Because he wouldn't save them.
e. From hell?

For a person behaving as literal-mindedly as Estragon is, 'from hell' would be the correct supposition, in view of Vladimir's explanation of 'saved' earlier; but:

v. Imbecile! From death.
e. I thought you said hell.
v. From death, from death.

Estragon now raises difficulties which stress the pointlessness of the story and of Vladimir's interest in it: 'Well what of it? . . . And why not? . . . Well? They don't agree, and that's all there is to it.' Under pressure, Vladimir becomes even more terse and difficult to follow: 'But one of the four says one of the two was saved.' The story peters out, and the two tramps move apart in disgust. The importance of the story, and of Vladimir's concern with its authenticity, is undermined by the incoherence of the telling, and the feigned incomprehension of the listener. The structure of the dialogue destroys the relevance of the content of the story: a central episode in Christian mythology fails to relieve the tramps' wait for Godot.

We now turn to the second of the two senses of 'dialogue' which were distinguished on p. 130 above: the implicit dialogue between different points of view in an apparently monologic text.

Whereas plays traditionally consist wholly of dialogue, other literary forms such as novels and short stories mix speech with monologic narrative and commentary. At first glance, there might appear to be a very sharp distinction between passages of dialogue, where the characters' voices seem to take the stage, and passages of prose writing, where the narrator takes charge. But in fact, narrative discourse engages in another class of dialogic interactions: between the narrator and the characters, and between the narrator and the reader. By 'dialogic' here I do not refer to text which has the superficial structure of dialogue, i.e. language which is set out as different 'speeches' attributed to different 'speakers'; rather, this is an *implicit* dialogue, where the language implies an interaction of views or values.

This topic of implicit dialogism has become extremely influential in modern literary theory and linguistic criticism since the 1970s, when, through translation, the work of the Russian theoretician Mikhail Bakhtin (1895–1975) became available in the West. The story of Bakhtin and his writings is a tangled one. He began publishing theoretical books on language in the late 1920s, under his own name, and under the pseudonyms V. N. Voloshinov and P. N. Medvedev. As Voloshinov, Bakhtin attacked the structural linguistics of Saussure for its conception of language as an abstract, static system; for its view of the sign as clear and unambiguous; and for its view of discourse as *monologic*—as presenting a single point of view. Bakhtin argued that language and language use were more dynamic than the Saussurean picture allowed, containing multiplicity of voice, tension, and contradiction. The key terms in Bakhtin's linguistics are *multiaccentuality, heteroglossia,* and *dialogism.* We have already met *multiaccentuality* in Chapter 6: it is the idea that a word (or other sign) does not have just one meaning, but is inherently double-valued. When words are used 'officially', there is a tendency for their meanings to be reduced or resolved in only one direction, one meaning suppressing others; but critical and creative practice can restore multiaccentuality, as we have seen. *Heteroglossia* is a relationship between different languages, dialects, styles, and registers (see Chapter 10). Most languages, and most utterances, are more of a mix of varieties than we usually imagine; official ideology prefers a monologic discourse where discord and tension are smoothed away. Finally, there is an inherent *dialogism* in language. When we speak or write, says Bakhtin, our words are always angled towards some other point of view: we anticipate the ideas of a hearer/reader, and we shape our own language accordingly, entering into implicit debate with an addressee.

Bakhtin is perhaps best known in literary studies for his application of these ideas to the novel in his book *Problems of Dostoevsky's Poetics.* According to Bakhtin, Dostoevsky's novels are *polyphonic* in character. Like a piece of music, the novel is woven from a number of interacting but independent voices. 'Polyphony' is Bakhtin's way of referring to heteroglossia and dialogism in fiction. For him, it is primarily a relationship between the author's and the characters' points of view: the characters in Dostoevsky are not submerged under the author's view of the world, they are allowed their own independent, 'fully-fledged' voices, they articulate views which can even, dialogically, challenge the world-view of the author.

Bakhtin's attitude to language and to the novel seems to be attractive and liberating. We cannot take on board all of its details, which in any case remain rather obscure, and difficult to grasp in concrete terms without knowing Dostoevsky in the original Russian. Enthusiasts for his ideas have rather tended to take up the spirit of dialogism, and use it to open up and pluralize literary texts in selected areas of structure. Three aspects of the rhetoric of narrative seem particularly appropriate subjects for dialogic treatment: (1) the relationships between a narrator and the characters in a fiction, not simply the permissive attitude Bakhtin finds in Dostoevsky, but some more restrictive, monologically expressed, controls on the characters; (2) the construction of an implied reader or addressee, 'dialogue' between author and reader or between narrator and narratee; (3) the interaction between different styles, and between different points of view, in texts which are heteroglossic to various degrees. Topic (3) will be the subject of Chapter 10, where I will try to clarify Bakhtin's views a little by interpreting them in sociolinguistic terms, particularly in the light of the concept of *register* drawn from Hallidayan linguistics. In the remainder of the present chapter, I will briefly discuss some simple examples of the processes classified under (1) and (2); there will be more extensive discussion of narrator-character relationships (1) in Chapter 9.

Let us look briefly at (1), narrator-character or author-character dialogic relationships, the principal subject of Bakhtin's Dostoevsky book. The basic theoretical point about narrative discourse is that it is never 'objective', but inescapably embodies attitudes towards its subject-matter. (This is the starting-point for my analysis of news discourse in my book *Language in the News*, where the theory is explained in greater detail.) In the novel, fictional humans or 'characters' in conventional terms are created, and they are coloured by the views of the author, who is bound to cause her narrator to speak of them from a certain point of view. In Chapter 9 we will look at some examples where the 'omniscient author' swamps the character with commentary, and some more complex cases in which we find a delicate dialogic interweaving of the narrator's and the character's voice. Some more obvious examples to make the point for the time being concern the narrator's treatment of characters' speech.

The words and phrases which are used to introduce speech inevitably indicate the narrator's comments on, and interpretations of, the utterances of the characters. Some novelists offer in this way a complete and explicit commentary on the motives and reactions of their characters. In Lawrence, for example, a 'third voice' is very obviously woven into the dialogue between two characters. For example, in Chapter 7 of *Sons and Lovers,* in addition to the routine 'he said', 'she replied' and the like, we find numerous more loaded speech-introducing expressions such as the following:

said Miriam, in her musical, caressing voice; said Miriam over-gently; laughed the farmer; she cried; replied the mother apologetically; asked Edgar, rather hesitatingly; he exclaimed appreciatively; she pleaded; he

called; she laughed in fear; he remonstrated; he said suddenly; she exclaimed; he persisted; she pondered; she sang; said the child, uneasy;
she murmured deep in her throat; repeated the child; she murmured;
she cried; she answered, low and intense; she said hesitatingly; she
said, soft and musical; he insisted; she faltered; etc.

These comments are more than 'stage directions' giving indications of the speech acts and behaviour of the speakers; cumulatively, they add an emotional colouring deriving from the
narrator's analysis of the relationship between the characters.
They make manifest an aspect of the narrator's ideology, in this
case the positive valuation of sexual behaviour which is soft and
unconfident in the woman, demanding and hypersensitive in the
man. It is more complicated than that, but a long analysis would
be necessary to refine that crude generalization. Of particular
interest is the way Lawrence directly juxtaposes narrative comment with characters' statements. Readers may care to examine
the chapter in question for the compatibility or otherwise of the
characters' statements and the narrator's comments.

The narrator's commentary on a character and his views can
also be indicated less directly, by stylistic infiltrations into the
character's speech itself. An extreme example would be stylistic
caricature, rendering a character's speech absurd and perhaps
passing more specific comment. Charles Dickens is famous for the
creation of memorable linguistic grotesques, for instance his treatment of the trade union demagogue Slackbridge in *Hard Times:*

'Oh my friends, the down-trodden operatives of Coketown! Oh my
friends and fellow-countrymen, the slaves of an iron-handed and a
grinding despotism! Oh my friends and fellow-sufferers, and fellow-
workmen, and fellow-men! I tell you that the hour is come, when we
must rally round one another as One united power, and crumble into
dust the oppressors that too long have battened upon the plunder of
our families, upon the sweat of our brows, upon the labour of our
hands, upon the strength of our sinews, upon the God-created glorious
rights of Humanity, and upon the holy and eternal privileges of
Brotherhood!'

This is obviously a caricature of oratory, but its specific features
are significant: repetition, parallelism, alliteration, excessive and
trite adjectives, worn-out and melodramatic metaphors, add up

to a hyperbolic language which is alien from his artisan audience and distant from workaday reality. Much more could be shown by a detailed analysis, but my intention here is merely to illustrate how a character can be criticized within the very language he is made to utter. (For a modern novelist's exploitation of grotesque speech, see my book *The Language of George Orwell* (London: Macmillan, 1995).

Implicit dialogue between author and character (dialogic category (1)) is discussed further in Chapter 9. We now turn to (2), dialogue between the author and the reader. This is an important type of dialogic rhetoric, in which the writer puts the opinions of a narrating voice into argument with his presumed *readers* or *narratees*. This author-reader discourse was a very prominent feature of eighteenth- and early nineteenth-century narrative. Laurence Sterne, who used the technique extensively and exuberantly, also described it aptly:

Writing, when properly managed, (as you may be sure I think mine is) is but a different name for conversation: As no one, who knows what he is about in good company, would venture to talk all;—so no author, who understands the just boundaries of decorum and good breeding, would presume to think all: The truest respect which you can pay to the reader's understanding, is to halve this matter amicably, and leave him something to imagine, in his turn, as well as yourself. (*Tristram Shandy*, 1759–67.)

'Conversation' with the reader is found throughout Fielding's *Tom Jones* (1749), from which I take my final example for this chapter: the first introduction of Miss Bridget Allworthy, Squire Allworthy's sister. Here is the paragraph in full:

1. He now lived, for the most part, retired in the country, with one sister, for whom he had a very tender affection. 2. This lady was now somewhat past the age of 30, an aera, at which, in the opinion of the malicious, the title of old maid may, with no impropriety, be assumed. 3. She was of that species of women, whom you rather commend for good qualities than beauty, and who are generally called by their own sex, very good sort of women—as good a sort of woman, madam, as you would wish to know. 4. Indeed she was so far from regretting want of beauty, that she never mention'd that perfection (if it can be

called one) without contempt; and would often thank God she was not as handsome as Miss such a one, whom perhaps beauty had led into errors, which she might have otherwise avoided. 5. Miss Bridget Allworthy (for that was the name of this lady) very rightly conceived the charms of person in a woman to be no better than snares for herself, as well as for others, and yet so discreet was she in her conduct, that her prudence was as much on the guard, as if she had had all the snares to apprehend which were ever laid for her whole sex. 6. Indeed, I have observed (tho' it may seem unaccountable to the reader) that this guard of prudence, like the trained bands, is always readiest to go on duty where there is least danger. 7. It often basely and cowardly deserts those paragons for whom the men are all wishing, sighing, dying, and spreading every net in their power; and constantly attends at the heels of that higher order of women, for whom the other sex have a more distant and awful respect, and whom (from despair, I suppose, of success) they never venture to attack.

Fielding here expresses, indirectly, a complex ironic judgement on Miss Allworthy. The complexity of statement and tone derives from the implicit presence of voices and opinions other than Fielding's: I want to show, briefly, how the language creates an impression of dialogue within a literally monologic text. I shall then demonstrate how the reader (who is centrally implicated in this 'dialogue') is called upon to interpret the text through a process which is constantly at work in understanding conversations: reference to general propositions or stereotypes which encode different views on social issues, in this case on sexual morality.

Fielding's standard mode of discourse is a kind of pretend-dialogue with an implied reader. This fiction is constructed by foregrounding interpersonal features of the language, including first- and second-person expressions ('I', 'you', and related forms) and other address and reference items which refer to the addressee who is invoked ('the reader', 'madam'); by verbs emphasizing the narrator's speech acts (not prominent in this particular paragraph, but I am thinking of verbs like 'acquaint', 'digress', 'desire', 'plead', which occur in the next one); by modal expressions of judgement as to values, and judgement as to narrative knowledge ('with no impropriety', 'perhaps', 'very rightly', 'unaccountable', 'I suppose'). The frequent presence of these devices in the text creates an impression of a vociferous and opinionated narrator, speaking his views and demanding response from a reader whom he appears to confront face-to-face. Readers should feel bombarded with assertions, and badgered to take up views of their own.

Often, Fielding's attitude to a subject is clearly announced, and whatever agreement or disagreement he expects from his reader is equally clear. But as often again, the attitudes involved are complex, and ironically expressed: and that is the situation in this paragraph.

The general drift of the critique is clear: Miss Bridget is attacked for an ostentatious, hypocritical, and self-deluding self-righteousness; for an envious and malicious contempt of beauty, and an unnecessary and excessive defence of her own virtue. But Fielding never *says* this; in fact, in some ways he appears to say quite the reverse—seems to approve of aspects of Miss Bridget's behaviour which he actually condemns. What he does is set up Miss Bridget as an instance of a category—'She was of that species of women'—and then insinuate his own views by citing other people's responses to that category (including Miss Bridget's). In this way he passes the burden of judgement from himself on to society. The sets of people cited are as follows:

  a. 'that higher order of women' of whom Miss Bridget is an instance
  b. 'their own sex'
  c. 'the men . . . the other sex'
  d. 'the malicious'

The voices and attitudes of these groups come through in various degrees of directness. Differences of style within the passage are instructive. Whereas the last two sentences, 6–7, are elaborately metaphorical, a literary signal of the narrator's presence, by contrast other sentences and phrases verge on the colloquial. In 3, 'called . . . very good sort of women—as good a sort of woman, madam, as you would wish to know' seems not only to report the opinion of the category 'their own sex', but their voice also: this could be felt to be a virtual quotation of one woman (from category b) speaking, probably sarcastically, about type a.

The next sentence, 4, quotes Miss Bridget—very damagingly, since what she is reported as saying habitually is extremely petty and slanderous, immediately undermining 'good' in the previous sentence so that it has to be read ironically. These quasi-quotations enhance the dramatic effect or verisimilitude of the dialogic style, but, more importantly, they complicate the rhetorical relationship between narrator and reader. Fielding is able to damn Miss Bridget not through his own words, but through the statements of others, including herself, while he, having established an ironic rhetoric, is even able to appear to approve attitudes which he in fact condemns: see 5 'Miss Bridget Allworthy . . . very rightly conceived . . . '. The reader has no voice quoted, but is faced with the task of locating, in this maze, Fielding's view.

We make sense of this passage by interpreting what is said (which is not what is meant) in terms of a series of implicit general propositions conveying sexual stereotypes. The generalizing phrase 'that species of women' in sentence 3 gives notice that such a stereotype is to follow. What characteristic properties does society attribute to this species? The relative clause does not really define their attributes without further interpretation, because it is doubly ambiguous: first, we need to be told what these 'good qualities' are; Fielding's vagueness here is crucial, because he can then proceed to bring us gradually to a realization that these good qualities are in fact vicious qualities. Second, 'rather than' in 'you rather commend for good qualities than beauty' does not clearly specify the nature of the option which is presupposed. Do we commend such women for their good qualities, ignoring their beauty because it is irrelevant? Or do we commend them for good qualities because they have no beauty for us to commend? In sentence 4, the phrase 'want ["lack"] of beauty' directs us to the second, unsympathetic, meaning, while not effacing the suggestion of innocent commendation first given by sentence 3. The proposition that supplies the ideological basis of the whole passage (even if it is strongly attacked) is, A, that sexual abstinence is commendable in women. There is a related stereotype, B, that beautiful women are sexually active (and are so outside the bounds of society's moral code) and therefore, by

A, are to be condemned. A more worldly proposition, C, alleges that men are only interested in beautiful women. Now C is obviously basic to sentences 6 and 7, but let us stay with the context of the opening of the paragraph for a moment. Acknowledging the possible validity of C—even if one dislikes its cynicism—casts unfavourable light on the motives of women who profess A: thus we derive the stereotype D, that plain women profess virtue because, being plain, they lack sexual opportunity. The protestation of virtue is not a good quality in itself (even if one applauds the idealism of A over the worldliness of C), because its motive is suspect: it is likely to be a type of compensatory behaviour. Interpretation in these terms helps with the slightly puzzling word 'assumed' in sentence 2: 'old maid' is not just a gibe at the sexual isolation of these ladies (in which case the title might have been 'given', not 'assumed'); it is a taunt at the willing assumption of the *role* of old maid. The behaviour associated with this role, and specifically Miss Bridget's behaviour, is sketched in the following sentences: it may be summarized as vicious slander masquerading as righteous comment; and ostentatious (and of course pointless) sexual aloofness ('prudence').

Fielding locates Miss Bridget Allworthy within a nest of ideological contradictions in the area of sexual behaviour and 'moral' behaviour. This ironic and ambivalent siting is functional in setting up her future role in the plot. But over and above this narrative relevance is the fundamental implication of the narrator and the reader in these ideological dilemmas, which are essentially dilemmas provoked by the *discourse* rather than by the story. As we have seen, the text of this passage does not say what it means, but can only be interpreted in the light of some unstated propositions, commonplaces of the culture, which the reader must supply. It is incriminating to entertain these stereotypes, which are variously naïve, malicious, and cynical, but readers must put themselves in the position of formulating the hidden propositions in order to make any sense of the passage. This gives Fielding the opportunity to cast his readers as people who might hold the propositions as convictions, rather than just imagine them as hypotheses. In sentence 3, Fielding directly invokes a class of female readers who are presumed to approve of proposition A (the virtues of celibacy) and then leads them on towards B in sentence 4 by suggesting, in the parenthesis '(if it can be called [a perfection])', that he agrees with this censorious attitude towards beautiful women; an illusion sustained in sentence 5 'very rightly'. The parenthetical comments in 6 and 7 convey a mock naïveté, a feigned innocence of the worldly proposition C, and the cynical conclusion D. But the metaphorical and hyperbolic language of these last two sentences, with the parody of romantic sentiment ('all wishing . . . '), makes it clear that Fielding is being ironic at the expense of any gullible and self-righteous reader. The emergence of the frankly critical proposition D revaluates what has gone before, and reinterprets the attitudes of sentences 3–4 as hypocrisy and unkindness; and damns any reader who has gone along with the surface meanings of the early part of the paragraph. Fielding's dialogue with the reader encourages the latter to approve of Miss Bridget, and to think that Fielding does, but subverts this position in the very process of expounding it.

References and Suggestions for Further Reading

The classic studies of sequencing in conversation and dialogue were those of the Americans Schegloff and Sacks. See, for example, E. A. Schegloff, 'Sequencing in conversational openings', *American Anthropologist,* 70 (1968), 1075–95; H. Sacks, 'An initial investigation of the usability of conversational data for doing sociology', in D. Sudnow, ed., *Studies in Social Interaction* (New York: Free Press, 1972). The method was developed by researchers at the University of Birmingham: see J. McH. Sinclair and R. M. Coulthard, *Towards an Analysis of Discourse* (London: Oxford University Press, 1975). For application to literary dialogue, see D. Burton, *Dialogue and Discourse* (London: Routledge & Kegan Paul, 1980). For an introductory account, see M. Coulthard, *An Introduction to Discourse Analysis* (London: Longman, new ed., 1985).

The originator of speech act theory or illocutionary act theory was the Oxford philosopher J. L. Austin, *How to Do Things with Words* (London: Oxford University Press, 1962); developed by J. R. Searle, *Speech Acts* (London: Cambridge University Press, 1969); for a simple brief explanation with an analysis of 'promising', see Searle, 'What is a speech act?', reprinted in P. P. Giglioli, ed., *Language and Social Context* (Harmondsworth: Penguin, 1972), pp. 136–56. A collection of relevant papers is P. Cole and J. L. Morgan, eds., *Speech Acts* (New York: Humanities Press, 1975).

Grice's theory of *implicature* was first proposed in his paper 'Logic and Conversation', reprinted in the Cole and Morgan volume, pp. 41–58. More recent work has suggested that Grice's theory may be replaced by a theory based on principles of *relevance*: see D. Sperber and D. Wilson, *Relevance* (Oxford: Blackwell, 1986). For Labov and Fanshel's account of implied 'general propositions', see W. Labov and D. Fanshel, *Therapeutic Discourse* (New York: Academic Press, 1977).

On one function of tag questions, see R. Lakoff, *Language and Woman's Place* (New York: Harper & Row, 1975).

The representation of speech in fiction is described in N. Page, *Speech in the English Novel* (London: Longman, 1973); also G. N. Leech and M. H. Short, *Style in Fiction* (London: Longman, 1981) ch. 9. See also R. Fowler, *The Language of George Orwell* (London: Macmillan, 1995) on grotesque and deviant speech.

For the work of Bakhtin, see references above, Chapter 6, p. 108.

Point of View

In traditional discussions of novels, short stories, epic, and other forms of narrative writing, it is usual to draw a distinction between the story and the point of view from which the story is narrated. For instance, the events of George Eliot's *Middlemarch* or *The Mill on the Floss* would be said to be narrated from the point of view of an 'omniscient' narrator who has privileged access to the thoughts and feelings of the characters in a way that an ordinary external observer does not; and who can foresee how events are going to turn out in the future. By contrast, the narrators in Hemingway's novels and stories say little about the characters' thoughts and feelings: from a psychological point of view, the telling is 'objective' or 'external'. A third type of point of view is represented in Virginia Woolf's novels: the events of the narrative are viewed from the perspective of one or more of the characters, with great emphasis on the characters' private responses to people and events: this is 'subjective' narration from a character's point of view. These three examples are merely illustrations from some familiar authors, and they by no means complete the range of types of point of view. In this chapter I have space to analyse only some of the more striking variations in point of view, with particular attention to defamiliarized perspectives; some other relevant materials are discussed in the following chapters.

In order to sort out what is evidently a very complex part of textual structure, we need to distinguish systematically among the various meanings of the notion 'point of view'. Fortunately, a great deal of the groundwork has been done by linguists and theoreticians in the French and Russian structuralist traditions, and our task in this chapter is to report the most useful of their conclusions, and to furnish their categories of point of view with an account of linguistic characteristics for critical linguistic description. This enterprise is admirably supported by some textbooks (listed pp. 183–4 below) which have appeared since the first edition of *Linguistic Criticism* was written, and which in some cases adopt, with improvements, the account of point of view which I gave in 1986.

The Russian and French founders of narrative theory all make the distinction which I phrased informally in the opening sentence of this chapter, i.e. between the story and the telling of it. The Russian Formalists distinguished between *fabula* and *sjuzhet*, in French structuralism we find *histoire* and *discours*; the ordinary English words *story* and *narration* will serve us here. The pairs of terms do not necessarily correspond exactly, but we will ignore the complications (which stem from their origins in different intellectual traditions). The important strategic move is to make a discrimination between the content of the story and its treatment in the narration: the same story-stuff may be treated to different temporal orderings, may be seen from the perspective of different narrating voices, may be suffused with various ideological colourings, and so on. It is in these areas of variation in narrative telling that 'point of view' is located.

The topic has been greatly illuminated by two theorists: the Russian semiotician Boris Uspensky and the French structuralist Gérard Genette. Genette's ideas have perhaps been more influential than Uspensky's, but Uspensky gives a more comprehensive framework, and this I will adapt as the basis of my exposition. Genette's work, based on a study of the French novelist Marcel Proust, was first published in French in 1972, and appeared in English translation as *Narrative Discourse* in 1980. It has contributed two major ideas to the theory of narration: the most widely acknowledged is the concept of *focalization*, which allows us to distinguish alternative viewing points from which a story might be told—for example, a novel may be narrated from the pervasive viewpoint of a single narrator; or it may be told in the third person as if by a narrator, but focalized through a character, the events related through the eyes of a character *within* the narrative. I have worked the idea of focalization into my account as appropriate. Besides focalization, Genette offers a very complete account of *time* in narration. Drawing on the analogy of the grammatical devices which handle time within the sentence, he studies temporal arrangements in the whole text under the headings of the *order* of events, including techniques such as flashback and preview; *duration*, the time taken by events in relation to the length of text in which they are narrated, and the presumed reading time; and the *frequency* of repetition in the narration of events. Genette's discussion of time in narration corresponds to, and details, Uspensky's *temporal* point of view. This is an area which will receive no further treatment in this book: it is expounded clearly in other accessible discussions of narration.

We turn now to the scheme offered by Boris Uspensky. He distinguishes between four 'planes' of point of view: (1) *ideological* point of view; (2) *phraseological*; (3) (a) the *spatial* and (b) *temporal* plane; (4) the plane of *psychology*. In this chapter, we will be concerned mainly with his 'psychological' point of view (which can include Genette's 'focalization'), leading to the analysis of ideology. The 'phraseological plane' seems to me not to be an independent level, but it includes discussions of how characters are named, and of the representation of characters' speech—a sign of Uspensky's debt to Bakhtin. The representation of speech and thought should actually be included under the 'psychological'. As I have said, the temporal plane will not be dealt with here, but we begin with an analysis of *spatial* point of view, which is the simplest 'plane' to grasp, and which calls very clearly on specific structures of language for its formation.

The *spatial* dimension of spatio-temporal perspective corresponds to viewing position in the visual arts. Just as a painting is composed structurally so that the viewer seems to see some objects close up, some in the distance, some focused, and some less clear; so that the eye moves from one part of the painting to another in an apparently natural succession—in the same way, someone who reads a novel which represents objects, people, buildings, landscapes, etc., is led by the organization of the language to imagine them as existing in certain spatial relation-ships to one another, and to the viewing position which he feels himself to occupy. In the following highly pictorial passage which sets the opening scene of a novel, we can see very easily what parts of language contribute to the building of spatial point of view:

The last of a hanger ran under the eastern ridge of the combe, where it had always been too steep and stony for the plough. It was now little more than a long spinney, mainly of beech. The field sloped from the wall of trees, westward, a gentle bosom, down to the open gate on to Fishacre Lane. The dark coats lay there in against the hedge, covering the cider-jar and the dinner-bundle, beside the two scythes that had been used to clear the still-dewed hedge swathe much earlier that morning. Now the wheat was half cut. Lewis sat perched behind the faded carmine reaper, craning into the sea of blond stems for stones, his hand on the mower-lever, always ready to lift the blades. Captain hardly needed the reins; so many years of plodding, just so, down the new stubble next to the still-standing ears. Only at the corners did Lewis cry, softly, coaxing the old horse round. Sally, the younger horse, who had helped on the steeper ground, stood tethered beneath a thorn not far from the gate, cropping the hedge, her tail intermittently swishing.

Bindweed ran up the stems of the corn; seeding thistles, red poppies; and lower, the little cornfield violets called heart's-ease; with blue speedwell eyes and scarlet pimpernel, shepherd's glass, herb of the second sight. The field's name was the Old Batch—batch from bake, some ancient farm's own annual bread was always grown there. The sky's proleptic name was California; the imperial static blue of August.

There are four figures in the field, besides Lewis on the reaper-binder. (John Fowles, *Daniel Martin*, 1977, pp. 7–8.)

This descriptive passage continues for another two pages, gradu-ally introducing four men, a boy, and two horses harvesting within the field, and a momentary onlooker outside it. If you read the whole passage, you will notice a wave-like alternation of visual perspectives, starting with an illusion of 'long shot', moving to 'close-up' as each of the people is introduced in turn, with distant views placed between the individual portraits. The opening four sentences give the broad outlines of the field: a ridge with a narrow belt of trees to the east, the field itself a more

gradual slope to the west, bounded by a hedge with a gate in it.
The general view is given by naming the features of landscape
themselves ('ridge', 'combe', etc.) and also by the metaphorical
use of other terms which have strong and clear geometrical
connotations ('wall', 'bosom', 'sea', and 'corners' later), with a
few adjectives of size and shape ('long', 'steep', 'steeper'). *Deixis*
(cf. pp. 79–80 above) is very prominent. The components of this
landscape are held together by prepositional phrases indicating
spatial relationships and directions: 'under the ridge', 'from the
wall', 'down to the open gate on to Fishacre Lane', etc. Such
locative phrases are exceptionally frequent throughout this and
similar descriptive passages, and they have a double function:
first, by sheer frequency, in co-operation with other types of
deictic ('where', 'westward', 'there', etc.), they insist on the
spatial content of the prose, they foreground the theme of
the representation of a place and its component parts. But the
prepositions and adverbs of place do not simply *refer* to locations, they also *relate* them, and as the text is organized in
sequence, the reader scanning it left-to-right is led from place to
place in a definite order, with a starting-point, and a subsequent
development, which suggest an initial viewing position, then a
chain of perceptions moving from that position. Here the
reader's eye is led from a vantage-point high in the field, along
the 'wall of trees', then down towards the hedge with the coats,
food, and tools stowed near it. The sequence offered by the
relational prepositions of place is helped by some unobtrusive
deictic verbs which indicate movement in a certain direction,
or a certain positioning: 'ran under', 'sloped from . . . down',
'covering'. Notice how 'covering', a very ordinary word, implies
vision from above: the observer sees the coats on top of the food.
When the observer's eye has reached the hedge, it is moved, by
implication, back into the centre of the field ('the wheat was half
cut') to focus on Lewis sitting high on the reaper. At this point
the emphasis is largely on his physical attitude—'perched',
etc.—but the verb 'craning' shifts to his perspective: he looks
down into the corn for stones, and what he sees, which is not
what the distant observer could see, is detailed in the microscopic
next paragraph: 'Bindweed . . . seeding thistles . . . and lower,

the little cornfield violets ... '. There is a striking difference of scale here, but soon the perspective moves out again to the wide view: 'There are four figures ... ' and in the following paragraph, 'They work in two teams, on opposite sides of the field, one clockwise, the other anti-clockwise, stooking' which is clearly the panoramic viewpoint of the high, distant, observer.

The whole passage is worth studying for the mechanics of these visual movements and transitions. The author's control of the reader's perception—focus, survey, and scanning of relationships—is strict, and dependent on linguistic artifices which, though unobstrusive, are clearly defamiliarizing, since the language instructs us to perceive carefully, clearly, slowly, and relevantly.

(Another rich source for the techniques of spatial perspective is the novel *Titus Groan* by Mervyn Peake—who was also a painter—from which illustrations are taken for other purposes later in this chapter.)

More fundamental than spatial point of view, and rather complicated because they overlap, are the *ideological* and *psychological* planes of point of view. I will introduce *ideology* first, briefly, reserving various parts of my treatment to the relevant categories of psychological point of view and to Chapter 11. The basic sense of 'ideology' has already been given in Chapter 2. I do not mean the derogatory sense of the word ('false consciousness' or 'delusion'), but simply the system of beliefs, values, and categories by reference to which a person or a society comprehends the world. As we have seen, language performs a crucial role in stabilizing, reproducing, and changing ideology. Now when we speak of point of view on the plane of ideology in a narrative text, we mean the set of values, or belief system, communicated by the language of the text. A novel, for example, gives an interpretation of the world it represents, a fact which is central to the interpretative descriptions offered by literary critics. The content of the ideology—Tolstoy's Christianity, Lawrence's celebration of sexuality, Orwell's denunciation of totalitarianism, and so on—is one thing to be identified, and linguistic analysis can be very effective in demonstrating the presence of such themes and ideas.

Other questions arise in considering point of view on the ideological plane. There are questions related to *focalization*. Who, within the compositional structure of the work, is the vehicle for the ideology? Is it the author speaking through the narrative voice, or is it a character or characters? And is there a single dominating world-view, or a plurality of ideological positions? The least interesting cases are those in which the text projects a single normative set of values according to which all the scenes, events, and characters are judged: such cases are rare, and among the major novels, potential candidates turn out to be complex or ironical—the perpetually commenting author-figure 'Fielding' in *Tom Jones*, the central consciousness Strether in Henry James's *The Ambassadors*. Plural ideological structure is more interesting, and particularly when the different value-systems articulated in the work are in some conflicting relationship. This is Bakhtin's *polyphony* or *heteroglossia*. In Dickens's *Hard Times*, for instance, various groups of characters represent and voice a number of different social theories: Gradgrind and Bounderby, the values of utilitarianism and manufacturing capitalism; Stephen Blackpool and Rachael, loyalty and affection; the circus people, spontaneity and gaiety; and so on. These points of view, which are expressed in many distinct and contrasting linguistic styles, are constantly challenging and contradicting each other, giving the novel an argumentative, dynamic structure. There is not one overall world-view subordinating every philosophy to a single point of view, but a range of alternative and interacting views of life.

Point of view on the ideological plane may be manifested in two fairly distinct ways, one direct, and one less so. Both ways of establishing ideological perspective are clearly identifiable in specific areas of linguistic structure.

In the first case, a narrator or a character may directly indicate his or her judgements and beliefs, by the use of a variety of *modal* structures. Modality (cf. pp. 78–9 above) is the grammar of explicit comment, the means by which people express their degree of commitment to the truth of the propositions they utter, and their views on the desirability or otherwise of the states of affairs referred to. Respectively, 'Sir Arthur *certainly* lost his fortune at the gaming table' and 'His gambling was *disastrous* for the family'. I have italicized the modal words: they come from a fairly specialized section of the vocabulary, and are easy to spot. The forms of modal expression include:

modal auxiliaries: may, might, must, will, shall, should, needs to, ought to, and a few others. These words signal either caution or confidence, to various degrees: something might happen, will happen, must happen. Notice that the strongly positive modals such as 'must' have the additional meaning of necessity or even obligation, so that a speaker using such a word to indicate his judgement of certainty or truth may simultaneously express approval of or a demand for the things that are being spoken of.

modal adverbs or sentence adverbs: certainly, probably, surely, perhaps, etc. There are also adjectival versions in such constructions as 'It is certain that . . . '.

evaluative adjectives and adverbs: lucky, luckily, fortunate, regrettably, and many others.

verbs of knowledge, prediction, evaluation: seem, believe, guess, foresee, approve, dislike, etc.

generic sentences: these are generalized propositions which claim universal truth, and are usually cast in a syntax reminiscent of proverbs or scientific laws: 'For loan oft loses both itself and friend, | And borrowing dulls the edge of husbandry' (Polonius in Shakespeare's *Hamlet*); 'At sixteen, the mind that has the strongest affinity for fact cannot escape illusion and self-flattery . . . '(George Eliot, *The Mill on the Floss*). Often generics are blatantly ironic, like the opening sentence of *Pride and Prejudice* quoted above p. 78). Where irony is not intended, the writer may vary her syntax somewhat away from the proverbial form, rendering the generic less obtrusive. George Eliot often does this: for instance, from the same chapter of *The Mill on the Floss*, 'It was a dark, chill, misty morning, likely to end in rain—*one of those mornings when even happy people take refuge in their hopes*' (I have italicized the modified generic). From sentences like this, the reader cumulatively builds up a picture of the stock of 'common sense' (i.e. ideology) on which George Eliot depends in presenting and evaluating the world of her characters.

(For a further instance of the relationship between modality and ideological structure, see the passage from Fielding's *Tom Jones* in the discussion of the author's dialogue with the reader, p. 153 above.)

There is a perhaps even more interesting sense in which language indicates ideology or, in fiction, the world-views of author or characters. This is what I referred to as a 'less direct' way. The modal devices just discussed make explicit (though sometimes ironic) *announcements* of beliefs; other parts of language, indirectly but nevertheless convincingly, may be *symptomatic* of world-view: it has traditionally been assumed in stylistics that the different ways in which people express their thoughts indicate, consciously or unconsciously, their personalities and attitudes. A writer may create a narrator, or a character, whose language expresses a characteristic or idiosyncratic point of view; and the style may be adjusted, as the book progresses, in order to express ideological development. Linguistic criticism, under the influence of M. A. K. Halliday's model of analysis, has developed sophisticated techniques for describing implicit ideology. This is such an important topic that I have reserved substantial discussion of it until Chapter 11, on language and world-view. I can, however, refer to two very familiar examples which will quickly demonstrate the point. In *A Portrait of the Artist as a Young Man*, Joyce changes the style gradually to reflect the intellectual development of Stephen Dedalus as he grows from infant to undergraduate, from the limited consciousness of the baby through the perplexity and isolation of the schoolboy, the fantasizing and emotionally self-indulgent 'adolescent, to the dogmatic, alienated college student. To focus a little more closely on a text, consider the famous opening sentences of Faulkner's *The Sound and the Fury:*

Through the fence, between the curling flower spaces, I could see them hitting. They were coming toward where the flag was and I went along the fence. Luster was hunting in the grass by the flower tree. They took the flag out, and they were hitting. Then they put the flag back and they went to the table, and he hit and the other hit. Then they went on, and I went along the fence. Luster came away from the flower tree and we went along the fence and they stopped and we stopped and I looked through the fence while Luster was hunting in the grass. (William Faulkner, *The Sound and the Fury*, 1931.)

The character from whose point of view this part of the narrative is focalized is Benjy, a 33-year-old man with the mind of a young child. It is obvious that Faulkner has designed the language to suggest the limitations of Benjy's grasp of the world around him. The style is not, however, disintegrated in a haphazard fashion, but is systematically patterned in certain areas of structure. Most striking is a consistent oddity in *transitivity*: there are almost no transitive verbs with objects, rather a preponderance of intransitives ('coming', 'went', 'hunting', etc.) and one transitive ('hit') used repeatedly without an object, ungrammatically. It is implied that Benjy has little sense of actions and their effects on objects: a limited notion of causation. Second, Benjy uses *circumlocutions* to designate objects that he has no name for: 'the curling flower spaces', 'where the flag was', 'the flower tree'. The implication of this is that he has command of only a part of his society's classification of objects. Third, he uses *personal pronouns* in an odd way—'them . . . they . . . They . . . they . . . they . . . he . . . the other . . . '— without identifying who he is referring to, and without varying the words he uses to refer to them. Fourth, his *deictic* words— 'Through . . . between . . . coming toward where . . . went along', etc.—do not add up to a comprehensible picture of the positions and movements of the golfers, himself, and Luster: Benjy is literally disoriented, with little sense of his location and his relationships within a context. The four areas of structure which characterize Benjy's world-view—transitivity, lexical classification, reference, and deixis—recur in other linguistic constructions of ideology, as we shall see in Chapter 11.

We come now to the third category of 'point of view', that which Uspensky calls 'psychological' or (better) 'perceptual' point of view. It corresponds broadly to Genette's 'focalization', and it allows us to discuss some issues in narration which have much preoccupied Anglo-American literary critics. This concerns the question of who is presented as the observer of the events of a narrative, whether the narrator or a participating character; and

the various kinds of discourse associated with different relationships between narrator and character. For clarity's sake, I have
divided the field into two categories, each with two subtypes; but
I must stress that probably no text exemplifies any single type
purely and consistently: such consistency would be an inconceiv-
able technical *tour de force* in a medium as complicated as
language. In any case, a great deal of the interest, in fictional
narrative texts, is in the shifts, contrasts, and tensions between
various modes of observation within the text, as we shall see in
the extract from Mervyn Peake's *Titus Groan* analysed at the end
of this chapter.

The basic distinction is between *internal* and *external* perspective. Uspensky introduces the distinction, without its further
complexities, thus:

> When an author constructs his narration, he usually has two options
> open to him: he may structure the events and characters of the nar-
> rative through the deliberately subjective viewpoint of some particular
> individual's (or individuals') consciousness, or he may describe the
> events as objectively as possible. In other words, he may use the *don-
> nées* of the perceptions of one consciousness or several, or he may use
> the facts as they are known to him. (*A Poetics of Composition*, p. 81.)

'Internal' narration is, then, narration from a point of view
within a character's consciousness, manifesting his or her feelings
about, and evaluations of, the events and characters of the story
(which I shall call Type A); or from the point of view of someone
who is not a participating character but who has knowledge of
the feelings of the characters—a narrator, or the so-called
'omniscient' author (Type B). 'External' point of view relates the
events, and describes the characters, from a position outside of
any of the protagonists' consciousnesses, with no privileged
access to their private feelings and opinions (Type C), and in
some cases actually stressing the limitations of authorial knowledge, the inaccessibility of the characters' ideologies (Type D).

The most subjective form of internal perspective, Type A,
consists of either *first-person narration* by a participating character, or *third-person narration* which is strongly coloured with
personal markers of the character's world-view, or which

includes *free indirect discourse* or *internal monologue* (see p. 173 and 173-7 below). The first-person variant is distinguished *deictically* by prominent use of first-person singular pronouns and perhaps some use of present tense, referring to the 'present time' of the act of narration (rather than referring consistently to the past time of the narrated events). The presence of a participating narrator may be highlighted by foregrounded *modality* stressing his judgements and opinions. There is reference to the character-narrator's feelings and thoughts by the use of *verba sentiendi* ('words of feeling', see below)—a very obvious subjectivity. Choices of *diction* may individualize the narrator as a certain psychological type or as a member of a certain social class. Finally, syntactic patterns, *transitivity*, etc., may endow the character with a certain ideological position (cf. the discussion of Benjy above, and Chapter 11 below). Most of these linguistic characteristics of my 'internal Type A' are found in Nick Carraway's introduction of himself in the opening pages of F. Scott Fitzgerald's novel *The Great Gatsby* (1925):

In my younger and more vulnerable years my father gave me some advice that I've been turning over in my mind ever since.

'Whenever you feel like criticizing any one,' he told me, 'just remember that all the people in this world haven't had the advantages that you've had.'

He didn't say any more, but we've always been unusually communicative in a reserved way, and I understood that he meant a great deal more than that. In consequence, I'm inclined to reserve all judgements, a habit that has opened up many curious natures to me and also made me the victim of not a few veteran bores. The abnormal mind is quick to detect and attach itself to this quality when it appears in a normal person, and so it came about that in college I was unjustly accused of being a politician, because I was privy to the secret griefs of wild, unknown men. Most of the confidences were unsought—frequently I have feigned sleep, preoccupation, or a hostile levity when I realized by some unmistakable sign that an intimate revelation was quivering on the horizon; for the intimate revelations of young men, or at least the terms in which they express them, are usually plagiaristic and marred by obvious suppressions. Reserving judgements is a matter of infinite hope. I am still a little afraid of missing something if I forget that, as my father snobbishly suggested, and I snobbishly repeat, a sense of the fundamental decencies is parcelled out unequally at birth.

Some form of the 'I' pronoun occurs in every sentence but one, often several times. Modality is very prominent in two areas: evaluative adjectives and adverbs, and generic sentences. Evaluative modalizers include 'more vulnerable', 'unusually', 'curious', 'veteran bores', 'abnormal', 'normal', 'unjustly', etc. Generics are extremely frequent: 'all the people . . . ', 'The abnormal mind . . . ', 'for the intimate revelations . . . ', 'Reserving judgements . . . ', 'a sense of the fundamental decencies . . . '. Ironically, Nick believes that he is 'inclined to reserve all judgements', but constantly makes pronouncements on life and on people in the most pompous way imaginable. His vocabulary—slightly staid, formal, and moralistic—fits this ironized self-characterization very aptly; the effect is cumulative, rather than locally salient, and derives from phrases such as 'unusually communicative', 'privy', 'feigned', 'intimate revelation', 'plagiaristic', 'fundamental decencies'. Also appropriate to Nick's view of the world is the rather literary, measured syntax. One is struck, for instance, by double adjective phrases such as 'younger and more vulnerable', and numerous balanced parallel phrases: 'curious natures . . . veteran bores', 'the abnormal mind . . . a normal person', 'as my father snobbishly suggested, and I snobbishly repeat'. The generics, too, are in a blatantly proverbial syntax; there is more than a touch of Polonius about Nick Carraway. Finally, Nick's language includes many *verba sentiendi*, as Uspensky calls them: words denoting feelings, thoughts, and perceptions, primary signals of a subjective point of view. Nick, being preoccupied with himself and his image, refers often to his own inner processes: 'turning over in my mind', 'understood', 'inclined', 'victim', 'realized', 'afraid'. Notice that a lot of these are words denoting reflection and judgement. In the ironic context which Fitzgerald has created, we are bound to suspect the objectivity of someone who is so self-conscious, so confident and considered in his pronouncements.

Benjy's language illustrates a different kind of first-person subjective perspective. As we saw, the emphasis there was less on explicit modality and personal judgement than on the construction of a radically transformed syntax and semantics imitating peculiar patterns of thought and perception. This shaping of language towards an illusion of directly experienced mental process is the central technique in the familiar type of internal point of view known as *stream of consciousness* or *internal monologue*. The Joycean variety associated with Leopold Bloom in Joyce's *Ulysses* (1922) provides the best-known examples; within third-person narration, there are sudden shifts into first-person discourse in which Bloom seems to speak his loosely associated, incomplete thoughts:

He walked on. Where is my hat, by the way? Must have put it back on the peg. Or hanging up on the floor. Funny, I don't remember that. Hallstand too full. Four umbrellas, her raincloak. Picking up the letters. Drago's shopbell ringing. Queer I was just thinking that moment. Brown brilliantined hair over his collar. Just had a wash and brushup. Wonder have I time for a bath this morning. Tara Street. Chap in the paybox there got away James Stephens they say. O'Brien.

Deep voice that fellow Dlugacz has. Agenda what is it? Now, my miss. Enthusiast.

The second type of internal perspective, Type B, differs from Type A in being consistently third-person narration by an 'omniscient' author who claims knowledge of what is going on in the characters' heads, reporting their motives and feelings. Deixis and modality are basically the property of the author-narrator, who can thus locate himself in an ideological and spatio-temporal position independent of the characters. But authorial modality is not prominent (contrast external Type D below), since the focus is on the characters, not on the position from which they are described. To a greater or lesser degree, the author gives an account of the mental processes, feelings, and perceptions of the characters, so the chief linguistic marker of this variant of internal narration is the presence of *verba sentiendi* detailing intentions, emotions, and thoughts. In the following extract from Mervyn Peake's *Titus Groan* (1946), the kitchen boy Steerpike, who is about to escape from captivity by scaling a wall, examines and plans his route; it is a moment of concentrated thought and intense response, and so there is a high density of *verba sentiendi* (italicized):

. Again he *fastened his gaze* upon the first dozen feet of vertical stone, *choosing* and *scrutinizing* the grips that he *would use*. His *survey* left him *uneasy*. It *would be unpleasant*. The more he *searched* the wall *with his intense eyes* the less he *liked* the *prospect*, but he could *see* that it was feasible if he *concentrated* every *thought* and fibre upon the attempt.

In this type of internal perspective, Type B, transitivity patterns and systems of lexical classification may or may not indicate the world-view of a character; to the extent that they do, they are framed by the authorial ideology. In the example just quoted, the verbs 'choosing' and 'scrutinizing' analyse rather than dramatize Steerpike's thoughts: they are the author's words for internal processes, part of an extensive lexical system by which Steerpike is characterized throughout the book as a deliberate, calculating entrepreneur. The point is that the words themselves are not manifestly part of any personal discourse attributed to Steerpike with a claim of psychological mimesis, such as we would expect in internal narration of Type A.

The difference between Type A (internal and wholly subjective) and Type B (internal but allowing an authorial phrasing of the character's feelings) provides the basis for an important style which throws Types A and B into what, in the previous chapter, I called an implicitly dialogic relationship. This style is *free indirect discourse* (FID): internal perspective in which the character's subjective feelings, which are given in Type A narration transformed into third person, are interwoven with and framed by the author's account of the character's inner state (Type B). By this device, a writer is able to juxtapose two sets of values, to imply a critique of the character's views, without the direct judgement which an external perspective would produce. Some particularly sensitive intermingling of the two internal viewpoints is found in Joyce's *Dubliners* stories (1914), from which I quote the opening of 'Eveline'. Eveline is a shop-girl who has agreed to elope to Buenos Aires with her boy-friend Frank; on the eve of her departure she weighs up the pros and cons of this adventure as against the ties of her admittedly hard family life, looking after her violent father and two younger children after her mother died insane. In the end, she cannot leave her mundane and unhappy family life, and does not depart with Frank. Like most of the Dubliners in this collection of stories, she is spiritually paralysed, bound to her trivial life by inaction and apathy. Her static and passive posture at the beginning of the story is symbolic of her inner state:

She sat at the window watching the evening invade the avenue. Her head was leaned against the window curtains, and in her nostrils was the odour of dusty cretonne. She was tired.

Few people passed. The man out of the last house passed on his way home; she heard his footsteps clacking along the concrete pavement and afterwards crunching on the cinder path before the new red houses. One time there used to be a field there in which they used to play every evening with other people's children. Then a man from Belfast bought the field and built houses in it—not like their little brown houses, but bright brick houses with shining roofs. The children of the avenue used to play together in that field—the Devines, the Waters, the Dunns, little Keogh the cripple, she and her brothers and sisters. Ernest, however, never played: he was too grown up. Her father used often to hunt them in out of the field with his blackthorn stick; but usually little Keogh used to keep nix and call out when he saw her father coming. Still they seemed to have been rather happy then. Her father was not so bad then; and besides, her mother was alive. That was a long time ago; she and her brothers and sisters were all grown up; her mother was dead. Tizzie Dunn was dead, too, and the Waters had gone back to England. Everything changes. Now she was going to go away like the others, to leave her home.

The first paragraph is third-person narration with some internal perspective—'she was tired'—but nothing that would indicate Eveline's precise feelings, indeed, quite the reverse, with the very literary metaphor of the evening 'invading the avenue'. Later, we find the phrasing of the opening paragraph repeated with slight variation after two and a half pages: 'The evening deepened in the avenue . . . she continued to sit by the window, leaning her head against the window curtain, inhaling the odour of dusty cretonne.' This repetition is another indication of the narrator's presence, but only in retrospect, so the first paragraph on first reading is more neutral than writerly. But as paragraph two progresses, the language develops in the direction of a style which can definitely be associated with Eveline. From 'One time . . . ', all the sentences can be transformed into utterances which might be spoken by Eveline, simply by changing some third-person pronouns into first-person—'in which *we* used to play'—and some past tenses into present—'Tizzie Dunn *is* dead'. At the end of the paragraph, the tense alternates between present and past: 'Everything changes. Now she was . . . '. 'Now' is repeated frequently in the story. It is the present tense of the character's reflecting consciousness, framed by the past tense of the author's narration. This mixture of two deictic spheres is very characteristic of FID.

Other signs of the character's voice are a general colloquialism tending towards the childish when she remembers her childhood experience: this is obvious both in the vocabulary, and in the opaque use of pronouns as if their referents were understood. The subjective and non-literary tone is given also by an exclamation immediately after our extract—'Home!'—and continues throughout the story: 'What would they say of her in the Stores when they found out that she had run away with a fellow? Say she was a fool, perhaps.' Eveline's voice is recognizable throughout the story, but the indirect third-person report (as opposed to the direct report of stream of consciousness) prevents her point of view from becoming alienated from that of the author, maintaining sympathy. Every now and then, Joyce intervenes, not with a judgement, but with a formulation of the shop-girl's dilemma which is patently not phrased in the language that the story has established as hers: 'Besides, the invariable squabble for money on Saturday nights had begun to weary her unspeakably', 'that life of commonplace sacrifices closing in final craziness'. The authorial voice reminds us that there are alternative ways of thinking about her situation; that, although Eveline 'tried to weigh each side of the question', the terms which she possesses for this self-examination are inadequate to the task: she cannot break out from her own limited ideology. The double voice of FID allows Joyce to present and to question her attitudes virtually simultaneously; to place two sets of values in an implicit dialogue with one another.

Turning now to external perspective, its basic characteristic is avoidance of any account of the thoughts or feelings of characters, or at least, avoidance of any claim to the fidelity of such an account. As with the internal modes, there are two chief variants. What I refer to as Type C is the most impersonal form of third-person narration, impersonal in two respects. First, in relation to the characters, it declines to report their inner processes, and so *verba sentiendi* are as much as possible banished from the discourse; it claims to be objective in not offering to report what an ordinary unprivileged observer could not see. Second, it is impersonal in relation to the author or narrator, declining to offer judgements on the characters' actions; this claimed authorial objectivity is indicated by avoidance of evaluative modalities. Type C is the formula for the most neutral, impersonal, type of third-person narration, which we associate with epic among the older literatures, and, in the modern period, with the ideal of objective realism proposed by Flaubert; and with news reporting. Hemingway is thought to be an extreme practitioner of this kind of writing, but close examination of his work reveals that the impression of objectivity comes from a foregrounding of action verbs and descriptions of physical states, with a relative scarcity but not a complete absence of modals and of words of feeling. In some of the more 'dead-pan' parts of his work, we find passages such as the following which are almost entirely sequences of action predicates and physical descriptions, with speech directly reported without comment:

Outside the arc-light shone through the bare branches of a tree. Nick walked up the street beside the car-tracks and turned at the next arc-light down a side-street. Three houses up the street was Hirsch's rooming-house. Nick walked up the two steps and pushed the bell. A woman came to the door.

  'Is Ole Andreson here?'
  'Do you want to see him?'
  'Yes, if he's in.'

Nick followed the woman up a flight of stairs and back to the end of a corridor. She knocked on the door.

'Who is it?'

'It's somebody to see you, Mr Andreson,' the woman said.

'It's Nick Adams.'

'Come in.'

Nick opened the door and went into the room. Ole Andreson was lying on the bed with all his clothes on. He had been a heavyweight prize-fighter and he was too long for the bed. He lay with his head on two pillows. He did not look at Nick. (Ernest Hemingway, 'The Killers', 1928.)

This is unusually close to pure Type C external, but the story as a whole does contain a few phrases indicating internal states, and a few modal judgements. It is virtually impossible to remove all modal and psychological indicators from a text, but they can, as above, be kept at a minimal level of prominence.

Finally, we come to Type D external perspective. By contrast with the impersonal Type C, the persona of the narrator is high-lighted, perhaps by first-person pronouns, and certainly by explicit modality. By these means, the impression is created of a speaker who controls the telling of the story, and who has definite views on the world at large (announced in generic sentences, perhaps) and on the actions and characters in the story (evaluative adjectives). Externality in relation to the characters emerges when the narrator's modal activity includes what Uspensky calls *words of estrangement:* words such as 'apparently', 'evidently', 'perhaps', 'as if', 'it seemed', etc., as well as metaphors and comparisons. These expressions pretend that the author—or often, one character observing another—does not have access to the feelings or thoughts of the characters. They emphasize an act of interpretation, an attempt to reconstruct the psychology of the character by reference to the signs that can be gleaned by external observation. *Verba sentiendi* may be used, but only if introduced by words denoting appearance or speculation: 'He seemed tired,' 'She was probably furious.' There is also, in texts which make extensive use of this technique, considerable reference to the physical characteristics and gestures of the characters. All of the linguistic signs of external

Type D narration are copiously present in the following extract, from the opening of a novel; I have italicized the 'words of estrangement':

On an autumn afternoon of 1919 a hatless man with a slight limp *might have been observed* ascending the gentle, broad acclivity of Riceyman Steps, which lead from King's Cross Road up to Riceyman Square, in the great metropolitan industrial district of Clerkenwell. He was rather less than stout and rather more than slim. His thin hair had begun to turn from black to grey, but his complexion was still fairly good, and the rich, very red lips, under a small greyish moustache and over a short, pointed beard, were quite remarkable in their *suggestion* of vitality. The brown eyes *seemed* a little small; they peered at near objects. As to his age, an experienced and cautious observer of mankind, without previous knowledge of this man, *would have said* no more than he *must* be past forty. The man himself was *certainly* entitled to say that he was in the prime of life. He wore a neat dark-grey suit, which *must have been* carefully folded at nights, a low, white, starched collar, and a 'made' black tie that completely hid the shirt-front; the shirt-cuffs could not be seen. He was shod in old, black leather slippers, well polished. He gave an *appearance* of quiet, intelligent, refined and kindly prosperity; and in his little eyes shone the varying *lights* of emotional sensitiveness. (Arnold Bennett, *Riceyman Steps*, 1923.)

This is very straightforward: the physique and dress are detailed, and the deductions from them which a stranger would make are suggested. A more extreme form of external Type D point of view uses the words of estrangement, usually accompanied by metaphors, to alienate the character, setting him at a distance, without sympathy. Grotesques and villains are often presented in this way. It is not only that the emphasis on their physical peculiarities presents them as bizarre and threatening; the exaggerated refusal to go *below* the surface, the ostentatious guesses at what unimaginable motives might lurk beneath, present the characters as inhuman, beyond the comprehension of an ordinary human belief system. Dickens uses this technique of sinister grotesquerie frequently, as does George Orwell, who learned it from Dickens. Examples of this alienating use of external Type D point of view are quoted in the discussion of switching perspectives in *Titus Groan* which follows.

Mervyn Peake's *Titus Groan* (1946) is a long, complicated novel, gothic and sinister, but also comic in an almost Dickensian fashion: there is a large cast of grotesque characters, all marked by strong idiosyncrasies including, prominently, peculiarities of physique, dress, and movement. The individual characters are presented as isolated within their own private worlds of motive and sensation; they are single-minded in the manner of 'humours'; Swelter is animated by his plotting of revenge on Flay, the Countess totally preoccupied with her birds and cats, Sourdust lives for the ritual of the community and its administration, Steerpike is ambitious to dominate the castle and its inhabitants for his own personal interest.

The mixture of isolation and detailed motivation is managed compositionally by constant and abrupt switches of perspective. The text focuses with precise concentration on one character at a time, but this focus is moved systematically from character to character. When a character is acting alone, s/he is often given exclusive attention; when a group is assembled, individuals are picked out one by one for their gestures and responses to one event, then the story develops, and Peake goes the rounds again. Both internal perspective (Type B, omniscient) and external perspective (Type D, estranged) are employed, with frequent sharp changes from one to the other. Internal Type B conveys knowledge of people's motives and reactions, whereas external Type D presents them as aliens, as caricatures. The source of Type B is, by definition, the framing narrative discourse; Type D sometimes emanates from the narrator's point of view, sometimes from that of one character watching another. There seems to be almost no trace of internal Type A ('mimetic'), so that, when we watch one person with another's eyes, the defamiliarizing metaphors used are as flamboyant and 'literary' as those of the narrator, and do not communicate a character's world-view distinct from that of the narrative voice.

I want to refer briefly to a crucial scene of the novel for some contrasting techniques: switches of perspective from internal to external; within internal perspective, switches from character to character; the defamiliarizing use of external perspective in the transformation of human to grotesque or to machine; and

accompanying alternations of spatial point of view. The scene is
a violent encounter between Swelter, the cook, and Flay, Lord
Sepulchrave's personal servant, just before the christening of
Titus, the infant heir to the Gormenghast estate. I cannot
quote the whole section, pp. 102–5 in the Penguin edition, and
must assume that it will be read carefully in its entirety. For ease
of reference, I have numbered the relevant paragraphs as
follows:

1. Great activity . . . 2. Suddenly the door opened . . . 3. 'Woah . . .'
4. The door knob moved . . . 5. Flay stiffened . . . 6. Swelter, as soon . . .
7. A voice came out of the face . . . 8. The line of . . . 9. Although
Mr Flay . . . 10. Swelter, as Mr Flay spat . . . 11. Into the room . . .
12. 'Mr Flay . . . ' 13. This was brought out . . .

Spatial point of view is foregrounded throughout the sequence:
para. 1 establishes the setting—'the cool room'—and an observation point—'in the room'. The room is empty, but from within
the room an invisible observer, a viewing point occupied by the
narrator and the reader, watches Flay enter; note the deictic
'came' indicating movement towards the viewer: 2 'Suddenly the
door opened and Flay came in.' Flay's external appearance and
his movements around the room are described, and then he is
located at the point of observation: 2 'he heard a voice beyond
the door.' Para. 4 presents the emergence of Swelter in the door
opening, from the psychological and visual viewpoint of Flay:
4 'For some time, or so it seemed to Flay, taut areas of cloth
evolved in a great arc and then at last above them a head around
the panels and the eyes embedded in that head concentrated their
gaze upon Mr Flay.' Through this estranged, metaphorical
language we feel that Flay sees Swelter as a shape, not as a
person; but the visual viewpoint switches from Flay to Swelter
at the end of the sentence. From now on we see Flay from
Swelter's point of view, and vice versa, in alternating perspectives. Both see one another as objects, and so does the reader see
both. Estranged external D narration is the dominant mode,
presenting both characters as grotesque automata. However,
some internal perspective is reserved for Flay, and some clauses
of active transitivity.

Paras. 2, 5, and 8 contain some phrases externalizing and estranging Flay: 2 'The negative dignity of the room threw him out in relief as a positive scarecrow', 2 'he shot his chin forward like a piece of machinery'; 5 'Flay stiffened—if it is possible for something already as stiff as a piece of teak to stiffen still further'; 8 'The line of Mr Flay's mouth, always thin and hard, became even thinner as though scored with a needle.'

The estranged external treatment of Flay is modest, however, compared with the externalization of Swelter. I have referred to para. 4, which presents him as a massive configuration of 'areas of cloth'. There are also classic markers of estranged external—diverse grotesque metaphors, modalizers such as 'as though', 'seem', evaluative adjectives—attached to Swelter in paras. 6, 7 ('a voice came out of the face'), 8 ('the white mountain'), 9, 10, and 13. Para. 6 illustrates the technique at its peak of intensity:

Swelter, as soon as he saw who it was, stopped dead, and across his face little billows of flesh ran swiftly here and there until, as though they had determined to adhere to the same impulse, they swept up into both oceans of soft cheek, leaving between them a vacuum, a gaping segment like a slice cut from a melon. It was horrible. It was as though nature had lost control. As though the smile, as a concept, as a manifestation of pleasure, had been a mistake, for here on the face of Swelter the idea had been abused.

Swelter receives virtually no internal treatment. The only *verba sentiendi* attributed to him in the whole passage are 'saw' (para. 6) and 'gazed' (10). Where an internal alternative would have been possible, an external expression is preferred: Swelter does not 'concentrate' on Flay, but wears 'an expression of comic concentration' (10). Flay's responses and perceptions, however, are frequently mentioned: for example, 2 'cared', 'to his mind', 'defiance', etc.; 9 'learned', 'ignore', 'his pride was wounded', 'learned', 'hatred'. For this reason we are 'on Flay's side' in his feud with Swelter: it is not only that Swelter is the more hideous of these two ogres—though that certainly is the effect of the estrangement devices piled on the cook—but also that Flay's feelings, through the reserving for him of internal Type B treatment, remain accessible to us. He could hardly be called sympathetic, but his actions are motivated and comprehensible:

as he suddenly strode past the chef towards the door . . . he pulled the chain over his head and slashed the heavy brass links across the face of his taunter. (para. 13.)

This narrative climax is signalled by the appropriate transitivity structure of action clauses, as happens at other crucial points in the narrative, for instance the moments of greatest effort and decisiveness in Steerpike's escape over the castle rooftops. Technically this is external narration Type C ('Hemingwayan'), but in the context it involves the reader with Flay by presenting him as determined and active.

References and Suggestions for Further Reading

The main sources for the account of point of view given in this chapter are Gérard Genette, trans. Jane E. Lewin, *Narrative Discourse* (Oxford: Basil Blackwell, 1980), and Boris Uspensky, trans. Valentina Zavarin and Susan Wittig, *A Poetics of Composition* (Berkeley: University of California Press, 1973).

Anglo-American literary theory and criticism concerning point of view has been dominated by the ideas and the techniques of the American novelist Henry James; for a classic 'Jamesian' statement see Percy Lubbock, *The Craft of Fiction* (London: Jonathan Cape, 1954 [1921]). The most influential modern book in this tradition is Wayne C. Booth, *The Rhetoric of Fiction* (2nd edn., Chicago: University of Chicago Press, 1983 [1961]).

Introductions to narrative analysis in the traditions of Russian Formalism and French Structuralism include Jonathan Culler, *Structuralist Poetics* (London: Routledge & Kegan Paul, 1975); Terence Hawkes, *Structuralism and Semiotics* (London: Methuen, 1977); Shlomith Rimmon-Kenan, *Narrative Fiction: Contemporary poetics* (London: Methuen, 1983). For a valuable introduction to narrative based on a synthesis of structuralist and other ideas, see Steven Cohan and Linda M. Shires, *Telling Stories: A theoretical analysis of narrative fiction* (London: Routledge, 1988).

Fiction and narration have been studied in a number of recent books which use a critical linguistic perspective: Geoffrey N. Leech and Michael H. Short, *Style in Fiction* (London: Longman, 1981); Roger Fowler, *Linguistics and the Novel* (London: Methuen, 2nd edn., 1983) (for discussion of internal and external perspective); Paul Simpson,

Language, Ideology and Point of View (London: Routledge, 1993); Michael J. Toolan, *Narrative: A critical linguistic introduction* (London: Routledge, 1988). Detailed linguistic commentary on individual novelists is to be found in Katie Wales, *The Language of James Joyce* (London: Macmillan, 1992) and Roger Fowler, *The Language of George Orwell* (London: Macmillan, 1995). See also R. Fowler, 'Polyphony and problematic in *Hard Times*', in R. Giddings, ed., *The Changing World of Charles Dickens* (London: Vision Press, 1983), pp. 91–108, reprinted in R. Carter and P. Simpson, eds., *Language, Discourse and Literature* (London: Unwin Hyman, 1989), pp. 77–93.

Both Wales's book, and that of Leech and Short, contain valuable material on the important topic of the representation of speech and thought in fiction. See also Brian McHale, 'Free Indirect Discourse: A Survey of Recent Accounts', *Poetics and the Theory of Literature*, 3 (1978), 249–87; and Dorrit Cohn, *Transparent Minds: Narrative modes for presenting consciousness in fiction* (Princeton: Princeton University Press, 1978).

CHAPTER TEN

Register and the Plural Text

Informally, it might be said that different points of view may be communicated by different *styles* of language. In the present chapter, I want to clarify some ideas which might be associated with the traditional notion of 'style', but I will introduce a more workable terminology. The term 'style' itself is extraordinarily slippery, and although linguistic criticism for a long time called itself 'linguistic stylistics' or even just 'stylistics', the stylisticians soon decided that 'style' was unusable as a technical term. Intuitively, in ordinary non-theoretical usage, the word makes sense, and is handy. We use the word in an enormous range of literary contexts, speaking of 'Milton's grand style' or 'the prose style of Henry James' (style of *author*), 'epic style', 'ballad style' (*genre*), 'seventeenth-century prose style' (*period*), 'Augustan style', 'Imagist style' (*movement*), 'florid style', 'plain style' (*impression*). 'Style' has similar usages in speaking about the non-verbal arts: 'baroque style' (painting, architecture, music as well as literature), 'pointillist style', 'Picasso's later style' (painting), 'fugal style', 'the style of Gregorian chant' (music). We also readily apply the word 'style' to language outside of literature: 'advertising style', 'lecture style', 'textbook style'; and to non-linguistic communication and other behaviour—'a relaxed style of driving', 'casual style (of dress)', 'authoritarian style'. Any horse-racing buff will recognize Piggott's style in the saddle. The applications of the term are endless, and they make perfect sense to their users.

To complicate this semantic picture further, there is a usage which is less descriptive, more evaluative, as when we say that someone has style or has no style, or is stylish or not at all stylish. Oscar Wilde devoted his life to style, and we can think of many contemporary examples of style dandies.

Setting aside the evaluative sense, the word 'style' seems to
mean roughly 'a recognizable and characteristic way of doing
something'. It is a generalization about regular conduct, particularly linguistic conduct. 'Style' would have to be more precise
than this, however, to be used descriptively and accurately, and
the fact is that the word has an inevitably blurring effect, because
the kinds of regularities referred to are so diverse in their nature.
An author's style in the sense of his or her linguistic fingerprints
is one kind of generalization; quite different in nature is the style
of advertising or of scientific writing, where we are talking about
linguistic arrangements which are far from unconscious, but
have been deliberately shaped to specific communicative purposes. The domain of style seems to be one for which, at the very
least, we need several distinct terms to divide up the field into
separate phenomena.

At this point I wish to explore the use in linguistic criticism of
the sociolinguistic term *register*. I hasten to say that 'register' is
not equivalent to the term 'style' (which has to be discarded as
a theoretical term, though it still has informal uses); 'register'
does some of the work of 'style', but can be defined more
explicitly, because it comes from a system of related technical
terms in sociolinguistics. These are all terms for linguistic *varieties*. 'Variety' is a very useful general, neutral concept, denoting
any distinctive and recognized form of language which has a
specific communicative role in a society. A variety is not necessarily something 'less' than a language, indeed the beauty of the
term 'variety' is that it can include whole languages if a culture
is diglossic or multilingual: French and Haitian Creole are
languages with distinct roles in Haiti; English, Malay, Chinese,
and Tamil are varieties in Singapore, each with its roles in
relation to the culture. For our purpose, however, the most
significant varieties are 'less than' a language, and specifically,
they may be used to define versions of the English language. The
relevant terminology may be set out as follows, to get all the
jargon out of the way at once:

dialect and accent
standard versus non-standard and antilanguage
sociolect

idiolect

register

Dialects are of course varieties which reflect the regional origins of speakers; they may be distinguished by features of syntax, and/or vocabulary, and/or pronunciation. An *accent* is the distinctive pronunciation of a dialect, the feature by which people generally recognize and name dialects: Cockney, Geordie, Scouse. In England, as in many countries, one regional dialect has attained the position of a *standard*. Standard English derives from the dialects of the south-east of the country, developing since the fourteenth century as a result of the domination by London and its environs in the spheres of government, commerce, education, and communications. The elevation of a regional dialect to a standard introduces complications. The standard is inevitably associated with and used by people who have enjoyed higher levels of income, education, and power, and its resultant prestige may lead people to regard it as 'not a dialect', unlike, in their view, Cockney or Northern dialects, which become seen as 'dialects' in a pejorative sense of 'nonstandard', therefore stigmatized. (The fact of the matter is that, contrary to prejudice, Standard English remains standard when spoken with a regional accent.)

Thus British Standard English is not only a dialect, but also a *sociolect*, i.e. a variety associated with a particular class or social group. It follows that the dialects which the standard defines as 'non-standard' are perceived as sociolects: thus, for example, the Cockney spoken by the characters in the television soap opera 'Eastenders' can be regarded in popular consciousness not simply as the regional dialect of East London but as a working-class sociolect. Sociolects have been extensively studied by modern 'urban dialectologists', notably William Labov and Peter Trudgill. Their research shows that, in complex urban areas (Philadelphia, Detroit, New York City, and Norwich have been studied), speakers possess finely-tuned mental models of the social values of speech varieties in the community. Speakers can be 'classed' by the recognition of minute phonological details, which can be regarded as *stereotypes*: in Britain, the presence of [r] in the pronunciation of words like 'car' and 'card', characteristic of dialects of the rural south-west, connotes a rustic character; [tʰ] or [t] in 'thing', 'three' stereotypes an Irish accent/sociolect. Sociolects are of great interest in the class-conscious English novel; not only class is involved, but occupational or professional groupings, which can reasonably be included under 'sociolect'. From the eighteenth century onward, the major English writers of fiction have been fond of representing non-standard speakers in their novels: Squire Western in Fielding's *Tom Jones,* the Cockney characters who populate Dickens's novels, Northerners in Mrs Gaskell, rustic characters in Hardy, a whole palette of diverse dialect speakers in Orwell. In general terms, the inclusion of non-standard speakers serves defamiliarizing ends: their speech suggests world-views which contrast with the thinking of the Standard English framing narrative voice or of other, cultivated, educated, characters. The topic of non-standard speech in fiction is beyond the scope of the present book, but has been discussed and illustrated in other criticism.

Dialect is a regional variety, sociolect a class or occupational variety; *idiolect* is the personal variety, the bundle of distinctive speech features which allow us to recognize an individual. It is a well-known fact that we can quickly identify our friends' voices when they telephone us; and a colleague speaking in another room or the corridor can be recognized on hearing just a few words. The idiolect is a compound of voice qualities which reflect a number of factors: the shape of the individual's speech organs; accent in the sociolectal/dialectal senses; other social markers such as signs of ethnicity and gender; idiosyncratic patterns of phrasing and choice of words. In recent years, the validity of the individual voice has even earned a degree of acceptance in *forensic linguistics,* with voice samples and 'voiceprints' being offered as evidence and analysed by expert linguists in courts of law. The more traditional counterpart of forensic linguistics in literary studies is the study of the personal styles of authors, in which the authorship of problematic texts has been debated on the basis of linguistic stylistic analysis and statistical methods. Idiolects also, like dialects and sociolects, are created for defamiliarizing effects in fiction: clear examples are found in the many grotesque individual caricatures which are found in Dickens's novels.

'Antilanguage' is a suggestive term which was coined by Halliday to refer to a type of sociolect which relates to the standard in a radically antagonistic way. Antilanguages are secret or canting languages invented and used by isolated, deviant groups such as prison inmates, thieves, and other underground or subversive communities. Halliday's pioneering article takes as instances of antilanguage the 'pelting speech' of Elizabethan thieves and vagabonds; the language of the Calcutta underworld; and what is called 'grypserka', the language of Polish prisons. An antilanguage probably originates as a *secret* language: a special vocabulary for the important objects and practices in the counterculture shields their activities from detection by the police, or from comprehension by members of the 'legitimate' or 'standard' culture. The jargon of truckers using Citizens' Band radio, the argot of a black community, and the slang of pop music culture would be modern examples. In expressing the concerns of the subculture, the antilanguage also becomes an instrument of *solidarity* or like-mindedness: not only a boundary around the group, but a bond within the group, a medium for talking about their defining preoccupations. Finally, Halliday points out that antilanguage is also a medium for verbal play and verbal art. Its basis is phonetic mutation of standard words, and metaphoric creation of a novel vocabulary, and it gives rise to word-games, verse, and repartee: this was evident as early as the sixteenth century in verse based on the vagabonds' 'pelting speech'; and exists today in such forms as rap, Cockney rhyming slang, and Rastafarian poetry. Antilanguages real or invented are also used—like non-standard English as mentioned above—within standard literary genres such as the novel to evoke deviant and antagonistic world-views: the most familiar example would be the teenage language 'Nadsat', based on Russian words, created in Anthony Burgess's *A Clockwork Orange*.

'Idiolect', 'sociolect' and 'dialect', and their sub-types such as antilanguage and occupational jargons, may be regarded roughly as varieties which reflect *who you are*. *Registers* are varieties which differ according to *how you use* language. The term 'register' (in this sense; and not to be confused with the musical sense of the pitch range of an instrument or voice) was introduced by T. B. W. Reid as follows:

> For the linguistic behaviour of a given individual is by no means uniform; placed in what appear to be linguistically identical conditions, he will on different occasions speak (or write) differently according to what may roughly be described as different social situations: he will use a number of distinct 'registers'. ('Linguistics, structuralism and philology', 1956.)

'Register' in this sense was then developed by Michael Halliday, whose contribution to a 1964 book *The Linguistic Sciences and Language Teaching* is the best-known exposition of the idea. Registers are distinctive varieties of language used in different *situation types* such as church service, lesson, textbook, sports reporting, etc. Situation types, and the registers associated with them, are, it was claimed, conventionally recognized in a society; registers are part of an individual's 'communicative competence' in the sense that s/he can write or speak a number of such varieties, and recognize many more originating from others including professionals. In the early years of register study, linguists proposed broad registers such as 'science', 'religion', 'instruction', 'advertising', 'law', 'sports commentary', 'weather forecasting', 'recipe', and the like, but it became clear that very much more specialized adaptations of language to situation type were generally encountered; that the boundaries between them were, however, fuzzy, so that no single complete classification was likely to be achieved; and that most texts were not in just one recognizable register, but contained a mixture of varieties. These complications do not invalidate the theory, however. Experience and research show that people can indeed produce, and identify, distinctive registers as appropriate to different types of situation. One of Halliday's most significant insights is that it takes only a scrap of language to cue recognition of a register:

> A sports commentary, a church service and a school lesson are linguistically quite distinct. *One sentence from any of these and many more such situation types would enable us to identify it correctly.* We know, for example, where 'an early announcement is expected' comes

from and 'apologies for absence were received'; these are not simply free variants of 'we ought to hear soon' and 'was sorry he couldn't make it'. (*The Linguistic Sciences and Language Teaching*, p. 87; my italics.)

A register is, then, a distinctive use of language to fulfil a particular communicative function in a particular kind of situation, but the text need not be saturated with consistent use of a typical vocabulary and syntax. It exists for language users as a model or schema, a package of sociolinguistic knowledge which can be activated by relatively slight textual cues. By this device a number of registers can be brought into play within a single text, the 'plural' kind of text of which the poem 'Street Song', analysed below, pp. 201–4, is an example.

On the other hand, some texts seem to be deliberately '*over-registrated*', absolutely full to the brim with signals which make it clear what kind of text we are faced with. Typically, these are formal and official documents such as legal contracts, prayers, and other religious set texts, instruction manuals, scientific and bureaucratic prose. The consistency, insistence even, of the style seems to have a symbolic function, saying to the reader that s/he must not mistake the purpose that the text is about: do not fail to recognize that I am an insurance policy, binding on both parties. Such registers might be called *hegemonic* registers: they aim at absolute authority in relation to the addressee, and they manage this by explicitness and by absolute clarity as to the register in which they are cast.

Registers seem to have a solid existence within the linguistic intuitions of people in a speech community. As far as *describing* them is concerned—as opposed to using them or recognizing them without analysis—students are able to talk readily about specific registers once they have got the general idea: simple examples such as an advertisement, or a scientific or legal text, can be easily characterized in impressionistic terms. The way Halliday developed the idea, however, provides more disciplined techniques for the use of registers in their social contexts: for describing their linguistic characteristics, and the way they relate to different situation types. He distinguishes three aspects in which situation types vary (with consequences for the linguistic organization of register) as follows:

Field: the activity associated with the language being used; subject-matter: this might be chemistry, politics, cars, cookery, or whatever. Quite clearly, different fields produce different language, most obviously at the level of vocabulary.

Tenor: the relationship between the people concerned in the speech act, e.g. solidary or power-distinguished, formal or casual; the intentions of the speaker, to persuade, inform, etc.

Mode: the way the text is organized in the chosen channel, speech, or print/visual, or a mixture of the two. Under mode we consider features such as typography, layout, use of colour, the marking-out of verse in lines, and so on; in speech, volume, speed, pauses, length of utterance, etc.

Each of these aspects of situation type corresponds to one of Halliday's three 'functions of language', and to each there relates a range of linguistic features to which the critical analyst may pay attention. These correspondences can be presented in tabular form, as shown on p. 193.

We may briefly illustrate the application of the categories presented in the table by considering a non-literary text, part of a whole-page magazine advertisement for a book club (see p. 194). The analysis is not meant by any means to be exhaustive: it is intended simply to illustrate how, by referring to the types of structure mentioned in the right-hand column of the table, we can rapidly and efficiently characterize the text as an example of a certain register of writing.

The *mode* of the advertisement as a whole is highly characteristic of this kind of register: it is a whole page on a bright yellow background; two-thirds of the advertisement consists of small photographs of dozens of books priced cheaply as an introductory offer, with a large section offering a cut-price video of the film *Jurassic Park;* the right-hand vertical third of the page has, at the top, the message ANY 5 FROM 50p EACH very large in reverse video on a red background; below it is the main text, with a red heading and then black on yellow, and in the bottom right-hand corner a cut-out box (in small black-on-white

Aspects of situation	Linguistic function	Features of linguistic structure
Field Associated activity, subject-matter	*Ideational* Representation of experience, categorization, and other structuring	Vocabulary Transitivity
Tenor Relationships between participants: power, solidarity; roles and purposes Formality of situation	*Interpersonal* Expression of roles, purposes, and relationships Linguistic contruction of addressor and addressee	Deixis: personal pronouns Modality, speech acts; mental processes Vocabulary as technical/formal/colloquial Syntax (e.g. hypotaxis v. parataxis)
Mode Type of channel, and organization of text within it	*Textual* Construction of text as medium: cohesion, development, emphasis, foregrounding Genre	Cohesive ties (anaphora, etc.) Thematization, parallelism Typography, voice qualities Genre-markers (e.g. rhyme)

print, offering a more formal appearance) for the reader to fill in and send to the book club. The main advertising text runs as follows:

TOP CLASS BOOKS AT ROCK BOTTOM PRICES!
Why pay high street prices when you can save money on **every** book you buy with World Books?

For a start, you can choose **any five books from just 50p each** as your special introduction to the club. That's a saving of up to £150 straight away!

Then, as a member, you'll receive a FREE colour magazine every month, packed with hundreds of top titles. All the books we sell are of the highest quality, being either original publishers' versions—identical to those you find in the high street—or our own superb hardback editions. And every book is offered at a discount of at least 25% off the published price—many are half price!

When you join World Books, you'll be joining two million other wise readers who profit from the fact that the club is part of BCA, a company with over 25 years' experience of providing them with great value and service. You couldn't be in better hands!

All we ask is that you choose four books in your first year of membership. It won't be difficult—the savings are so good and the selection so wide, you'll probably buy more!

So waste no time. Join today. But send no money now! We **know** we're the best but we want you to see the proof **before** you pay!

Some further observations might be made about the mode of this part of the advertisement: the division into very short paragraphs, the liberal use of capitals, bold typeface, and exclamation marks. These features are characteristic of this kind of popular advertisement, and more broadly, of public, printed media texts of an informal kind: they are found, for example, in editorials in tabloid newspapers. Further analysis of the mode would show that it is designed to give the impression of a speaking voice directly addressing the reader: the bold print suggests emphasis, the short sentences and paragraphs the organization of speech; and this impression of orality brings us to consideration of *tenor*.

The illusion of a speaking voice fits in with other features of tenor which give the register of this advertisement a kind of 'personal' flavour. Pronouns mention the 'speaker' and, particularly, the addressee, with great frequency: the source of the advertisement is signalled by repetition of the corporate 'we' (World Books), while the reader/potential book club member is pinpointed by repeated uses of the second-person pronoun 'you'—one or two mentions in almost every sentence serve to delineate a place for the reader to occupy in this persuasive interaction. The next aspect of the writing to study—and one central to this advertising register—is the *speech acts* which occur. The text is full of speech acts which build a demanding, manipulatory relationship between the advertiser and the reader. It begins with a rhetorical question, i.e. a question with a predetermined answer. The presupposition of 'Why pay high street prices . . . ' is that it is not sensible to pay more when the reader can buy from World Books for less: the reader is required to accept this, and this is the justification and motive for reading on. The next three paragraphs consist of a series of promises and offers, speech acts which are reinforced by appropriate *modality*: 'you can', 'you'll', etc. The final paragraph, as is customary for this type of advertisement, consists of requests—'All we ask . . .' —and apparent imperatives—'waste no time', one of which ('But send no money today!') is surely the kind of sentence which Halliday had in mind when he remarked that 'One sentence . . . would enable us to identify [a situation type] correctly' (cf. p. 190 above).

The *field* is entirely straightforward, and can be represented as the union of three sets of lexical items that are prominent in the text:

money and saving money: 'prices', 'money', '50p each', 'saving', etc.

books and publication: 'books', 'colour magazine', 'titles', 'books', 'publishers', 'hardback', etc.

club and membership: 'club', 'member', 'join', 'club', 'membership', etc.

Note that the field is not simply 'books', but 'saving-money-by-buying-books-through-a-club'. Some other commodity—records, clothing, or whatever—could be substituted for books without materially altering the register, and indeed this register is widely associated with a range of products in British newspaper and magazine advertising.

Listing the linguistic features associated with the field, tenor, and mode of a text is an easy and organized way of characterizing the register; it only makes sense, of course, if we can relate the complex of features to the situation type which gives meaning to the register—in this case, we need to be aware of the function and conventions of magazine advertising of certain commodities. What is the status of these features for the reader? For the reader, they must serve as *cues* which activate this register as a scheme of stored sociolinguistic knowledge. Though the majority of readers would not be able to write in this register of popular magazine advertising, they know the conventions through experience, and the textual signals or cues bring the register to awareness, to tacit recognition.

The advertising text—which I have included just to illustrate the application of the terminology associated with 'register'—is an example of a hegemonic text as defined above. It is clear and consistent: no reader could mistake its purpose; no one who is communicatively competent in English would have to pause in order to work out what sort of response is called for. As far as sociolinguistic description is concerned, the text is unproblematic: it represents the register of advertising, or at least, one of the range of clearly identifiable types of register associated with the differing styles of advertising found in the English mass media. This advertisement illustrates the kind of straightforward text which tends to be used to teach the principles of register theory (others might be scientific articles, sermons, legal documents, sports commentaries, cookbooks, etc.). I selected it because it is a clear, obvious, and familiar kind of text; but its simplicity is untypical of much of our language experience. Most texts are much less indeterminate as to a particular register, or alternatively, they contain cues which signal the presence of a mixture of registers—they are 'plural' in character. Discussing this situation in an earlier book on newspaper discourse, I commented that:

The traditional way of looking at this matter seems to me to put the cart before the horse. I would prefer to say, not that a text is in a certain . . . register, but that . . . registers . . . are 'in' texts. (*Language in the News*, p. 60.)

Texts (other than hegemonic texts) are often plural, containing a mix of registers, dialects, and sociolects woven together, represented economically by significant details of structure (our 'cues') which encourage readers to construct a fuller picture of each whole variety in their imaginations. Where the mixture is obvious and explicit, and there appears to be a purpose to mixing the varieties, a text may be called—using a term from Bakhtin's dialogic theory of literature—**heteroglossic.**

Where the signals of two or more varieties are juxtaposed in a text, the reader cannot rest in a state of untroubled certainty, as s/he does when processing an advertisement, a legal contract, or a recipe. The point of the association has to be worked out, and very often, we are looking at a critical relationship between two registers, a dialogue between the world-views implicit in the two varieties. Thus, heteroglossia is intrinsically connected with *defamiliarization*. It is no accident that the most strikingly defamiliarizing texts are most committed to variety-mixing as a structural principle of composition: Lawrence Sterne's *Tristram Shandy,* James Joyce's *Ulysses,* T. S. Eliot's *The Waste Land,* George Orwell's *Nineteen Eighty-Four.* Let us, however, take some simpler heteroglossic texts as examples. The following three texts, by Henry Reed, Fleur Adcock, and W. H. Auden, are all very accessible, popular texts. Note that they will be discussed only as examples of some types of heteroglossic constructions; no claim of anything like a complete analysis will be made, but readers will easily be able to take the analysis further by private study or by discussion in class.

'Naming of Parts' by Henry Reed is one of a pair of poems with the collective title 'Lessons of the War', in which Reed presents the experience of a conscript soldier under training in such a way as to attack war and military values. Contrast of register is the dominant structural principle; each stanza contains two distinct 'voices', the second offering an implicit critique of the first:·

Naming of Parts

To-day we have naming of parts. Yesterday,
We had daily cleaning. And to-morrow morning,
We shall have what to do after firing. But to-day,
To-day we have naming of parts. Japonica
Glistens like coral in all of the neighbouring gardens,
    And to-day we have naming of parts.

This is the lower sling swivel. And this
Is the upper sling swivel, whose use you will see,
When you are given your slings. And this is the piling swivel,
Which in your case you have not got. The branches
Hold in the gardens their silent, eloquent gestures,
    Which in our case we have not got.

This is the safety-catch, which is always released
With an easy flick of the thumb. And please do not let me
See anyone using his finger. You can do it quite easy
If you have any strength in your thumb. The blossoms
Are fragile and motionless, never letting anyone see
    Any of them using their finger.

And this you can see is the bolt. The purpose of this
Is to open the breech, as you can see. We can slide it
Rapidly backwards and forwards: we call this
Easing the spring. And rapidly backwards and forwards
The early bees are assaulting and fumbling the flowers:
    They call it easing the Spring.

They call it easing the Spring: it is perfectly easy
If you have any strength in your thumb: like the bolt,
And the breech, and the cocking-piece, and the point of balance,
Which in our case we have not got; and the almond-blossom
Silent in all of the gardens and the bees going backwards and forwards,
    For to-day we have naming of parts.

According to Halliday, a register allows us to identify a situation
type. In a poem, the situation is of course fictional: there is no
real place or participants, and the language is all we have to go
on. In the present case, the register of the first voice evokes a
situation type very effectively: an instructor taking a class of
trainees through the parts and the handling of a rifle. There are
many deictic forms anchoring the situation in time and space:

'to-day', 'yesterday', 'to-morrow morning', and the repeated 'this ... this ... this' pointing to the parts of the gun in the instructor's hands or on the table in front of him. The tenor contains typical features of the language of instruction. There is, for example, the inclusive pronoun 'we' by which most teachers gather their pupils into the shared activity of the current lesson: 'To-day we have naming of parts,' just as I would say in a seminar or lecture 'This morning we're going to discuss heteroglossia.' There is repetition of phrase and sentence, a stock part of lecturing technique. There are set phrases for the sections of instruction, which could have come out of a manual: 'naming of parts', 'daily cleaning', 'what to do after firing'. The field is further specified by technical terms for the various parts of the gun: 'lower sling swivel', 'upper sling swivel', etc. The vocabulary generally is plain and utilitarian, even the technical terms being based on common words; verbs are simple—'have', 'see', 'given', and the like—nouns are mundane, there is an almost complete absence of adjectives, and word-length is short, generally one or two syllables (the reader can readily confirm this analysis). There is absolutely nothing literary about this register—it is what Orwell would have called 'demotic' English, plain and direct. Note that this demotic verges on the vernacular and uneducated. It takes only one cue to suggest this, the non-standard 'easy' for the adverb 'easily' in the third stanza.

Towards the end of the fourth line of each of the first four stanzas there is an abrupt shift out of the instructor's register into a style which is markedly poetic. The very first of these transitions makes the point strikingly:

Japonica | Glistens like coral in all of the neighbouring gardens.

The very first word, 'Japonica', an exotic-sounding four-syllabled word for an ornamental shrub, is a marked enough signal of poeticity; it is immediately developed by a metaphor 'Glistens like coral' which is entirely foreign to the instructor's register: for an experienced reader of literature, the sentence would cue the genre of landscape description. Different, and almost equally poetic, evocations of landscape occur at the equivalent points of the other stanzas. The contrast with the first register could hardly be greater, and we are presumably meant to imagine the presence of a second 'speaker': better, a second *focalizer,* to make use of Genette's term (Chapter 9, p. 161 above). This consciousness is distinct from the instructor's, and gives the impression of being that of an educated conscript who dissociates himself from the gun-assembly lesson, day-dreaming and gazing out of the window.

A full analysis of this poem would go further than merely demonstrating that there are two contrasting registers in the text, one pedagogic, matter-of-fact, and military, the other literary, educated, and reflective. The poetic day-dreamer, who in fact has less to say than the gun instructor, is appealing to the beauty and life-creating powers of Nature to make a critique of the military position embodied in the instructor's language. There is a conventional theme implied, one that will be familiar to readers who know the work of the earlier generation of poets of the First World War (notably Wilfred Owen, Rupert Brooke). It is the reader's role initially to find this theme in the contrast of registers, but it is developed in the specific details of the interaction between the two voices, not in the sheer contrast itself. Reed has the second voice echo the first, taking up a phrase or a sentence of the instructor's speech and repeating it in the prominent refrain-like position of the last line of each stanza. These phrases are, then, appropriated and translated into another register, where they are reinterpreted by the changed context. Each matter-of-fact segment of the instructor's speech is ironized by being quoted in the 'literary' register: 'To-day we have naming of parts' which first appears in the mundane classroom context (lines 1, 4) assumes the status of a complaint in line 6, communicating an unfavourable contrast between the deadness of the lesson and the spectacular vitality of the japonica. In the second stanza, 'Which in our case we have not got' in line 6 becomes an explicit indictment of the dumbness of the rifle class. Similar critical reinterpretations occur in the remaining stanzas, in which, cumulatively, the 'poetic' consciousness pokes fun at the unrealized sexual imagery in the way the instructor refers to the parts of the gun and how they are to be 'eased';

outside the window, the natural processes of procreation proceed with more discretion and beauty.

In 'Naming of Parts' the juxtaposition of two sharply distinguished registers is used to make a point—in a somewhat laboured way, it might be felt—about war as an affront to nature, life, and beauty. The next poem to be considered, 'Street Song' by Fleur Adcock, is more radically heteroglossic, more unsettling because less diagrammatic.

Street Song

Pink Lane, Strawberry Lane, Pudding Chare:
someone is waiting, I don't know where;
hiding among the nursery names,
he wants to play peculiar games.

In Leazes Terrace or Leazes Park
someone is loitering in the dark,
feeling the giggles rise in his throat
and fingering something under his coat.

He could be sidling along Forth Lane
to stop some girl from catching her train
or stalking the grounds of the RVI
to see if a student nurse goes by.

In Belle Grove Terrace or Fountain Row
or Hunter's Road he's raring to go—
unless he's the quiet shape you'll meet
on the cobbles in Back Stowell Street.

Monk Street, Friars Street, Gallowgate
are better avoided when it's late.
Even in Sandhill and the Side
there are shadows where a man could hide.

So don't go lightly along Darn Crook
because the Ripper's been brought to book.
Wear flat shoes, and be ready to run:
remember, sisters, there's more than one.

I gather that the street names mentioned in 'Street Song' are from the city of Newcastle-upon-Tyne—however, the words would have their own connotations even if the reader did not know anything about that city. The 'Ripper' is presumably a

reference to the 'Yorkshire Ripper', Peter Sutcliffe, who mur-
dered and mutilated a number of women in the West Yorkshire
area in the 1980s; beyond that, there is a reference to 'Jack the
Ripper', a notorious but unidentified mass murderer of women
in the late nineteenth century. The poem voices a familiar theme
of modern feminism, the threat men pose to women and the need
for vigilance, particularly in the streets of cities. This much is
stated explicitly in the final stanza, which draws on a 'women's
register':

> Wear flat shoes, and be ready to run:
> remember, sisters, there's more than one.

'Sisters' is a powerful lexical cue to a register of feminism. What
is notable about the poem, however, is that this register surfaces only at the end: the main body of the text is registrated in
a range of other voices. If the poem had been cast wholly in a
feminist voice, it would have risked being flat, and sounding
like a political statement or a harangue: it would have been
monologic. Being heteroglossic, the poem feels dynamic and
disturbing.

A first and striking impact is made by a feature of *mode,* the
metrical organization of the text as verse. Each line, variously
eight, nine, or in one instance ten syllables in length, has a
pounding four-beat rhythm, unmistakable from the second line:

> Pínk Lane, Stráwberry Lane, Púdding Cháre:
> Sómeone is wáiting, I dón't know whére;
> híding amóng the núrsery námes,
> he wánts to pláy pecúliar gámes.

What verse form is this? The four-beat pulse is associated with
popular oral verse and, particularly, verse for children. You
could skip or play jumping games to the rhythm of 'Street Song',
and this of course gives a first interpretation to 'games' in line 4.
The street names in the first line reinforce the suggestion of a
register of childhood: they are indeed 'nursery names', adding up
to the pink strawberry blancmange which is a staple party treat
for young children. The cheerful rhythm and party-tea reference
are ironical in relation to the menace and perversion of the

vocabulary that follows. In the context of the poem and of contemporary society, the play situation evokes danger: it is not safe for children to play in the street. 'Waiting', 'hiding', and 'games' have thus a double meaning: the game is not only hide-and-seek, but the perverse ('peculiar') sexual play of the adult predator.

'Leazes' suggests 'sleaze', and a murky sexuality is sketched by a series of verbs which are all associated by their present participle '-ing' form. The Jakobsonian principle of equivalence (Chapter 6 above) should lead the experienced reader of poetry to link together the series of words and their meanings:

waiting, hiding, loitering, feeling, fingering, sidling, stalking, raring to go.

The poem is unified by this series, but there are noticeable transitions of register as the text proceeds. 'Loitering' is a uniaccentual word from the register of police observation. A person can only loiter with bad intent; and in this context the intent is sexual assault on children and young women, or gratification watching them: 'fingering something under his coat' is clear enough. Then 'stalking', 'Hunter's Road', and 'raring to go' have connotations of animals and hunting. 'Quiet shape', 'cobbles', 'Back', 'Monk', 'Friars', 'Gallowgate' are sinister or medieval in their connotations; Chaucer's readers know about the bad morals of the monks of olden times.

There are many more observations that could be made about register and shifts of register: the vernacular, colloquial mode of stanza 3, as if some local people are talking about a voyeur or rapist; then the elevated tone of the street names in stanza 4, which spreads the threat to a 'better-class' residential area. Readers may for themselves notice and reflect on the register differences cued by slight signals, which produce unsettling changes of tone. After all of this fluctuation, the register settles at the end to a 'woman's voice'. It is not marked in the penultimate stanza, which is, however, moving to a tone of direct statement. The last stanza, as we have seen, contains explicit cues which would allow us to construct a situation of, say, someone addressing a local support or self-defence group. The urgency of the message is enhanced by the troubling register-mix of the body of the poem.

The two poems which I have just discussed illustrate the way in which literary texts tend to mix registers to produce a defamiliarizing effect, restoring the multiaccentual nature of crucial words by confronting differences of meaning which exist in different styles of language. Register-mixing is a feature of non-literary texts as well—apart from hegemonic texts—but in the texts which feature on the usual literature courses the mixing is often deliberate and pointed. There are a number of other remarks that could be made, in conclusion, about register and literature. One central observation is that literary texts are *fictional*, or at least are read as fictional. Granted, a play or a novel does stem from, and is read in, a real communicative situation: someone has written it, used a certain technology of production, is paid for it, it is published with all the complexities that that entails. The writer has a certain readership and circulation in mind, the readership or audience buys or borrows the book, buys the theatre ticket or pays their television licence fee. But the literary text is fictional in that it is not 'about' that relationship of textual production and consumption. In the world of the fiction, an Irish airman foresees his death, or Lear divides up his kingdom, Jimmy Porter rants at his flat-mates, and so on. The literary text's language is not embedded in a real context of situation, as an advertisement or an insurance policy is, but it creates its own situation, topic, and world for the reader to enter. As Ronald Carter and Walter Nash express it in an important paper,

The literary text makes its own universe of discourse; the reader does not come to it with the prior purpose of mending his car or taking out insurance or pursuing any other social aim. It is not 'used' for any practical purpose; it teaches its own use; it is sovereign in its own domain of language. ('Language and Literariness', p. 130.)

This property which Carter and Nash call *sovereignty* has not been discovered by them; what is novel in their account is that they ground its understanding in the concept of register. In practical terms situationless, the literary text creates its own fictional situation by drawing on registers of language which are outside the writer-reader communication link. This is a major part of what modern literary theorists call *intertextuality*, the process of allusion to other texts and discourse. Carter and Nash provide the very useful term *re-registration* for this process. A register which forms part of the reader's pre-existing communicative competence is appropriated for new use within the literary textual world.

When an 'external' register is transported within a text and a situation in which it is not normally used, it is of course no longer the same register. The integral link between register and situation gets broken in fictional texts; the external register is therefore in the new text for some purpose other than its original function. Inevitably, it becomes 'estranged'; it is framed by the new context of poem or novel, offered for critical attention. What would be familiar and practical—thus unnoticed—in a real setting stands out and is scrutinized. As a striking example of re-registration, the final text to be considered in this chapter, here is a poem by W. H. Auden:

The Unknown Citizen
(To JS/07/M/378 This Marble Monument is Erected by the State)

He was found by the Bureau of Statistics to be
One against whom there was no official complaint,
And all the reports on his conduct agree
That, in the modern sense of an old-fashioned word, he was a saint,
For in everything he did he served the Greater Community.
Except for the War till the day he retired
He worked in a factory and never got fired,
But satisfied his employers, Fudge Motors Inc.
Yet he wasn't a scab or odd in his views,
For his Union reports that he paid his dues,
(Our report on his Union shows it was sound)
And our Social Psychology workers found
That he was popular with his mates and liked a drink.
The Press are convinced that he bought a paper every day
And that his reactions to advertisements were normal in every way.
Policies taken out in his name prove that he was fully insured,

And his Health-card shows he was once in hospital but left it cured.
Both Producers Research and High-Grade Living declare
He was fully sensible to the advantages of the Installment Plan
And had everything necessary to the Modern Man,
A phonograph, a radio, a car and a frigidaire.
Our researchers into Public Opinion are content
That he held the proper opinions for the time of year;
When there was peace, he was for peace; when there was war, he went.
He was married and added five children to the population,
Which our Eugenist says was the right number for a parent of his
      generation,
And our teachers report that he never interfered with their
      education.
Was he free? Was he happy? The question is absurd:
Had anything been wrong, we should certainly have heard.

The title, and the bracketed sub-title, provide an intertextual reference to the official genre of celebrations and monuments dedicated to 'unknown soldiers' or 'unknown warriors' who have died on behalf of their country. Such symbolic figures are real, but unidentified: the remains of a man killed in war, his individuality unrecoverable, stand for the thousands who have anonymously lost their lives for their country, and are honoured on behalf of the many other heroic victims. The irony in this title for this poem is that the man celebrated in its text is not really 'unknown': the State claims to know everything about him. He has been the object of bureaucratic surveillance and documentation. The sub-title anonymizes him with a number instead of a name, 'JS/07/M/378', triggering the well-established British distaste for tagging people by numbers (as soldiers are), a process which, we feel, effaces their individuality and affirms the power of the State over the person.

The text which follows is a thorough re-registration into officialese, or more accurately, a register of bureaucratic language which contains banal fragments of ordinary mundane discourse; both the bureaucratic and the mundane are, of course, ironically inappropriate to a 'poetic' text. I have no space to offer a full analysis of the register or registers in this poem, but this is a simple opportunity for the reader to investigate the poem further through the 'field-tenor-mode' model of register which we have just explored. The bureaucratic register can readily be charted in the vocabulary which matches the field: 'Bureau of Statistics', 'official complaint', 'reports', 'Health-card', 'researchers into Public Opinion'. There are also indications of the impersonality of officialese in the syntax, beginning with the opening passive 'He was found . . . ' and continuing with a number of nominals as subjects: 'reports . . . agree', 'reactions . . . were normal', 'Policies . . . prove', and so on, a stereotypical form of impersonal official English. In the middle of the poem there is a low or demotic register associated with trades union jargon or working men's speech: 'scab', 'paid his dues', and 'popular with his mates and liked a drink'. The official register continues with lines of banal prosiness which swamp the rhythm of the free verse metrical form: 'And that his reactions to advertisements were normal in very way', 'He was fully sensible to the advantages of the Installment Plan'. In the verse context, this style connotes bureaucratic insensitivity, a theme which prepares for the unselfcritical and callous pseudo-questions and answers at the end voiced in a new interpersonal manner, asserted by the official all-powerful 'we' which surfaces in the last line.

The effect of these re-registrations is in general terms as follows (a more delicate critical statement can be made with further analysis). Official and mundane registers have been inserted in a poetic context and are foregrounded or framed by that context. They are also subjected to a critique, making the point that the nation's attitude to individual people is callous and unappreciative—a particularly poignant critique, given that the genre offered by the state 'we' is a poetic celebration of the life of an individual. This ironic interpretation can be expressed in other words if we return to the title 'The Unknown Citizen'. The effect of this re-registration within the sovereignty of a verse form is, like other examples of defamiliarization which we have studied, to restore the multiaccentuality of the key word of the title, 'unknown'. The State claims to know everything about JS/07/M/378, but its kind of knowledge does not, in the message of the poem, count as a valid form of personal knowledge. Biographical facts and statistics, for all their claim of completeness and insight, leave the citizen precisely as the title puts it— 'unknown', unexperienced as an individual person; therefore the ostensible appreciation of his life is insincere and ignorant.

Reference and Suggestions for Further Reading

The problems of defining *style,* and of handling the concept within linguistic criticism, are discussed in N. E. Enkvist, J. Spencer and M. J. Gregory, *Linguistics and Style* (London: Oxford University Press, 1964); G. N. Leech and M. H. Short, *Style in Fiction* (London: Longman, 1981), chs. 1 and 2. The writings of S. Ullmann are helpful on the older traditions of stylistics: e.g. *Meaning and Style* (Oxford: Blackwell, 1973). See R. Wellek and A. Warren, *Theory of Literature* (New York: Harcourt, Brace & World, 1956), ch. 14 for literary stylistics. A pioneering study of functional linguistic variation in which 'style' approximates to 'register' is D. Crystal and D. Davy, *Investigating English Style* (London: Longman, 1969).

For references to introductory books on *sociolinguistics,* see Chapter 7, p. 129 above. The classic research studies by Labov and by Trudgill mentioned above, p. 187 are W. Labov, *Sociolinguistic Patterns* (Philadelphia: University of Pennsylvania Press, 1972) and P. Trudgill, *The Social Differentiation of English in Norwich* (Cambridge: Cambridge University Press, 1974). On English accents and dialects see S. Gramley and K.-M. Pätzold, *A Survey of Modern English* (London: Routledge, 1992), part 3; A. Hughes and P. Trudgill, *English Accents and Dialects* (London: Edward Arnold, 1979); J. C. Wells, *Accents of English,* (Cambridge: Cambridge University Press, 1982).

On *Standard English,* see J. Milroy and L. Milroy, *Authority in Language* (London: Routledge, 2nd edn., 1991). For its antithesis, *antilanguage,* see M. A. K. Halliday, 'Antilanguages', *Language as Social Semiotic* (London: Edward Arnold, 1978), ch. 9. Antilanguage is also discussed by M. Montgomery, *An Introduction to Language and Society* (London: Routledge, 1986), ch. 5. Applications of 'antilanguage' to literature include R. Fowler, 'Antilanguage in fiction', *Style,* 13 (1979), 259–78, reprinted in *Literature as Social Discourse* (London: Batsford, 1981), ch. 8; G. Kress, 'Poetry as antilanguage: A reconsideration of Donne's "Nocturnall upon S. Lucies Day" ', *Poetics and the Theory of Literature,* 3 (1978), 327–44. To the list of modern antilinguistic varieties given on p. 189 might be added Angloromani, a variety of English with distintive 'secret' vocabulary spoken by gypsies in the British Isles. See I. Hancock, 'The Romani Speech Community', in S. Alladina and V. Edwards (eds.), *Multilingualism in the British Isles* (London: Longman 1991), ii. 89–106.

The original source of *register* in its current usage is T. B. W. Reid, 'Linguistics, structuralism and philology', *Archivum Linguisticum*, 8 (1956), 28, quoted and discussed in J. Ellis and J. N. Ure, 'Language varieties: Register', in A. R. Meetham, ed., *Encyclopaedia of Linguistics, Information and Control* (Oxford: Pergamon Press, 1969). For Halliday's earlier treatment of the concept, see M. A. K. Halliday, A. McIntosh and P. Strevens, *The Linguistic Sciences and Language Teaching* (London: Longman, 1964), ch. 4; his *Language as Social Semiotic* develops 'register' into a much more powerful concept: registers are now 'ranges of semantic potential'—modes of meaning, not just styles.

For the source of *re-registration* and *sovereignty* see R. A. Carter and W. Nash, 'Language and literariness', *Prose Studies*, 6 (1983), pp. 123–41.

CHAPTER ELEVEN

Meaning and World-View

In Chapter 2, I argued that language is of great importance in shaping speakers' classification of experience: as Halliday puts it, language has an *experiential* or *ideational* function. Applying this notion to a whole language, one might claim that English as a whole, or French, or Arabic, encodes two sorts of meanings which are accessible to speakers: on the one hand, *natural* meanings such as 'red', 'greater than', 'square', 'up/down' which are necessarily coded because all human beings are biologically equipped to make such discriminations; and on the other hand, *social* meanings which reflect the organization of a society and its relationship with its environment: 'Prime Minister', 'son', 'doctor', 'democracy', 'landscape', 'Spring', etc. It is obviously in the—vast—area of social meanings that differences between languages are greatest; and, if the ideational theory is correct, speakers' world-views differ most in this socially constructed field of significances.

Just one point to emphasize here is that, when I speak of 'social meanings', I am not referring only to terms like 'aunt' or 'vote' which are obviously directly defined in terms of social organization. The point about the social construction of reality is that it extends to many concepts that we normally regard without question as natural and fundamental: 'common-sense' terms like 'home', 'anger', 'food' (cf. my discussion of 'weed' and 'pet', Chapter 2, p. 25 above). Languages vary considerably in what meanings they encode, even in what one might regard as basic areas and structures of experience.

I referred above to the ideational resources of 'the whole language'. This broad generalization allows us to say that English differs from French ideationally, an obvious fact which emerges from the well-known difficulties of translation between languages. But comparing whole languages is an unmanageable task, and is anyway remote from the particularity of real language-use. In specific uses of language, the ideational differences of which we are conscious are differences between speaker and speaker, text and text. This is how Halliday relates his 'ideational function' to the experience of the individual:

> Language serves for the expression of content: it has a representational, or, as I would prefer to call it, an *ideational* function ... the speaker or writer embodies in language his experience of the phenomena of the real world; and this includes his experience of the internal world of his own consciousness: his reactions, cognitions, and perceptions, and also his linguistic acts of speaking and understanding. ('Linguistic function and literary style', p. 332.)

Now experience, and its coding in language, differ from individual to individual: not absolutely, nor randomly, but according to conventions which govern the individual's roles in the social and economic system. S/he is born into a family at a specific place in a much wider social network, with access to some patterns of interaction, but not to many others; similarly, specific limitations of experience and contacts extend through school, work, and the social affiliations of maturity. In consequence, our experience, and thus what we know about and need to have coded in our semantic resources, is personal; but is also a product of our position in socio-economic relations. Under these constraints, our semantic repertoire and the structure of our language are similar to the resources of people who have had similar paths through life, but significantly different from those of others.

The same ideational variation distinguishes text from text: according to the theory of *register,* each act of language is formed for a specific purpose and in a particular setting, and the text's structure reflects these circumstances. The social setting and the purpose of the communication produce a characteristic set of meanings, and these are coded in a characteristic structure of the text, with the relevant ideational shaping for the persons concerned. Again, differences are not random: a text's structure, and thus its perspective on its subject-matter, follow the *conventions* for that particular type of communication in that type of setting. To offer an extremely simplified example, the ideational structure of a love-letter is likely to be very different from that of a sociological paper on courtship, even though the subject-matter might be similar. The differences would reflect conventional contrasts of goals, social roles, assumptions about the reader, assumptions about other relevant discourse, etc. Differences of world-view would be relatable to conventionalized, socially based, perceptions of communication.

Now the same person might well write a love-letter and an academic article; and many other types of discourse. The point is that every person's sociolinguistic abilities are diverse, so that their language-use incorporates a repertoire of ideational perspectives. It would be incorrect to think that each individual possesses one single, monolithic, world-view or ideology encompassing all aspects of his or her experience; rather, the ideational function provides a repertoire of perspectives relative to the numerous registers of discourse in which a speaker participates. When I say 'X's point of view' or 'X's world-view', I am using a shorthand for 'the viewpoint constituted for X in this register'.

This pluralism is part of the reason why, as Halliday observes, the extreme version of the Whorf hypothesis of linguistic determinism (that one is absolutely constrained, conceptually, by the structure of one's own language) cannot be correct. A language embodies alternative ways, not *one* way, of looking at the world, and in these circumstances it is obvious that speakers are not going to be trapped within one overriding system of beliefs. Because speakers constantly make ideological shifts as they change registers (and are frequently involved in contradictions—which can readily be brought to consciousness) they can experience a creative relativity of view. As Halliday puts it: 'The speaker can see through and around the settings of his semantic system; but he is aware that, in doing so, he is seeing reality in a new light, like Alice in Looking-glass House' ('Linguistic function and literary style', p. 333). Obviously, knowledge of more than one language must help speakers to be aware of ideational restrictions imposed by their native linguistic competence. So must experience of a multiplicity of modes of discourse within their own language: an experience which should be a prime objective in critical education. Finally, if we recall the argument about language and defamiliarization presented in Chapter 4, it should be clear that texts in 'literary' modes of discourse are expected to help us see around the settings of our semantic systems, to be aware of new ideational orderings, 'reality in a new light'. In particular, the function of *metaphor,* which has been given especial prominence in literary studies, and is generally regarded as the presentation of one idea in a perspective normally associated with another, is precisely to cast a new light on experience and thought.

Ideational processes may be significant either at some specific point in a text (a *local* effect) or by a *cumulative* building of a world-view. I will be primarily examining the latter case. That is not to say that locally effective ideational processes are not important. Local processes include some of the most powerful of traditional rhetorical devices, the 'figures of thought' ranging from the complex concept-forming apparatus of metaphor to surprising and challenging lexical choices, as when T. S. Eliot opens a poem with the conundrum 'polyphiloprogenitive'. Local devices may suggest specific reinterpretations of experience at particular points in the text; many examples have already been given in this book. Cumulative ideational structuring depends on regular and consistent linguistic choices which build up a continuous, pervasive, representation of the world. This is the major source of point of view in fiction. Cumulative ideational structuring is of course a property of all discourse, not just those modes which are regarded as 'literary'. We may notice a distinctive style in a speaker, a newspaper, a writer, a novel, etc. (or we may not notice it—it may register automatically and unconsciously, if habitualized) and this is the product of regularly repeated choices of linguistic structure. Such regularities establish particular varieties or *registers* of discourse such as legal language, scientific writing, popular journalism, romantic fiction, etc., or more specifically the style of an author or of a school of writers. Within the context of the present argument, the point is that such stylistic or register differences, correlating with social and ideological circumstances, carry differences of ideational significance. So the distinctive linguistic style of, say, a political speech necessarily implies a particular perspective on the topics treated: that politician's view of the world, as shaped for that particular occasion of discourse. Concrete examples of how different styles shape reality differently can be found in Tony Trew's analyses in *Language and Control* of news-reporting styles. Different papers' treatments of the same events, he argues, reflect and express contrasting theories of the causes, nature, and significance of the events.

Discussing this phenomenon in literary fictions, I have called it *mind-style*: the world-view of an author, or a narrator, or a character, constituted by the ideational structure of the text. From now on I shall prefer this term to the cumbersome 'point of view on the ideological plane' which I borrowed from Uspensky in Chapter 9: the notions are equivalent. The basis for the idea, and much of the linguistic analysis required to make it concrete, are provided by M. A. K. Halliday in a pioneering article 'Linguistic function and literary style: An inquiry into the language of William Golding's *The Inheritors*'. Here Halliday demonstrates how foregrounded patterns of *transitivity*—the structure of the processes, participants, and circumstances which feature in clauses—are used by Golding to suggest cognitive limitation, a diminished sense of causation, and an imperfect understanding of how humans can control the world, on the part of the central character, Lok, a Neanderthal man whose world is being taken over by a more advanced people. Halliday's article is absolutely essential reading for this part of linguistic criticism.

I will illustrate ideational structuring involving three different types of linguistic feature: *vocabulary, transitivity,* and certain *syntactic structures.*

As we have seen, the *vocabulary* which speakers have at their command is a strong influence on, and an indicator of, the range and structuring of their experience. The ideational and thematic importance of vocabulary in texts has long been recognized by literary critics, so I am not going to treat it at length; the contribution of linguistics to the study of vocabulary is to ground it in the semantic and psychological theory sketched in the early chapters, and to suggest a system of terms for lexical analysis.

Once we look at vocabulary or *lexis* as the encoding of ideas or experience, it becomes a good deal more dynamic than a dull list of words in a dictionary. The lexical structure of a text, or of a person's mental lexicon, can be thought of as a distinctive, but changing, set of relations and processes.

The basic process, the background against which the others work, is *lexicalization*. This is simply the existence of a word for a concept—'magnolia' for magnolia—and of sets of words for families of concepts—'bush', 'shrub', 'tree'. Normal lexicalization has been adequately discussed in Chapter 2, where it was argued that the lexis of a person, or of a discourse, or of a society, can be regarded as mapping the conceptual repertoire of the person (etc.) concerned. If we do not know the term 'magnolia', we are likely not to know the concept which it denotes; if we designate the woody part of the plant kingdom with a different set of terms from 'bush', 'shrub', and 'tree', it is likely that we classify that part of our experience differently. Before moving on to variations on the normal situation, I want to make one further point: that different terms are available for referring to the same object. They may differ in a number of dimensions.

First, pairs of words which can denote the same thing or process may differ in *connotation* or tone and suggestivity. Lexical alternatives have their origins in different registers: 'house' versus 'domicile', or 'knackered' versus 'tired', come from texts which are used in different contexts of situation, and therefore the alternatives gather different associations from the contexts. Stylistic differences stemming from differences of connotation are well understood in literary studies and need no further comment here.

A second dimension of variation may be less familiar in stylistics, and that is variation in *generality* of terms. 'Shrub' is a more general term than 'magnolia', and conversely 'apple' is a more specific word than 'fruit', 'fruit' more specific than 'thing', and so on. It would be possible for a writer consistently to choose general terms, or specific terms, in a text, with consequent differences of effect. This is a possibility which I have not investigated thoroughly in textual analysis, but it seems likely

that consistent over-generalization would create the impression
of mind-styles tending to childishness, naïveté, coyness, or evas-
iveness. One example that comes to hand is Mr Tulliver's
repeated use of 'thing' in his shy and unfluent consultation with
Mr Riley about his son's education: 'There's a thing I've got in
my head . . . It's a very particular thing . . .' and so on; see
George Eliot, *The Mill on the Floss* (1860), Bk. I, Ch. 3. On the
other hand, consistent use of very specific terms would evoke
specialist knowledge, pedantry, obsession, etc.; examples should
not be hard to find. Such effects would be akin to those of
underlexicalization and *overlexicalization*, respectively.

Matters of connotation, the effects of generality/specificity and
the related distinction abstractness/concreteness, are amply discussed in stylistics, and form major preoccupations in hand-
books for writers. Two less familiar aspects of vocabulary usage
which are established in critical linguistics are *underlexicalization*
and *overlexicalization*.

Underlexicalization is the lack of a term or of a set of terms.
The psycholinguistic theory of vocabulary that we have been
assuming would suggest that such gaps, in an individual's lexical
repertoire, mean that the individual does not have access to the
concepts concerned, or has difficulty of access. In deliberately
formed 'literary' texts such as we have been considering, underlexicalization is marked by two alternative linguistic devices:
either the noticeable suppression of a term, or the substitution
of a noticeably complex expression for what in other registers
would be a simple term. The former procedure, suppression, is
the basis of Swift's shocking presentation of the Yahoos as
animals rather than humans (pp. 58–9 above). The latter, substitution of a complex expression, is a standard device for the
evocation of naïve consciousness, as we have seen already in
Benjy's 'curling flower spaces' and 'flower tree'. (Note that
lexical suppression is also at work in the opening of *The Sound
and the Fury*: the game of golf which Benjy is watching is never
named.) Lok in the text discussed by Halliday is assigned phrases
like 'white bone things', 'a lump of bone', 'sticky brown stuff'.
In Kingsley Amis's *Take a Girl Like You* (1960), the inexperi-
enced heroine Jenny Bunn, taken to a pretentious restaurant,

contemplates the 'huge pink fish', 'raw fish' (smoked salmon?), 'sort of meat fritter' (pâté?), 'curly iron fences' (wrought iron) incomprehendingly.

In such cases, the concept or object which is presumably unfamiliar to the perceiving subject is rendered by a circumlocution, a noticeably complex phrase where we would have access to a simpler term securely coding the concept. The complexity of the circumlocution foregrounds the device, signals the reader to be alert for implied significance. Now the circumlocution conveys, not just the lack of a securely coded concept, but an *analysis* in the cognitive area where the gap lies. In this respect, circumlocutions with their different internal structures can function very differently. Benjy's 'flower tree' and Jenny's 'raw fish' are simple cases: the naming is done by an accurately applied noun of higher generality preceded by a mundane descriptive modifier. Neither of these phrases precisely specifies the nature of the entity referred to, leaving the concept vague and unprocessed. Benjy's 'curling flower spaces', on the other hand, does not simplify, but attempts to analyse a complicated geometrical concept: 'Through the fence, between the curling flower spaces, I could see them hitting.' Read in context, the noun phrase 'curling flower spaces' seems not to be a laborious struggle to a concept for which there might be a simple word which Benjy does not know, but the creation of a perception which Benjy has and which is unusual (a strangely shaped space edged by the shapes of the flowers); the phrase is thus defamiliarizing, for 'normal' speakers of English. This creative effect shows that underlexicalization, avoidance of the simple and most efficient term, is by no means always a case of a cumbersome second best.

For a clearly poetic use of this 'analytic' type of circumlocution, consider lines 4–6 of Wallace Stevens's poem 'Disillusionment of Ten O'Clock' (1915):

> The houses are haunted
> By white night-gowns.
> None are green,
> Or purple with green rings,
> Or green with yellow rings,
> Or yellow with blue rings.

5

> None of them are strange,
> With socks of lace
> And beaded ceintures.
> People are not going   10
> To dream of baboons and periwinkles.
> Only, here and there, an old sailor,
> Drunk and asleep in his boots,
> Catches tigers
> In red weather.   15

The white night-gowns, in this context, symbolize a humdrum
lack of imagination, the failure of the solid citizen to experience
'strangeness' as the drunken sailor does. The alternative
imaginations are symbolized by, first, a simply coded but presumably extravagant colour, green, and then by a series of colour
combinations which are not lexicalized in English: 'purple with
green rings', etc. The reader must exercise his or her imagination
to work out the appearance of these striking garments, and here
the internal structure of the phrases is significant: notice how the
colour of the rings in line 4 adopts the background green of
line 3, while lines 5 and 6 reverse the process by adopting the
colour of the rings as the colour of the background. The reader's
attention is carefully led back and forth between figure and
ground, with heightened consciousness. The unsettling underlexicalization is accompanied by other defamiliarizing lexical processes which have ideational implications: the double meanings
of 'disillusionment' and 'haunted', the odd syntax of 'socks of
lace', the archaism 'ceintures', and so on. Although this is not an
obscure poem, its lexis is sufficiently unfamiliar to lead the reader
into an estranged perception of the world (one which the wearers
of plain white night-gowns do not share).

Overlexicalization is, as its name suggests, the opposite process: the availability, or the use, of a profusion of terms for an
object or concept. The term was introduced by Halliday in his
paper on antilanguages. Strictly speaking, overlexicalization is
the existence of many synonyms or near-synonyms, but it is
useful to generalize from the specialized phenomenon of syn-
onymy to include other, similar, lexical processes. There are
cases where a text makes extensive and repetitive use of sets of

terms for related concepts, so that particular lexical systems, and the ideas they symbolize, become foregrounded. Fairly straightforward literary examples abound, and have been amply discussed in 'literary criticism. A proliferation of terms in some semantic field indicates an unusual preoccupation with a part of the culture's, or the writer's, experience. Shakespeare, and other writers, have been virtually psychoanalysed by the critics on the basis of recurrent lexical preferences; other critical notice of cumulative vocabulary patterns has been more moderate, interpreting them as indicators of theme or point of view.

I can illustrate the specific working of overlexicalization by referring briefly to a poem which everyone knows: Keats's 'To Autumn' (1820). Here the writer draws repeatedly on a restricted lexical stock in the area of experience which is the poem's central preoccupation.

> Season of mists and mellow fruitfulness,
>   Close bosom-friend of the maturing sun;
> Conspiring with him how to load and bless
>   With fruit the vines that round the thatch-eaves run;
> To bend with apples the moss'd cottage-trees,
>   And fill all fruit with ripeness to the core;
>   To swell the gourd, and plump the hazel shells
>   With a sweet kernel; to set budding more,
> And still more, later flowers for the bees,
> Until they think warm days will never cease,
>   For Summer has o'er-brimm'd their clammy cells.

The rhetorical device here is hyperbole: celebratory, praiseful overstatement. The key word for Keats's theme of the abundance of autumn is repeated three times: 'fruitfulness', 'fruit', 'fruit'; and the fruits of autumn are particularized in 'vines', 'apples', 'gourd', 'hazel', 'flowers'—admittedly, not closely related fruits of nature, but nevertheless a dense set of similar references for a short stretch of text, and clearly forming a coherent class in Keats's mind. Among the attributes emphasized are the centres of the fruit, mentioned in two near-synonymous words, 'core' and 'kernel'; notice how the lexical relationship is underlined by phonetic parallelism in the consonants /k/ and /r/. The maturing of the fruits is extensively lexicalized, using three pairs of words which convey three processes: weighing down ('load', 'bend'), swelling ('swell', 'plump'), and filling with liquid ('fill', 'o'er-brimm'd'). As with 'kernel' and 'core', two of these are so close in meaning as to be almost synonyms—'plump', 'swell'; for another example of near-synonymy, cf. 'maturing' and 'ripeness'. The fullness of the vocabulary in these lexical fields (working with phonological and syntactic repetitiveness) draws attention to, and imitates, the natural plenitude which is Keats's theme.

We now move from *vocabulary* to a 'deeper' level of meaning. In Chapter 5 (pp. 73–4) I mentioned some basic semantic relations in terms of which the propositions conveyed by sentences are organized: concepts such as 'agent', 'object', 'action', 'mental process'. These (and others) form what Halliday calls the *transitivity* system of a language: they are a small set of presumably universal categories which characterize different kinds of event and process, different types of participants in these events, and the varying circumstances of place and time within which events occur. In the article on Golding's *The Inheritors* referred to above, Halliday has shown how consistent selections from the transitivity system can suggest different world-views, including, as in the example he discusses, highly defamiliarized mind-styles. I shall follow the broad outlines of Halliday's system, without adopting all the specific terminology of his analysis, which is somewhat idiosyncratic.

I have explained that the semantic nucleus of a proposition is a predicate and one or more nouns associated with it. Predicates convey some sort of activity or state in which the associated nouns are concerned. They divide into several contrasting types. A fundamental type is *action* proper, a movement or deliberate action with consequences, under the control of the principal noun:

1. The horse *swam* across the river.
2. John *slammed* the door.

These contrast on the one hand with *states* which simply attribute properties to objects:

3. The road is *wide*.
4. This music is too *loud*.

and contrast in another dimension with *processes* which are events or changes which 'happen' to things without their control:

5. John *fell*.
6. The road *widened*.

There are also *mental processes* and *mental states*; respectively,

7. Henrietta *listened*.
8. Brian was *blissful*.

These simple distinctions between different types of events and states of affairs convey different pictures of what is going on in the world. It is easy to imagine the types of mind-styles associated with a dominance of one sort of pattern: predominant action predicates may go with strong physical activity, foregrounded mental processes with an introspective mind-style, and so on. But to complete such an analysis we need also to make reference to the kinds of nouns which occur with predicates.

Nouns designate individual concepts and entities; and in propositions, they do not only designate or refer, but also have their referents performing different *roles* relative to predicates. There is a fundamental contrast of role between *agent* and *object*; respectively,

9. *John* jumped twenty feet.
10. *John* fell twenty feet.

In 9 John is treated as a person acting deliberately, in 10 as a mere physical object to which something outside his voluntary control happens. Both agent and object roles occur in 11:

11. The kitten chased a butterfly.

It is useful to distinguish sub-types of 'object', including *beneficiary*:

12. Mary sent *Henrietta* a Christmas card.

and *experiencer*:

8. *Brian* was blissful.
13. *Helga* is in love.
14. *We* heard an explosion.

Another role needed in this type of analysis is *instrument*:

15. I picked the lock with a *hairpin*.

Now for some complications. In 15 the word 'with' gives an indication of the role of the noun. However, while some roles are marked by prepositions, as here, and some by the position of the noun in the sentence, as in 9, and 16 below, English does not invariably identify roles, unlike Latin which, with both prepositions and case-endings, is much more informative in this respect. This lack of explicit role-marking can have ideationally interesting consequences when a noun with one role is made to appear as if it had another. For instance, the classic position for the agent role is the left-hand noun phrase in a clause:

16. *John* slammed the door.

But none of the italicized nouns in the following examples 17–21 are agents; the syntax makes them *appear* to be, by the placing to the left of the sentence, and cumulatively this sort of construction might suggest an analysis of depicted events as more active than might be:

17. The *door* slammed.   (Object)
18. A *hairpin* picked the lock.   (Instrument)
19. *John* loves Mary.   (Experiencer)
20. *I* received a telegram.   (Beneficiary)
21. The *gale* blew down the fence.   (Force)

Such 'pseudo-agentive' structures are important in the passage from *Melmoth the Wanderer* to be analysed shortly.

Finally, to complete the account, I will mention the nouns which perform as 'circumstances'. The principle is simple: to the basic structure of a proposition can be added noun phrases which specify times and places:

22. Mary sent Henrietta a card *last Christmas*.
23. I'd like to be a fly *on the wall*.

There is a 'pseudo-locative' construction which depersonalizes people by representing them as places:

24. *In the majority of babies* there is a strong sucking instinct.

With this basic apparatus at hand, we can now examine how transitivity patterns determine mind-style. I have chosen a characteristic extract from Charles Maturin's Gothic novel *Melmoth the Wanderer* (1820) in which an estranged mind-style is constructed by peculiar transitivity.

As Melmoth leaned against the window, whose dismantled frame, and pieced and shattered panes, shook with every gust of wind, his eye encountered but that most cheerless of all prospects, a miser's garden— walls broken down, grass-grown walks whose grass was not even green, dwarfish, doddered, leafless trees, and a luxurious crop of nettles, and weeds rearing their unlovely heads where there had once been flowers, all waving and bending in capricious and unsightly forms, as the wind sighed over them. It was the verdure of the churchyard, the garden of death. He turned for relief to the room, but no relief was there—the wainscotting dark with dirt, and in so many places cracked and starting from the walls—the rusty grate, so long unconscious of a fire, that nothing but a sullen smoke could be coaxed to issue from its dingy bars,—the crazy chairs, their torn bottoms of rush drooping inwards, and the great leathern seat displaying the stuffing round its worn edges, while the nails, though they kept their places, had failed to keep the covering they once fastened,—the chimney piece, tarnished more by time than by smoke, displayed for its garniture half a pair of snuffers, a tattered almanack of 1750, a time keeper dumb from want of repair, and a rusty fowling piece without a lock . . .

The Gothic genre indulges its heroes and heroines in morbid feelings and sensational imaginings. The most straightforward way of indicating their broodings and forebodings would be a foregrounding of mental state and mental process predicates, with overlexicalization of morbid sentiment, and that is the pattern of many works in this genre. But this passage works in a linguistically more complex fashion; and this may be the reason why its style can still be experienced as alert and defamiliarizing rather than (as is much Gothic) stale and formulaic. Melmoth's mental state is not described, but is to be inferred from his perception of the objects around him. His surroundings are perceived as active, sentient, like living beings, whereas he is inactive, a mere register of impressions. Melmoth is subject of only two verbs ('leaned' and 'turned') and these are simply

movements which reorient his body, first to the window and then
to the room. His survey of the garden seems not to be a
conscious looking, but an accident of vision: 'his eye encountered', Melmoth performs no action which causes a change
to any object; he does not control his environment, nor even
interact with it.

By contrast, the objects in his environment engage in a welter
of activity; action predicates abound: 'frame, and . . . panes,
shook', 'weeds rearing their . . . heads . . . waving and bending',
'the wind sighed', 'wainscotting . . . starting from the wall'; 'the
. . . seat displaying the stuffing', 'the nails . . . kept . . . failed to
keep', 'the chimney piece . . . displayed . . . '. The obvious linguistic point is that there is a large number of clauses in which
a noun referring to an inanimate object serves as the subject of
an action predicate: the sheer quantity of these clauses is the
basis for our impression of an unexpectedly vigorous objective
world. The individual clauses might be quite ordinary ('panes
shook') or contain dead metaphors ('the wind sighed'); but the
effect is cumulatively grounded. However, there is much more
going on in this passage, for many of the individual clauses are
unusual. Particularly notable are the subject-verb combinations
in the section describing the room: the wainscotting is not just
loose but 'starts' from the wall; the seat, nails, and chimney-piece
are all given verbs which denote purposeful actions, implying
conscious intention (e.g. 'displayed'). This is in a context which
contains other indications of consciousness or feeling in objects—'cheerless', 'capricious', 'unconscious', 'sullen', 'crazy'—or
words which in some respect might be associated with humans—
'dwarfish', 'doddered', 'heads', 'dumb'. It is not surprising that
the plants and furniture that occupy the garden and the room
are sensed to be animate: the weeds rearing their heads like
aggressive wild beasts, the 'time keeper' (with its *-er* suffix
ambiguous between agent, as in 'teacher', and instrument, as in
'screwdriver') felt to be more like a chronicler than a clock.

Other aspects of the language contribute to the world-view
embodied in this passage. One is the prevalence of negation and
paradox. The passage is full of explicitly or implicitly negative
words: 'dismantled', 'cheerless', 'unlovely', 'unsightly', etc.

Paradoxes are salient: the walks are not walks because they are overgrown with grass; the grass is not grass because it is not green; the crop is a crop of noxious nettles (this would be less striking for a reader who knew that nettles used to be cooked, and brewed into tea!); fittingly, it is a garden which denies the expected values of vitality, productivity, brightness—a garden of death. So the actions and motions which are ascribed to the trees and weeds and other objects are fruitless, even destructive; this paradox of actions which are goalless compounds the paradox of a world in which humans are inert, and inanimate things move of their own accord. Finally, many of the destructive processes are not assigned an agent or cause: there are quite a number of passive past participles denoting actions but with no specified agent—'dismantled', 'pieced', 'shattered', 'broken down', 'doddered' (?), 'cracked', 'coaxed', 'worn', 'tattered'. By whom, or by what? These unexplained processes, added to the unnatural quasi-human activities of the plants and the furniture, increase the portentous and threatening atmosphere of this world. Or rather, of this world-view or mind-style, for what Maturin is doing is making his language construct a point of view which systematically transforms our common-sense world into one which is negative, perverse, and portentous: a world over which humans have little control, and little understanding of the controlling forces. This is obviously a technique for defamiliarization; it requires the reader to set an unusual perception of the world against her or his own habituated assumptions about loose wainscotting, plants blown by the wind, or the comforts of the hearth. The dominant transitivity patterns of this passage reverse our assumptions about human control over a secure and comprehensible domestic world.

It must be acknowledged that the distinctiveness of this text does not lie merely in the foregrounding of inanimate agents and inanimate experiencers. This pattern interacts with other estranging structures such as the negatives and paradoxes; the surreal separation of the eye from the beholder; the bizarrely assorted references at the end; the hints of archaism in the vocabulary ('verdure', 'garniture'). Above all, what I called the 'alertness' of this style comes from complications *within* the basic transitivity

structure. There is progression from the more to the less familiar—weeds after all are living things which can easily be imagined moving, but grates, seats, and clocks are much more
startling candidates for human qualities. Then there is the fact
that the mental state predicates attached to the objects are not
all drawn from the gloomy or sensational vocabulary of Gothic:
'cheerless' and 'sullen' perhaps are, but the majority of these
state predicates work more delicately: 'capricious', 'unconscious', 'crazy', etc. These animations progressively prepare for
the strikingly complete humanization of the clock as a dumb
time keeper.

A comparison with some simpler and more stylized passage of
Gothic would have been instructive here, if there had been space.
The Gothic mode became enormously popular in the late eighteenth–early nineteenth century, and is still recognizable in much
popular romantic fiction today. It relied on few distinctive
features (mostly the use of non-human subjects with human
verbs, and a characteristic vocabulary of architecture, landscape,
and morbid sentiment) and rapidly became stilted and formulaic.
We have glanced at the effects of such stylization in the case of
eighteenth-century landscape poetry (pp. 69–70 above): the language—hence the mind-style—became habitual and uncritical. It
is exactly this cognitive degeneration of the Gothic style that
Jane Austen satirizes in *Northanger Abbey* (published 1818 but
probably written twenty years earlier): Catherine Morland's
expectations about life at the Abbey are absurdly distorted by
her reading of sensational Gothic novels, a gullibility which
earns her a parody-Gothic teasing by Henry Tilney in Bk. II.
Ch. 5.

The passage just analysed might be described as 'abnormal' or
'deviant' in language and mind-style; in a sense it is, but we must
carefully qualify the implications of calling it such. First, it is
unusual—somewhat original—by comparison with many works
in its genre, and so potentially defamiliarizing for consumers of
the genre. Second, it embodies a theory of causation, and a
classification of agents, which departs from certain deeply held
assumptions about the power of humans, and the ineffectuality
of inanimate objects. That plants do not move because they

decide to do so; but that we humans can deliberately cause them
to move, are two aspects of a very basic lesson that all babies
must learn. Does this mean that there must be a mind-style of
'normal' causation in relation to which the style of *Melmoth the
Wanderer* is a kind of deformed antithesis? By no means. A style
which foregrounded deliberate human actions might also seem
unusual; we will look at such a case in a moment.

A crude contrast of normal versus abnormal does not completely explain the particular impact of a specific text. While
Melmoth is undoubtedly odd ideationally in its theory of causation, its overall character is derived from other circumstances as
well, specifically the place of the text in the system of other,
relevant, modes of discourse. It is situated historically and
socially, as well as cognitively, in relation to the dispositions of
the human mind. I will return to this question of the historical
situation of discourse in my final chapter.

Bearing in mind, then, that we should not expect it to feel
ideationally neutral and normal, let us examine briefly a text
which embodies a different theory of causation. This is a quite
ordinary extract from 'Big Two-Hearted River: I', one of Hemingway's stories from the collection *In Our Time* (1924). Here
Nick is setting up his solitary camp:

1. The ground rose, wooded and sandy, to overlook the meadow, the
stretch of river and the swamp. 2. Nick dropped his pack and rod-case
and looked for a level piece of ground. 3. He was very hungry and he
wanted to make his camp before he cooked. 4. Between the two jack-
pines, the ground was quite level. 5. He took the axe out of the pack
and chopped out two projecting roots. 6. That levelled a piece of
ground large enough to sleep on. 7. He smoothed out the sandy soil
with his hand and pulled all the sweet fern bushes by their roots.
8. His hands smelled good from the sweet fern. 9. He smoothed the
uprooted earth. 10. He did not want anything making lumps under the
blankets. 11. When he had the ground smooth, he spread his three
blankets. 12. One he folded double, next to the ground. 13. The other
two he spread on top.

14. With the axe he slit off a bright slab of pine from one of the
stumps and split it into pegs for the tent. 15. He wanted them long
and solid to hold in the ground. 16. With the tent unpacked and
spread on the ground, the pack, leaning against a jack-pine, looked

much smaller. 17. Nick tied the rope that served the tent for a ridge-pole to the trunk of one of the pine-trees and pulled the tent up off the ground with other end of the rope and tied it to the other pine. 18. The tent hung on the rope like a canvas blanket on a clothes line. 19. Nick poked a pole he had cut up under the back peak of the canvas and then made it a tent by pegging out the sides. 20. He pegged the sides out taut and drove the pegs deep, hitting them down into the ground with the flat of the axe until the rope loops were buried and the canvas was drum tight.

There is one dominant transitivity structure: the majority of clauses present Nick as an agent of a physical action affecting a material object in some way:

> 2. Nick dropped his pack . . .
> 5. He took the axe out . . .
> 7. He smoothed out the sandy soil . . , etc., cf. 9, 11, 12, 13, 14, 17, 19, 20.

All the predicates designate manipulatory actions literally speaking, i.e. using the hands (which are mentioned in 7 and 8); the objects affected are items of his kit, parts of his makeshift tent, and detailed features of the site. The effect is of close focus on a sequence of precise, small-scale activities. Other predicates emphasize the deliberateness of Nick's actions: 'looked for', 'wanted to', 'did not want', 'wanted'. Purposiveness is indicated in a number of phrases at the ends of sentences: 'large enough to sleep on', 'into pegs for the tent', 'down into the ground . . . until the rope loops were buried'. Apart from these indications of Nick's conscious intentions, there are almost no mental state or mental process predicates—only the straightforward 'hungry' (3). Other state predicates are physical descriptions: 1 'wooded', 'sandy', 4 'level', etc.; only 8 'smelled good' and 'sweet' express Nick's evaluation of his surroundings, and they relate directly to sensory perceptions: in this passage the physical is physical, and not a projection of the character's state of mind. All in all, the passage is minimally introspective and minimally evaluative.

Syntax is of a simplicity associated with straightforward narrative. Because all the sentences are declarative, the clause elements Subject, Verb, Object occur most often in the order

SVO, the order which is normally associated with the expression of actions in narrative. All clauses are in active voice; there are no passives to disturb the SVO order. The agent (Nick) is almost always designated by the first word or phrase of a sentence; rarely is any other element of clause structure shifted to occupy the first syntactic position (see, exceptionally, sentences 12–14). The sequence of clauses and sentences is organized by *parataxis* rather than *hypotaxis*, that is to say, it is a sequence of clauses of similar status linked by 'and' or 'then' or merely an implied temporal link, with very few subordinate clauses or non-temporal cohesive ties (see pp. 88–90 above). This simple parataxis is *not* neutral, but a definite literary style, traditionally and widely associated with plain, simple, often naïve narration (primitive narrative such as the *Anglo-Saxon Chronicle,* children's stories, etc.). Readers are likely to bring to their response to this passage their experience of other instances of the style, the values which have become attached to this form of syntax in the history of narrative writing.

Interestingly, there is one potential significance which seems not to emerge from this passage. A text which, like this one, contains many transitive SVO structures with human agents, might be associated with a tough, action-packed style. One might imagine that this would be particularly likely to materialize with Hemingway, given his preoccupations and his image; but in this passage, presumably the relatively domestic actions Nick performs cancel any suggestions of energy or violence. This situation is a reminder to the linguistic critic to be cautious in assigning significances to particular linguistic structures without consideration of context and content.

Just as a foregrounding of SVO structures does not automatically mean a mind-style preoccupied with physical activity, so energy and violence might be encoded in some quite different type of structure. Here is an instance, from Dashiel Hammett's *The Maltese Falcon* (1930); the sinister Joel Cairo has just pulled a gun on investigator Sam Spade:

1. Cairo went around behind him. 2. He transferred the pistol from his right hand to his left. 3. He lifted Spade's coat-tail and looked under it. 4. Holding the pistol close to Spade's back, he put his right hand

around Spade's side and patted his chest. 5. The Levantine face was then no more than six inches below and behind Spade's right elbow.

6. Spade's elbow dropped as Spade spun to the right. 7. Cairo's face jerked back not far enough: Spade's right heel on the patent-leathered toes anchored the smaller man in the elbow's path. 8. The elbow struck him beneath the cheek-bone, staggering him so that he must have fallen had he not been held by Spade's foot on his foot. 9. Spade's elbow went on past the astonished dark face and straightened when Spade's hand struck down at the pistol. 10. Cairo let the pistol go the instant that Spade's fingers touched it. 11. The pistol was small in Spade's hand . . .

. . . 12. Spade by means of his grip on the Levantine's lapels turned him slowly and pushed him back until he was standing close in front of the chair he had lately occupied. 13. A puzzled look replaced the look of pain in the lead-coloured face. 14. Then Spade smiled. 15. His smile was gentle, even dreamy. 16. His right shoulder raised a few inches. 17. His bent right arm was driven up by the shoulder's lift. 18. Fist, wrist, forearm, crooked elbow, and upper arm seemed all one rigid piece, with only the limber shoulder giving them motion. 19. The fist struck Cairo's face, covering for a moment one side of his chin, a corner of his mouth, and most of his cheek between cheek-bone and jaw-bone.

The point of view is external perspective (pp. 177–8 above). There are very few mental process predicates indicating the protagonists' motives or feelings, or the narrator's judgements (only 9 'astonished', 13 'puzzled', 15 'gentle', 'dreamy'). A few estrangement devices emphasize the conjectural nature of judgements (13 'look', 18 'seemed'). But the externality derives largely from the insistently physical character of the nouns and predicates of the passage. To take the predicates first, they designate actions—4 'patted his chest'—and, to a large extent, movements: either movements of the subject—1 'Cairo went around behind him'—or changes of location caused to the object—2 'transferred the pistol'. These characteristic predicates are so prominent in the passage that it would be superfluous to offer further illustration; but readers are advised to check the verbs one by one to confirm just how movement predicates dominate the text. Now these predicates are accompanied by locative prepositional phrases, and some locative adverbs, in virtually every clause in the extract; 1 'behind him', 2 'from his right hand to his left', 3 'under it', and so on. Some of the phrases indicate movement—6 'to the right'—and the others meticulously document positions—5 'six inches below and behind Spade's right elbow'. Cumulatively, the impression is one of continuous spatial movement within precisely defined points in a small space: to that extent it is like the Hemingway passage, but it is vitally different in other respects. One is the sheer density of movements and directions and locations, and their diversity (as opposed to the essential congruity of Nick's integrated series of purposive actions): these factors produce an atmosphere of frenzied, unpredictable activity in *The Maltese Falcon*. A further, crucial, difference is in the treatment of agency. In the Hemingway extract, of 26 noun phrase subjects, no fewer than 18 refer to Nick as agent. Of 27 in the Hammett, only 10 refer to Spade or Cairo as agents (at transitions in the narrative when the initiative shifts); 13 refer to parts of their bodies *as if* these were agents; the 4 remaining are subjects of state predicates, and again refer predominantly to body parts—5 'The Levantine face', 11 'The pistol', 15 'His smile' and 18 'Fist, wrist, forearm, crooked elbow, and upper arm'.

Another relevant statistic is the total number of noun phrases referring to body-parts or clothes, that is to say counting those that occur in prepositional phrases, and as objects, as well as subjects. The breakdown of all noun phrases is as follows:

Humans	17
Objects	7
Body-parts, clothes	47
	71

This amounts to a remarkable foregrounding of parts of the body and a backgrounding of the whole human as agent and as consciousness. The impression of frenzied physicality more or less out of conscious control derives from this focus on bits of the body moving rapidly in diverse directions.

I have commented elsewhere on the use of body-parts as pseudo-agents: in *Linguistics and the Novel* I related it to a context of what I called 'alienated sex' in D. H. Lawrence's *Sons and Lovers*. It is also a stock feature of pornography. Once again, we have an example of how the context changes the significance of a construction, though having said that, one might speculate that there is a key, in this peculiar use of noun phrases, to the link between violent texts and pornographic texts, and between their associated mind-styles.

References and Suggestions for Further Reading

This chapter depends very much on M. A. K. Halliday's paper 'Linguistic function and literary style', in S. Chatman, ed., *Literary Style: A Symposium* (New York and London: Oxford University Press, 1971) (see p. 20 above for books where it may be found reprinted). It may be read at this point for the general account of the ideational function, and for the application of *transitivity* analysis to a literary text. For this approach, D. Burton's 'Through glass darkly: through dark glasses', in R. Carter, ed., *Language and Literature* (London: Allen & Unwin, 1982), pp. 195–214, is especially recommended. Burton's analysis of a passage from Sylvia Plath's *The Bell Jar* is a model of systematic analysis which has important implications for educational practice.

R. Fowler, *Linguistics and the Novel* (London: Methuen, 2nd edn., 1983) introduces the idea of *mind-style*, and contains further discussion of some materials briefly alluded to here, e.g. Kingsley Amis's *Take a Girl Like You* (pp. 216–17) and 'alienated sex' in D. H. Lawrence (p. 232).

For a summary of traditional theories of metaphor, see T. Hawkes, *Metaphor* (London: Methuen, 1972); for a stimulating collection of modern essays treating metaphor from linguistic and other points of view, A. Ortony, *Metaphor and Thought* (Cambridge: Cambridge University Press, 1979).

Tony Trew's analyses referred to on p. 214 are chs. 6 and 7 of R. Fowler, R. Hodge, G. Kress and A. Trew, *Language and Control* (London: Routledge & Kegan Paul, 1979). See also R. Fowler, *Language in the News* (London: Routledge, 1991).

Overlexicalization (on the analogy of which I have coined *underlexicalization*) comes from M. A. K. Halliday, 'Antilanguages', in *Language as Social Semiotic* (London: Edward Arnold, 1978), pp. 164–82.

CHAPTER TWELVE

The Role of the Reader

A literary text, like any other text, is primarily the realization of a mode of discourse or a number of modes of discourse. That is to say, its basis can be found in ways of writing (styles, registers, genres) that precede it and are found more widely than in just the individual work. Whatever is created by the individual writer, it is not the whole being of the text, because nothing is possible without the pre-existing discourses: and they are rooted in social, economic, political, and ideological conditions which go far beyond the consciousness and control of the writing subject, 'the author'. This is not a matter of linguistic 'styles' only; styles of discourse encode the systems of ideas of the cultures which produce them: they are 'registers'. In effect, the author is constituted by the forms and the ideas of the discourses which (with their social conditions) s/he has experienced. Creativity is founded on the author's critical consciousness of these resources of discourse, and the practical skill to deploy language to a defamiliarizing effect. Because the whole process of production and reception of texts is essentially historical, defamiliarization must be transient, regularly requiring a secondary application of critical consciousness: the consciousness of the linguistic critic.

In this short book, I have not developed as fully as I might have done the implications of these claims, because of the pressure of other topics. I wanted to introduce the reader to a good range of types of linguistic construction; to visit several useful topics in literary criticism; and to illustrate the practice of analysis by reference to a wide variety of literary examples. None could be discussed very fully, and certainly not set properly in its historical context. In this final chapter I would like to draw together some of the implications of the theory of literature as social discourse; and particularly with reference to the view of the *reader* which the theory suggests.

In the pioneer years of linguistic stylistics, the 1960s, the advocates of the approach took a more are less orthodox line about literary communication, conforming to the conventional literary criticism of the time. We assumed that the author shapes the language of his work, chooses patterns of syntax, of vocabulary, metre, metaphors, sound symbolism, etc., and that those patterns exist in the work as real structures which can be described by the critic, whether linguistic or of any other school of criticism. Textual structure consisted of language patterns which were *in the text,* objectively there and empirically describable. The modest, elementary claim of stylisticians was that our discipline, founded on the efficient methods of linguistics, could provide a solid, unambiguous and illuminating account of a literary text, a good basis for criticism. This claim was, of course, my starting-point in Chapter 1; it is neatly expressed in the stipulation by Michael Halliday quoted on p. 3 above. However, this is only the first move in a linguistic account of literary communication and literary criticism.

To say that there are objective structures of language in literary texts, and that these can be precisely described using linguistics, is a big advance, but it leaves some important questions unanswered. How is it that a piece of language comes to be accepted as a literary work? What is *poetic* about a poem? Roman Jakobson was convinced that he had the answer. In Chapter 6 above, I quoted Jakobson at length: his demonstration that equivalence and parallelism make a major contribution to structure in literary texts provided us with an important analytic tool. I showed that parallelism not only creates formal patterns of metre and syntax, but also highlights meaning in a special way. Foregrounded regularities of the kind which we observed in Blake and in Lawrence can be deployed to restore the multiaccentuality of words, thus recuperating the critical significance of texts which may become habitualized when they are read as part of the familiar, 'official' canon of English literature. However, this is an extension of Jakobson's argument, not part of his basic contention. Jakobson claims only—though this is a bold claim!—that foregrounded linguistic regularities define the essence of literature; he does not consider their semantic or ideological effect, or their relationship with the activity of reading.

The issues came to a head in the early years of linguistic poetics. In 1962, Jakobson joined forces with the anthropologist Claude Lévi-Strauss to produce a famous or infamous linguistic analysis of Charles Baudelaire's poem 'Les chats' ('Cats'). In their article they exhaustively charted the syntactic, metrical, and lexical symmetries of the poem, offering raw linguistics with very little commentary or interpretation. The analysis is a virtuoso demonstration of the Jakobsonian principle that linguistic correspondences define the poetic essence of a text—or, that is what it is intended to show. The substance of the analysis need not concern us. What made Jakobson and Lévi-Strauss's treatment of 'Les chats' historically important was the exhaustiveness of the technical analysis, and the response which their display provoked. In a trenchant and plausible critique, first published in 1966, the stylistician Michael Riffaterre raised the question

whether unmodified structural linguistics is relevant at all to the analysis of poetry. The authors' method is based on the assumption that any structural system they are able to define in the poem is necessarily a poetic structure. Can we not suppose, on the contrary, that the poem may contain certain structures that play no part in its function and effect as a literary work of art, and that there may be no way for structural linguistics to distinguish between these unmarked structures and those that are literarily active? Conversely, there may well be strictly poetic structures that cannot be recognized as such by an analysis not geared to the specificity of poetic language. ('Describing poetic structures,' p. 191.)

Riffaterre makes it clear that he does not reject the poetic potential of the principle of equivalence itself, only the indiscriminate display of linguistic symmetries some of which are not even *perceptible to the reader*. Jakobson and Lévi-Strauss have produced a model of the poem which is

inaccessible to the normal reader, and yet the structures described do not explain what establishes contact between poetry and reader. No

grammatical analysis of a poem can give us more than the grammar of
the poem. (p. 202.)

There is, let us add, another way of putting Riffaterre's point: if
we imagine ourselves reading (or, more dramatically, trying to
translate) a poem supposing that we are equipped only with a
knowledge of the grammar and word-meanings of the poem—
the syntax, phonology, word-meanings, and semantic conventions of French, in this case—it is obvious that this is an
unnatural and impossible task. Clearly, an adequate reading
calls on much more knowledge than simply knowledge of the
structures of the language (Chomsky's 'linguistic competence').
Riffaterre proceeds in his article by showing how the *significant*
formal regularities of the Baudelaire poem would be identified
by a 'superreader' who is equipped with appropriate cultural and
literary knowledge.

Riffaterre in this paper made what was a decisive move in
linguistic criticism: he established that the reader must be at the
forefront of critical attention, because the poem as language does
not come to life without the active participation of an informed
reader. Elsewhere, the role of the reader came to be acknowledged in other critical schools during the 1970s: in the 'reception
theory' of Wolfgang Iser, the 'affective stylistics' of Stanley Fish,
and by Roland Barthes who most clearly led the move from
'structuralism' to 'poststructuralism' in France (for references,
see pp. 253-4).

The problem for the linguistic critic is how to incorporate a
major role for readers in our overall approach while retaining a
primary attention to the objective structures of language. The
issue is addressed by Jonathan Culler in his 1975 book *Structuralist Poetics*; Culler proposes that

To read a text as literature is not to make one's mind a *tabula rasa*
and approach it without preconceptions; one must bring to it an implicit understanding of the operations of literary discourse which tells
one what to look for. (pp.113–14.)

One must be prepared to read a literary text as *literature,* and
this involves a knowledge of conventions which determine literary ways of reading: this knowledge Culler calls, on analogy

with Chomsky's 'linguistic competence', *literary competence.*
Now there are a lot of problems with the word 'competence' in
linguistics, and I prefer not to rely on it as a technical term.
However, the point is clear: that a text communicates not simply
through its objective structures of language, but only in so far as
the structure is activated and made significant by an adequate
reader (that is, presumably, what literary education is all about,
and why it is so difficult). Jakobson and Lévi-Strauss's fellow
structuralist Roland Barthes puts the point in an extreme but
memorable form: 'in the text, only the reader speaks'.

At this stage we might seek to progress our theoretical understanding by posing the question 'What is literary competence?'
This awesome question would, however, bring our enquiry to a
halt as surely as, in the past, the unanswerable question 'What
is literature?' inhibited rather than progressed literary theory—
both questions contain the presupposition 'Literature exists',
which puts a complete stop to unprejudiced enquiry.

Fortunately, linguistic criticism is able to bypass this particular
intellectual hurdle. At the end of Chapter 1, I indicated that
linguistic criticism accepts as its first principle that, whatever
'Literature' is, it is a fact that the texts which are regarded as
literary are in any case *language.* Thus, we may take whatever
linguistics can tell us about language, in its broadest sense, as
applicable to literary texts, and to the processes of literary
communication. It is essential to construe this proposal in a very
inclusive sense. If linguistics were regarded as no more than the
structural study of syntax, semantics, and phonology, the contribution of linguistics would be very limited: I take it that
Riffaterre's criticism of Jakobson and Lévi-Strauss's procedure
identifies one case of such a limitation. However, the scope of
linguistics has broadened considerably in the last twenty to thirty
years, to include sophisticated investigations of *sociolinguistic,
psycholinguistic, pragmatic,* and *text-grammatical* aspects of
communication in language. Linguistics has progressed substantially in areas which can throw light on difficult theoretical
questions such as the one raised in the present chapter: what is
the role of the reader in relation to the objective structural
characteristics of texts?

The grandiose question 'What is literary competence?' must give way to the less exotic but still crucial question 'How do people make sense of texts and utterances?' Psycholinguistic research into the comprehension and interpretation of texts and utterances (for simplicity, we will refer to them as just 'texts') has in recent years established that understanding language is not just a simple decoding process based on 'what is there' in the text. It might be thought that a listener or reader understands a text by hearing the sounds or reading the letters, building them into words, recognizing the meanings of the words, which are then constructed into phrases and sentences, which are finally understood. This would be a 'bottom-up' model of text comprehension, in which the reader's or listener's comprehension, and thus what s/he could get out of the piece of language, would be restricted to what s/he could find 'in' the text through receiving it and analysing it. The reality is much more 'top-down'. As Jean Aitchison puts it,

decoding is not the simple matter it was once thought to be. People do not passively 'register' the sentences uttered by a speaker. Instead they hear what they expect to hear. They actively reconstruct both the sounds and syntax of an utterance in accordance with their expectations. (*The Articulate Mammal*, p. 205.)

In listening or reading, the top-down process, powered by 'expectations', runs alongside, and indeed drives, the bottom-up recognition of units of the text. Aitchison demonstrates how this works at the levels of phonology and syntax. If you are processing a text which you know to be about cats, you do not need to recognize every sound or letter when you come to a sequence which could spell the word 'paws'. The subject-matter, and our knowledge of the world, permit us to dispense with a full analysis of the spelling. Similarly at the level of syntax, as soon as we encounter a definite article we start looking for a noun, then a verb, and so on, continuously working with expectations formed in advance of meeting the actual words which fulfil them. And we use our semantic knowledge to resolve syntactic uncertainties: we make guesses at meaning even before we finish working out the grammar.

The most important factors in this reader-driven (or hearer-driven) process of comprehension are *pragmatic* ones. Readers making sense of texts are not only reacting to the objective features of the language of the text, deploying their linguistic competence, they are also blessed with a vast amount of knowledge of the world. In pragmatics this is generally known as *encyclopaedic knowledge* as opposed to 'linguistic knowledge': a neat terminological distinction, but of course encyclopaedic knowledge does include knowledge of texts, and knowledge derived from texts. It is this dimension of knowledge of the world, and experience of texts, which Michael Riffaterre adds when he reanalyses Baudelaire's poem; it is this which is missing from Jakobson and Lévi-Strauss's formalist account. Riffaterre imagines what he calls a 'superreader', composed of a store of historical, philological, and cultural references, knowledge which guides the reader through the poem, 'holding him up' at significant points ('Describing poetic structures', p. 204). This is the answer to the stumbling-block which floors the objective linguistics of the structuralists, that linguistics in itself (or, linguistic competence strictly speaking) gives no guidance on which parts of the form are significant.

Riffaterre's 'superreader' is one example of a number of 'ideal reader' proposals which were offered and debated in the 1960s and 1970s, the general claim being the somewhat élitist one that every poem (for example) has a right reading, which will only be realized by a very narrow class of suitable readers who are somehow equipped to receive the poem's message. The evaluative connotations of such terminology are distracting. Interestingly, in a French translation of his essays a few years later, Riffaterre substituted the expression *lecteur moyen,* 'average reader', which brings the discussion back to earth again. What I want to say about the reader of literary texts is based on principles which apply to *all* readers—'a reader' or 'the reader'— and indeed, to anyone who understands any piece of language addressed to them, or overheard. People understand language by imposing on it interpretations which are based on their previous experience of the world (and of language). The problem in communication is that everyone's experience is different. Are we then admitting a principle of chaos, or the *laissez-faire* doctrine that anyone's reading is as good as anyone else's? Certainly not: communication generally takes place unsubverted by such anarchy, and when someone misunderstands, it is generally obvious, and correctable; and in literary criticism, there are clearly some interpretations which are patently *wrong* because inappropriate encyclopaedic knowledge has been brought to bear.

Although our individual experience is unique, we share conventional *representations* of it in our minds. This is understandable, since we live in highly structured societies, and are very communicative: when we talk about objects and places and experiences and ideas, we make the assumption that we have much in common—we assume that two people's quite distinct experiences are in some sense instances of 'the same thing'. As I explained in Chapter 2, we sort the world of our perception and consciousness into *categories;* these categories are largely social in origin, and they are very solidly represented in the vocabulary of a language.

This 'packaging' of experience is referred to in cognitive psychology under the general term *scheme,* often cited in its Greek form *schema* (plural *schemata*). According to the originator of the idea, F. Bartlett, a scheme is 'an active organization of experience'. Schemata are the mechanisms by which memory is facilitated and ordered: we store our ideas and experiences in terms of what is *typical,* what we take to be the usual attributes of an event or an idea. So, for example, most of us possess a schema for the features that usually characterize a child's birthday party: cards, presents, games, a special tea culminating in a decorated cake with candles, the blowing out of the candles, departure of the guests bearing party bags of goodies. Such a cluster of typical features is generally referred to by the specific term *frame:* a frame is the set of typical features in terms of which we represent our knowledge of, in this case, birthday parties. Other kinds of schema are *scripts* and *plans.* A script has a sequential ordering, either temporal or logical: in fact, I reported the birthday party frame more or less as a script, since I listed the typical features in the order in which they usually occur at a party. Scripts are stories, and they have an obvious and immediate relevance when we are talking about literary structure. Finally, a plan is an ordered script which progresses toward some deliberate end, for instance the way in which you mentally represent your usual route to work by car.

We can regard readers, then, as possessing vast stores of knowledge of the world—'encyclopaedic knowledge' as I called it above—but knowledge which is not stored in bits and pieces, and which is not randomly different from person to person. It is packaged in schemata which are shared by members of a community. Quite obviously, schemata are acquired in the processes of socialization which begin from the cradle. They are acquired in the course of interaction with others, in structured social settings: in the family, the peer group, at school, in church, at work, in relationships with institutions such as banks, libraries, insurance companies, and so on. In this lifelong process of socialization into schemata, the most important medium is language, the individual's experience of talk, letters, books, newspapers, and so on.

The social nature of the processes involved here explains how different individuals come to share a common stock of schemata; and also how *differences* in people's repertoires develop. Almost everyone possesses the schematized knowledge which is necessary for reading newspapers, because newspaper consumption is a very widespread daily activity in our culture. Similarly, most adults have the knowledge which is appropriate to making sense of bills for tax and public services, and letters demanding payment of debts. A great many fewer individuals can write letters, and in some cultures there are professional letter-writers who will do the job for you for payment. In these ways, depending on their experiences within social practice, people's *communicative competence* varies—not so much their knowledge of the rules of the language, but their access to the banks of schemata which allow them to construct (as consumers as well as producers) different kinds of texts. It is as a section of 'communicative competence' that the idea of 'literary competence' is to be understood: literary competence is schematized knowledge possessed by those people who have had a literary education. It is not a special, superior, 'aesthetic' knowledge, but it has, logically, the same unremarkable status as the competence which allows us to make sense of advertisements, to decode weather forecasts as weather forecasts, obituaries as obituaries, to recognize and respond appropriately to letters requiring us to pay our debts, and similarly for many other genres of discourse. Just which ones we are competent in depends on our experience and education, and this is by no means the same for everyone; however, the sharing which comes from socialization within communities ensures that there are considerable areas of overlap, so that common schematic 'packages' permit effective communication and considerable agreement on response to and interpretation of linguistic texts.

If 'literary competence' is regarded as a part of communicative competence, and as culturally relative, it loses the absolute and universal character which is implied by Culler's discussion, by the analogy with Chomsky's 'linguistic competence', and by Jakobson's theory, which is explicitly in quest of a universal principle of 'literariness'. What then does 'reading a literary text *as literature'*, a phrase I used above (p. 236), mean within this redefined context of communicative competence? What I want it to mean is that, given a specific text, readers will recognize, through cues, what kind of text it is, and deploy appropriate conventional schemata. These are going to be highly diverse, but, as we have seen, they are not random or idiosyncratic. Some schemata will include, for example, a knowledge of typical story-lines (scripts) for different kinds of narrative: family history, novel of psychological development, thriller, romantic fiction, adventure at sea . . . ; there will be frames to be produced for typical narrative situations and settings, e.g. weddings, parties, battles, strikes, duels, the countryside, school, courtroom, prison . . . ; conventions govern narrations from different points of view; a rhyming text, or one with other sorts of parallelism, will (by the competent reader) be read for extra connections of meaning between the rhymed or paired units; and so on.

In part, this is a question of factual knowledge: knowing about Keats's life and his sufferings, about the systems of scientific thought that were available to John Donne, the marriage laws and practices in Hardy's time, and so on. But in large part what is involved is experience of, and acuteness in deploying, conventional manners of reading particular modes of discourse: learning and practising ways of reading. These are 'packaged' as schemata for the 'ideal reader' of a text, but less securely established for others. Students who are 'stuck' when Keats's 1820 Odes, or *Much Ado about Nothing,* or *The Rape of the Lock,* confronts them as part of a syllabus, have not yet learned the range of reading conventions appropriate to these modes of discourse—conventions which are of course blessed by the examination system within which the student is competing.

One more example from Pope will readily illustrate some of the processes involved. I have chosen Pope—with whom in a sense our argument started on p. 22—because of the manifest artificiality, the obvious distance from our twentieth-century linguistic competence, and therefore obvious reliance, for the text's interpretation, on non-linguistic information. Here is a very famous passage from the *Essay on Man* (1733-4):

> Know then thyself, presume not God to scan;
> The proper study of Mankind is Man.
> Plac'd in this isthmus of a middle state,
> A being darkly wise, and rudely great:
> With too much knowledge for the Sceptic side,   5
> With too much weakness for the Stoic's pride,
> He hangs between; in doubt to act, or rest,
> In doubt to deem himself a God, or Beast;
> In doubt his Mind or Body to prefer,
> Born but to die, and reas'ning but to err;   10
> Alike in ignorance, his reason such,
> Whether he thinks too little, or too much:
> Chaos of Thought and Passion, all confus'd;
> Still by himself abus'd, or disabus'd;
> Created half to rise, and half to fall;   15
> Great lord of all things, yet a prey to all;
> Sole judge of Truth, in endless Error hurl'd:
> The glory, jest, and riddle of the world!
> 　　　　　　　　　　　(Epistle II, 1-18)

These lines recapitulate an extended argument in Epistle I to the effect that man, in the hierarchical order of things, is paradoxically placed between the higher rational beings (God, angels) on the one hand and the beasts and inanimate objects on the other: man's make-up contains elements from both the higher and the lower ranges of the hierarchy. These are contradictory elements, and Pope's verse builds a picture of man as anomalous and vulnerable because of the contradictions.

The summary which I have just given is very awkward because its content is not really expressible outside Pope's eighteenth-century verse discourse. One problem of the précis is that modern academic prose cannot accommodate the ideas with which Pope is juggling. I felt like putting everything in 'scare quotes': 'hierarchical order of things', 'man', 'God', etc. The difficulty of expression in modern prose is not simply that atheism and feminism have prohibited these terms, but that the whole system of cosmological and metaphysical beliefs presupposed by Pope's poem is not ideationally encoded in any contemporary mode of discourse which we habitually experience. The modern reader of *An Essay on Man,* therefore, needs to become familiar with seventeenth-and eighteenth-century discourse on 'the great chain of being' and other relevant concepts. More specifically, the modern reader has to be able to cope with the unfamiliar verse form. For example, the discipline of rhyming pentameter couplets requires, among other linguistic constraints, syntactic inversions which could throw completely off course any reader who did not expect them. In the first line, the word 'God' must be parsed as the object of 'scan'—which is not possible in modern English. A reader who had not internalized this rule of eighteenth-century verse syntax would be tempted to misconstrue the whole line and so the ensuing argument. A correct parsing settles the meaning of 'presume' as 'be presumptuous', not 'assume'. It also establishes a contrastive parallelism between the words 'thyself' and 'God', which occupy equivalent stressed positions in the two halves of the line. Here we encounter a major linguistic system which characterizes this mode of discourse: the use of parallel rhythmic positions to effect contrasts and other links of meaning (recall 'husbands' and 'lap-dogs', p. 22). Rhymes are also significant: 'scan ... Man' summarizes the first two lines; 'rest ... Beast' in 7–8 is part of a little symmetry—

```
act   :   rest
 ↓         ↓
God   :   Beast
```

—by which Pope implicitly defines man's predicament in terms of initiative versus passivity. Such formal devices of contrast and linkage are a major dimension of the meaning potential of this mode of discourse. Pope's 'ideal reader' must be continuously alert to them and to their significances. He utilizes them in every line throughout the text to shape his theme, to give a specific structure to his argument. This parallelistic verse form encodes a binary, oppositional, mode of thinking which transforms the linear, stepped structure of the 'Great Chain of Being' into a system of contrasts in which 'man' always occupies the disadvantaged position. The main theoretical point to note here is that the form of the discourse actively influences the logical structure of the argument—an insight that Pope seems to have been conscious of, since, in the prefatory note to the poem, he speaks of the advantages of writing in verse rather than prose: not only memorability but also 'force', 'conciseness', 'precision', an unbroken 'chain of reasoning'.

The Pope example demonstrates the *historicity* of the practice of linguistic criticism if done thoroughly. The modern reader has to work out what values to associate with the unfamiliar structures of a mode of discourse of nearly three hundred years ago, and that in itself is a considerable exercise in the history of ideas and the social semiotic of a past era. But more is involved, because the theory of defamiliarization encourages us to make ourselves aware of parts of ideology that were under question, unstable, changing at a given time: to what extent was the 'Great Chain of Being' problematic for Pope? And more still is required in linguistic criticism, for there is the question of why and how Pope is read in the latter part of the twentieth century. The conventional answer, that great works of art survive because they treat matters of timeless importance, just will not do, as anyone who has thought about Pope in the light of contemporary social assumptions, or, say, Shakespeare in relation to current sexual ideologies, will rapidly realize. There must be a multiplicity of answers to such questions, all involving complex and subtle ideological relationships.

The complexity of these discursive processes, even when no great historical distance exists between the period of writing and the period of reading, was wonderfully illuminated by one student when we were discussing in class the Hemingway passage treated in Chapter 11 above. I had, as above, contrasted it with *Melmoth* from the point of view of transitivity, and raised the question whether we should regard the one as neutral and natural, and the other as deviant and unnatural. This question was of course designed to elicit the theoretical insight that no matter how 'natural' in appearance, language always invites the reader to construct a *version* of reality. The person who took this question on board commented that the Hemingway transitivity, the foregrounded patterns of goal-directed activity, was indeed a construct, and not 'natural': and she referred it to the myth of 'the American Dream', the drive in that country to mould and exploit the land for man's purposes, and the peculiarly manipulative and aggressive role of the male in the conquest. Now this is an empirical thesis: writings of that period could be examined for corroboration, and, if it turned out that these transitivity patterns did commonly serve the ideological functions proposed for Hemingway, we would be interested in looking for further evidence of this mode of discourse in other, comparable, conditions. (As Benjy's discourse in *The Sound and the Fury* consists of linguistic selections elsewhere associated with naïve or defective consciousness: see pp. 168–9 above.) Then there is the question of whether these values are simply reproduced by Hemingway, or whether they are problematic and critically defamiliarized. On this question, it was suggested that we might look for the presence and the effects of linguistic structures distinct from the purposive, male, agent-action-goal dominant paradigm. Are there, for example, 'female' structures, say adjectives indicating reflective mental processes and judgements, troubling the uniformity of the general pattern and drawing attention to an alternative mind-style which has *not* been quantitatively foregrounded? Armed with this hypothesis, one could easily go back to the whole story and check; perhaps the reader would like to do this.

Finally, the third question I raised hypothetically about Pope and his modern readership may be considered in relation to the Hemingway extract: why and how does a reader who is socio-historically distinct from Hemingway's contemporaneous 'implied readers' reconstruct such a discourse? The point about this case is that Hemingway's insistence on males organizing the world has become a widely unacceptable attitude today; and thus the linguistic coding of it has become highly salient for modern readers—particularly for women, presumably. Modern readers have reconstituted Hemingway's text as a different discourse, insisting on its significance within the framework of today's social semiotic for sex roles.

Let us return to a more general consideration of the role of the reader. The approach taken in this book chimes with other contemporary literary theories in giving a privileged position to the reader. Who is 'the reader', who the 'we' I have so frequently invoked in this book? Certainly I do not intend or advocate a purely subjective, individualistic notion of the reader, with every individual reader licensed to respond to and interpret texts according to their personal fancies. Individuals do of course respond subjectively, but the practice of literary criticism is to engage in discussion towards agreement on interpretation and judgement; where disagreement persists, critics generally occupy differing positions within one overall framework of debate. Thus critical response is not subjective but *intersubjective*, something worked out within a community, and going beyond the level of the individual subject's consciousness. 'The reader' whom I have invoked is a participant in and representative of this process within a literary community (and of other processes) and is therefore genuinely 'we'.

Let us speculate on the kind of intersubjective knowledge involved by recalling the argument put forward by Jonathan Culler. He hypothesized that readers of literature possess a skill called *literary competence* analogous to Chomsky's 'linguistic competence'. As linguistic competence is knowledge of the properties of sentences, so literary competence is knowledge of the nature of literature, and so of the properties of literary texts.

We have reinterpreted this knowledge as part of *communicative competence.* Equipped with this knowledge, an author can write, and a reader can read, texts *as literature.* Culler demonstrates what such reading entails by showing how a literary-critical interpretation of Blake's poem 'The Sunflower' differs from a common-sense paraphrase of the words and sentences on the page: literary competence directs us to read for metaphor, symbolism, allegory, for significances communicated by indirection. Now it is certainly true that people who have enjoyed a literary education, and/or have plenty of reading experience, can make distinctive special statements about those texts which are classified as 'literary', statements which would never occur to people of a non-literary background. The question is whether there is some single, universal, literary competence which is the same for all readers in all periods, and which works equally for any genre of literature. I have argued in *Literature as Social Discourse,* and here, that there is not. It is an empirical fact that the formal linguistic characteristics of 'literary' texts vary enormously; and so do the circumstances of their production and reception. What is more, the texts that count as literature vary from age to age—works and authors being admitted to or expelled from the canon—and this is one facet of a general changeability in the reception of literary works. The examples already briefly discussed in this chapter show how readers of different periods constitute texts as different discourses: 'literary competence' must vary from age to age. It also varies at any single point of time: groups of people from different sub-communities within a whole language community respond differently to particular texts. A dramatic example, for me, was when I served as a GCE A level examiner in English both for students educated in British schools and for candidates from Malaysia and from the Caribbean. Systematically different kinds of answers were furnished by different groups of candidates, varying no doubt in accordance with differences in their educational and cultural milieux.

Anyone who has had experience of the variability of literary response among groups of educated people will realize that 'literary competence' is not one single skill, but is variable relative to cultural circumstances—as communicative competence is generally. This is to be expected, for two general reasons. First, literary education takes place within a precise social, economic, and political context. In Great Britain, for example, students are introduced to a standard canon of accepted English literary texts (from Chaucer to Ted Hughes) from an early age in primary school. Then they are worked through a hierarchical, and very selective, sequence of public examinations—GCSE at 16, A level at 18, university degree at about 21, perhaps advanced study or research after that. At each stage, only a small minority passes through, so at the end of the process an élite has been selected: this is the source of teachers for coming generations, and thus the process is reproduced historically. The selectivity of the process also ensures that the majority of the population do not have access to or practice in the reading of literary modes of discourse. The overall point is that both groups, the included and the excluded, as well as the different levels of more-or-less qualified people in between the extremes, obtain their communicative competence, and their knowledge of literature, within an educational system: and an educational system is very much the product of the economic, political, social, and ideological conditions of its time. So the literary competence we acquire changes as historical conditions change.

I mentioned *two* general reasons for the cultural relativity of literary competence. The second is, quite simply, that, if we define literary competence in terms of knowledge of modes of discourse, then its acquisition is just a particular instance of the acquisition of sociolinguistic competence generally. The educational practices which I sketched above illustrate how different groups of people acquire knowledge of different discourses during the process of socialization. The same principles apply as we acquire experience and expertise in the multitude of other modes of discourse which structure the culture: the various languages of the classroom, the media, the law, commerce, entertainment, advertising, family conversation, and so on. These sociolinguistic varieties are what Halliday calls *registers* (see above, Ch. 10). It is an elementary fact about socialization that, as people grow into and are moulded into the society they inhabit, they acquire active or passive competence in a vast range of these linguistic varieties, each with its own distinct semantic possibilities. People's sociolinguistic repertoires differ considerably, according to the nature of their roles and relationships in society, and the details and the breadth of their experience and activities. A journalist will have a different repertoire from a doctor: the former must be able to write in the house style of his newspaper, while the latter must be capable in the special discourse doctors use in interviews with patients. This mode of speech is expected by society, and especially by its unwell members: indeed it is part of the definition and the qualification by virtue of which a person counts as a doctor. Of course doctor A and doctor B are likely to have different linguistic repertoires according to their individual social and professional affiliations. Journalists and doctors alike—journalists particularly—can be expected to include some degree of literary competence within their sociolinguistic abilities. The journalist may well have passed through a literary education, and certainly works with books as part of his job; the doctor has been exposed to literature through having been long at school and at university (though not *directly* educated in literature), and continuing knowledge of literature is (like theatre, painting, and 'quality' newspapers) part of the means by which the doctor maintains his social position in the professional middle class.

These brief and highly simplified examples illustrate how knowledge of literary styles fits readily into the overall sociolinguistic abilities of individuals; and how this knowledge is, like other knowledge of discourse, part of the process of socialization and social reproduction. Quite simply, the competent reader of literature, through participating in the educational and social processes described above, has come to possess knowledge of 'literary' varieties of discourse within her or his sociolinguistic repertoire—and the various systems of ideas that go with these linguistic varieties.

Let us finally return, briefly, from the reader to the critic and the student critic. The critic's task is to comprehend texts as discourse: to realize them as transactions within society, to understand how they represent the dominant or the problematic beliefs which are current within a historically specific society. That is to say, linguistic criticism has a goal which is compatible with a traditional aim of literary criticism: to understand the transmission and the transformation of values in a culture. However, the linguistic critic, unlike many literary critics, is not concerned simply to reproduce dominant values, but to come to a reflexive understanding of the values of a time and a culture. I have insisted that linguistic criticism is necessarily a historical discipline: it must regard the texts it studies not as isolated and timeless artefacts, but as products of a time of writing and of a time of reading. The significance of the text changes as cultural conditions, and beliefs, change, and so criticism is a dynamic process.

It follows that the critic's basic qualification is a store of knowledge about the practices and the ideas of the periods which produce and consume the texts to be studied—a historical and social knowledge of relevant schemata. The knowledge that critics possess, and that they study, is embedded in discourses: in documents, poems, treatises, manuals, newspapers, letters, etc., etc. These are the background reading and the research materials for the practising critic. For the student, there is really no short cut to the amassed experience of discourse and its values which is acquired by the mature critic. But there are some educational practices which foster, and some which inhibit, the relevant experience. Inhibiting are lecture and tutorial teaching formats: lectures encourage passivity in the student and authoritarianism in the lecturer; tutorials promote indulgence and subjectivism when they are the sole medium for the student. By contrast, seminar groups (of say eight to fifteen students) diminish the authority of the lecturer and encourage sharing of experience; they are a classroom model of the *intersubjective* principle of social knowledge of which I have often spoken in this book. In this context, students can pool and compare the range of discourses of their collective experience, and discuss their significance. One of the teacher's major roles is to introduce a good range of varieties of language, so that the authors being studied are seen in relation to other relevant discourse of the time of writing and of the time of reading. It goes without saying that the language studied in the literature classroom should not be restricted to the 'literary'; but the language of 'literary' texts taught in the context of 'non-literary' modes of discourse will feel more accessible, more like a natural part of one's communicative competence.

The same principle of teaching literature in a historical context and in the context of a variety of modes of discourse applies to exercises and examinations as much as to classroom practice. A crucial task in most literature syllabuses is 'Practical Criticism', which requires critical commentary on short texts which are new to the candidates. This exercise was invented by I. A. Richards when he was teaching at Cambridge in the 1920s. In his hands it was a kind of detective guessing game: unattributed and often arcane poems were placed before candidates; those did well who avoided being caught out, making informed and pertinent guesses; the crass mistakes of the others were ridiculed in Richards's book. It was a test to separate sheep˙ and goats. But this test can easily be modified so that it becomes a positive instrument in the development of literary competence in the sociolinguistic sense defined above: all that is required is a syllabus which contains a socially and historically varied mix of texts (including 'non-literary' ones); with no preference for recherché work or misleading parodies designed to trip up the candidates; all the passages to be precisely titled, attributed, and dated; and the kind of commentary expected of candidates to be requested in technically explicit instructions. Furthermore, student activity should not be restricted to detached forms of 'commentary' and 'analysis' which assume that the text is sacrosanct and unchangeable. We have seen that it is in the nature of texts that their status and meaning change as the language and the culture change, and as the assumptions of readers change. Roland Barthes speaks of the text as a 'methodological field' within which the reader explores and plays, shaping structures and meanings. It is increasingly acknowledged in literature teaching that reading is a participatory, even manipulative, activity. Students can be empowered by being encouraged to perform different kinds of operations on the text: by rewriting exercises which, for example, render a narrative passage so that it is represented from the point of view of a different focalizer; or which substitute a new vocabulary or metaphors; or which modify the syntax of verse so that the balance of a line is changed. The writings of Deirdre Burton and of Rob Pope (references pp. 232 and 19) discuss and exemplify the application of such techniques.

Which brings me to my final point about the qualifications of critics, and their education. I said that the basic qualification of critics is a store of historical knowledge—knowledge of the beliefs and values of cultures and periods; and that this knowledge is embedded in discourses. This book has shown, I hope, that the mechanisms of coding of social meanings in discourse are complicated, and by no means obvious on the surface. Hence the need for a technique to analyse carefully the relationships between textual structure and the text's discourse meanings: a technique, a terminology, and a theory best drawn, I have argued, from an appropriate linguistic model. My entire book has been devoted to exposition of a technique of linguistic criticism, and demonstration of how it works. To make the link with the end of my previous paragraph, linguistics is an excellent source of technically explicit instructions—for essays, research projects, rewriting exercises, examination questions, and topics for class discussion. If you set people to study agency, or cohesion, or nominalization, or over-lexicalization, etc., in a text, you are giving them something practical and achievable to do. What is more, this analysis is not simply a mechanical exercise: guided by exploratory hypotheses, it will lead to a refined understanding of the significances of a text. I conceded in my introductory chapter that linguistics *by itself* is not a discovery procedure: that analysis has to be guided by knowledge and theory. No one becomes a critic simply by learning linguistic analysis; scholarship and sensitivity, wide reading, and membership of a literary culture are called for. But then, no one becomes a critic simply by reading; analytic technique is essential, and linguistics answers this need best of all techniques.

References and Suggestions for Further Reading

On *linguistic competence,* see the writings of Noam Chomsky, and discussions of his theory: for references, see p. 20 above. *Communicative competence* is a term first proposed in a critique of the limitations of 'linguistic competence' by the ethnographer of communication Dell Hymes: see his 'On communicative competence', in J. B. Pride and J. Holmes, eds., *Sociolinguistics* (Harmondsworth: Penguin, 1972), pp. 269–93. *Literary competence* seems to originate with Jonathan Culler: see his *Structuralist Poetics* (London: Routledge & Kegan Paul, 1975).

Psycholinguistic introductions to text interpretation, including discussion of 'top-down' processing, are contained in J. Aitchison, *The Articulate Mammal* (London: Routledge, 3rd edn., 1989); M. Garman, *Psycholinguistics* (Cambridge: Cambridge University Press, 1990); A. Garnham, *Psycholinguistics: Central Topics* (London: Methuen, 1985). On schemata, see F. C. Bartlett, *Remembering* (Cambridge: Cambridge University Press, 1932). For frames, M. Minsky, 'A framework for representing knowledge', in P. H. Newton, ed., *The Psychology of Computer Vision* (New York: McGraw Hill, 1975). On the use of schemes in text processing, see R. de Beaugrande and W. Dressler, *Introduction to Text Linguistics* (London: Longman, 1981), ch. 5.

The debate on analysing Baudelaire was initiated by R. Jakobson and Cl. Lévi-Strauss, ' "Les chats" de Charles Baudelaire', of which different translations may be found in M. Lane, ed., *Structuralism: A reader* (London: Jonathan Cape, 1970), pp. 202–21 and R. DeGeorge and F. DeGeorge, eds., *The Structuralists from Marx to Lévi-Strauss* (New York: Doubleday, 1972), pp. 124–46. For the reply, see M. Riffaterre, 'Describing poetic structures: Two approaches to Baudelaire's *les Chats'*, in J. Ehrmann, ed., *Structuralism* (New York: Doubleday, 1970), pp. 188–230. Another 'exhaustive' Jakobsonian analysis which raises the same issues is R. Jakobson and L. G. Jones, *Shakespeare's Verbal Art in 'Th'Expence of Spirit'* (The Hague: Mouton, 1970). For further commentary on the issues, see R. Fowler, 'Language and the reader', in R. Fowler, ed., *Style and Structure in Literature* (Oxford: Blackwell, 1975), pp. 79–122.

Roland Barthes's dictum 'in the text, only the reader speaks' (p. 237 above) is to be found in *S/Z*, trans. R. Howard (London: Cape, 1975), p. 151. On text as a methodological field (p. 251), see his article 'From work to text' in J. V. Harari, ed., *Textual Strategies: Perspectives in post-structuralist criticism* (London: Methuen, 1979), pp. 73–81. See also Barthes, 'The death of the author', in R. Barthes, *Image-music-text*, ed.

and trans. S. Heath (Glasgow: Fontana, 1977), pp. 142–8. Also reprinted in Harari is a related discussion by M. Foucault, 'What is an author?', pp. 141–60.

Some important works of various schools of reader-oriented criticism are W. Iser, *The Act of Reading: A theory of aesthetic response* (Baltimore and London: Johns Hopkins, 1978); S. Fish, *Is there a Text in this Class? The authority of interpretive communities* (Cambridge, Mass.: Harvard University Press, 1980); N. Holland, *The Dynamics of Literary Response* (New York: Oxford University Press, 1968); U. Eco, *The Role of the Reader* (Bloomington: Indiana University Press, 1979). For a survey dealing largely with the German school of *Rezeptionsästhetik* which Iser's work represents, see R. C. Holub, *Reception Theory: A critical introduction* (London: Methuen, 1984). For a broader critical survey, see E. Freund, *The Return of the Reader* (London: Methuen, 1987).

The Great Chain of Being is the title of a pioneering book by A. O. Lovejoy (Cambridge, Mass.: Harvard University Press, 1936) which gives extensive background to this scheme. Selections of debate on the poem are reprinted in J. Barnard, ed., *Pope: the Critical Heritage* (London: Routledge & Kegan Paul, 1973), pp. 278–316. A valuable critical and scholarly account of the poem is Maynard Mack's Introduction to his edition of the *Essay on Man* (London: Methuen, 1950), reprinted in Mack, *Collected in Himself: Essays . . . on Pope* (Newark: University of Delaware Press, 1982), pp. 197–246.

Index

The Oxford World's Classics Website

www.worldsclassics.co.uk

- Information about new titles
- Explore the full range of Oxford World's Classics
- Links to other literary sites and the main OUP webpage
- Imaginative competitions, with bookish prizes
- Peruse *Compass*, the Oxford World's Classics magazine
- Articles by editors
- Extracts from Introductions
- A forum for discussion and feedback on the series
- Special information for teachers and lecturers

www.worldsclassics.co.uk

American Literature

British and Irish Literature

Children's Literature

Classics and Ancient Literature

Colonial Literature

Eastern Literature

European Literature

History

Medieval Literature

Oxford English Drama

Poetry

Philosophy

Politics

Religion

The Oxford Shakespeare

A complete list of Oxford Paperbacks, including Oxford World's Classics, OPUS, Past Masters, Oxford Authors, Oxford Shakespeare, Oxford Drama, and Oxford Paperback Reference, is available in the UK from the Academic Division Publicity Department, Oxford University Press, Great Clarendon Street, Oxford OX2 6DP.

In the USA, complete lists are available from the Paperbacks Marketing Manager, Oxford University Press, 198 Madison Avenue, New York, NY 10016.

Oxford Paperbacks are available from all good bookshops. In case of difficulty, customers in the UK can order direct from Oxford University Press Bookshop, Freepost, 116 High Street, Oxford OX1 4BR, enclosing full payment. Please add 10 per cent of published price for postage and packing.